"When King David reflected on humanity, he concluded that people are 'fearfully and wonderfully made.' In that same spirit, Bill and Kristi Gaultiere use a Christ-centered Enneagram to help you understand that your emotions are a gift from God, given to draw you into richer relationships with others, yourself, and your Creator. We have been studying the Enneagram for two decades, and *Healthy Feelings, Thriving Faith* is unlike any other Enneagram book we have read because it offers unique insights into the emotional life of each of the nine types. This book has become an essential tool for us personally and professionally."

Beth and Jeff McCord, Your Enneagram Coach

"If, like me, you've ever found yourself having certain emotions hijack a moment or sabotage a relationship, then *Healthy Feelings, Thriving Faith* is for you. Bill and Kristi Gaultiere beautifully help you better understand your emotions, the energy and motion connected to them, your unique personality, and what the way of Jesus has to offer you. This is a must-read!"

Steve Carter, pastor and author of *The Thing Beneath the Thing*

"In this truly unique resource, Bill and Kristi combine decades of biblical study, formal education, and clinical practice to give readers the most impactful Enneagram-related resource I have read to date. With refreshing candor and clarity they take readers beyond good information and fun stories to practical ways of seeing ourselves and others through new eyes. Their unique insights on our core emotions, including anger, shame, anxiety, sadness, and empathy, are immediately applicable. *Healthy Feelings, Thriving Faith* truly is one of those books that you'll want to read more than once and recommend to your friends."

Gary J. Oliver, ThM, PhD, psychologist and author of *Mad About Us*

"Many Christ followers misunderstand or are afraid of their 'negative' emotions. Bill and Kristi show us how all our emotions are valuable gifts from God by eloquently intertwining emotional intelligence (EQ) tips, the dynamic Enneagram personality inventory, and the Bible. They make complex spiritual and psychological principles understandable and easily applicable both for your personal transformation and so you can be a healing catalyst for someone else's growth. I enjoyed the compassionate, transformational therapy and mentoring session Drs. Bill and Kristi blessed me with for my Type 8 struggles."

Karl Benzio, MD, board-certified psychiatrist, founder and medical director of Honey Lake Clinic, and medical director of the American Association of Christian Counselors

"*Healthy Feelings, Thriving Faith* will help you get unstuck from unhealthy personality patterns so you can truly blossom in God's grace and best purposes for your life. I'm especially excited about this book as a tool for life coaching, spiritual direction, and discipleship to Jesus. Bill and Kristi make the Enneagram so personal, engaging, and powerfully transformational for Christians. They weave together Scripture, psychology, and practical soul care guidance to help you make the changes that will positively impact your personal and professional relationships."

Georgia Shaffer, professional certified coach, licensed psychologist, and author of *Coaching the Coach*

"*Healthy Feelings, Thriving Faith* is a must-read for those who want to grow in self-awareness as well as for those who want to hold space for others on the journey of healing. This book is packed full of information and practical tools to help activate the new emotional and spiritual awareness for real life change."

Jackie Brewster, certified Enneagram coach

"Engaging with others and going on an inward journey are both fundamental to the health of our personalities. Through an in-depth look at each of the nine Enneagram types and their emotions, Bill and Kristi have given us an opportunity to dive deeper into the exploration of our souls. In these pages we saw not only ourselves but every relationship we have. This is a must-read in your spiritual formation journey."

Vince and Allison Hungate, founders of Intentional Marriage

"*Healthy Feelings, Thriving Faith* brings together Enneagram wisdom, sound psychological insight, and a deeply biblical framework to lead us in spiritual direction and soul care. It has given us many moments of delight and personal insight, especially in the teaching and practical exercises to help with anger, shame, anxiety, and sadness. The stories of different people were so relatable and helpful. It made us feel like we were sitting in Bill and Kristi's office receiving spiritual direction and soul care."

John and Evelyn Lo, lead pastors of Epicentre Church

"Emotions are at the heart of our trials and our transformation into the image of Christ. In *Healthy Feelings, Thriving Faith*, Bill and Kristi Gaultiere adeptly use the Enneagram as a tool to help readers understand their emotional life so they can grow in love for God and others. By weaving together personal stories, psychological theory, and biblical truths, they guide readers on a journey of inner healing and deep growth. This book will help readers better understand themselves and the people in their life, fostering healthier relationships. You will come away with many aha moments. I highly recommend it!"

Todd W. Hall, PhD, author of *The Connected Life* and professor of psychology at Rosemead School of Psychology

"By inspiration of the Holy Spirit and through their personal journey, Bill and Kristi have engineered a tool to aid us in becoming both spiritually and emotionally healthy. Within the pages of this well-thought-out work, you will learn how to tether feelings with faith and discover God's presence in your personality. I can't wait to get this book to our churches and other pastor friends!"

Bishop Sheridan McDaniel, pastor and spiritual director

"Bill and Kristi have given us a tremendous resource with which to navigate our manifold emotions. In *Healthy Feelings, Thriving Faith*, they help us own that the human experience is fraught with circumstances that our personalities tend to suppress. We must each learn—in our own way—to receive life as it comes and permit ourselves the grace and time to process if we are to progress. Read this book and follow these wise guides into the depths of life."

AJ Sherrill, Anglican priest and author of *The Enneagram for Spiritual Formation*

HEALTHY
FEELINGS,
THRIVING
FAITH

HEALTHY FEELINGS, THRIVING FAITH

Growing Emotionally and Spiritually
through the Enneagram

BILL AND KRISTI GAULTIERE

Revell

a division of Baker Publishing Group
Grand Rapids, Michigan

© 2023 by Soul Shepherding, Inc.

Published by Revell
a division of Baker Publishing Group
Grand Rapids, Michigan
www.revellbooks.com

Library of Congress Cataloging-in-Publication Data
Names: Gaultiere, William, author. | Gaultiere, Kristi, author.
Title: Healthy feelings, thriving faith : growing emotionally and spiritually through
    the Enneagram / Bill and Kristi Gaultiere.
Description: Grand Rapids, Michigan : Revell, a division of Baker Publishing Group,
    [2023] | Includes bibliographical references.
Identifiers: LCCN 2022060086 | ISBN 9780800745066 (casebound) | ISBN
    9780800742812 (paperback) | ISBN 9781493443499 (ebook)
Subjects: LCSH: Personality—Religious aspects—Christianity. | Enneagram—
    Religious aspects—Christianity.
Classification: LCC BV4597.57 .G38 2023 | DDC 155.2—dc23/eng/20230217
LC record available at https://lccn.loc.gov/2022060086

The proprietor is represented by the literary agency of The Gates Group, www.the
-gates-group.com.

The names and details of the people and situations described in this book have been
changed or presented in composite form in order to ensure the privacy of those with
whom the author has worked.

In many cases when the author identifies the possible Enneagram type of a public figure,
it is the author's opinion and may not be how that public figure would self-identify.

Baker Publishing Group publications use paper produced from sustainable forestry
practices and post-consumer waste whenever possible.

23   24   25   26   27   28   29   7   6   5   4   3   2   1

For our students earning a certificate
in spiritual direction or coaching
from the Soul Shepherding Institute:
It's a joy to follow Jesus with you!
Here's the book you asked for.

Contents

PART 3 ANXIETY: A BUSY BRAIN

PART 4 SADNESS: A HEALING PATH

Where's Your Hurt?

Even at night my heart instructs me.

Psalm 16:7

Emotions—we love 'em and hate 'em.

E-*motions* move us, motivate us, ignite our passions, and bring us pleasure, excitement, and connection. But they also stump us, stress us, cripple us, and hurt us and others. Many of us are controlled by our emotions, or we have learned to shut them down by numbing or distracting ourselves.

Have you considered that your emotions are a gift from God? A source of intelligence, faith, and love? God has emotions, and he created us in his image, which includes the ability to feel emotion (Gen. 1:26; 2:9).

Bill and I (Kristi) are blessed to have four little grandchildren. We've been reminded that children develop the capacity to feel before they develop the capacity to think rationally. Their emotions alert us to their needs and compel us to take action to care for them.

I am the youngest in my family, with two sisters who are almost five and seven years older than me. My parents and sisters were strong thinkers and had control over their emotions. But

I was born with the opening to my stomach closed. Whenever I was fed, I would projectile vomit. I cried in hunger, screamed in rage, and was inconsolable. My mom took me to the doctor, and I had life-saving surgery. But the trauma of the abandonment I experienced as an infant alone in the hospital added to my highly sensitive nature as a feeler.

As I grew, I continued to experience strong emotions, and when I expressed them it overwhelmed my parents. They tried everything they could to shut down my emotions: reasoning with me, telling me to snap out of it, making threats, isolating me. Nothing worked. I could not help but feel my feelings. I felt tremendous shame about being so emotional. How were they able to be so logical all the time? How could they be so even-keeled and unemotional? Why couldn't I be like them?

I began to *hate myself* for being so emotional. To cope with all my emotions and the stress they caused for me and those around me, I learned to put my energy into being sensitive to the desires and needs of others so I could help them and secure their love. I was not conscious that I was doing this—I just knew that caring for others made my life go better. I had found a way to secure myself in my relationships, feel better about myself, and earn people's love.

Largely, my personality seemed to work for me until I hit a wall in my late thirties. I suddenly realized how unloved I felt, even by God. I had taught that the Lord was good and loving, but then I was no longer able to really trust this to be true. I didn't want to admit it, but I was angry at God for allowing me and the people I loved to suffer. Due to repressing my emotions, I found myself buried in shame, horrified by the pride and hypocrisy in my soul, questioning my faith, dissatisfied with my life and relationships, and suffering from depression.

Bill and I write about hitting a wall spiritually in our book, *Journey of the Soul*. To get through The Wall, we need to go on an inner journey of getting emotionally honest with ourselves, God, and others. As we do, we grow into a deeper intimacy with God and greater spiritual and emotional health to be formed in Christlikeness.[1]

Deeper Understanding of Emotions and Personality

I sought help from Jane Willard (wife of Dallas Willard), who introduced me to a tool she was learning in her spiritual direction training called the Enneagram. Friends had told her that it had saved their marriage. Some of our friends were also learning it and reported that the Lord was using it to reveal deep truths and lead them into greater growth and freedom in their lives. This included an Al-Anon sponsor who found it very valuable in her work with codependents in recovery.

At first we were skeptical. The Enneagram diagram looked like a pagan or occult symbol. It had not yet been scientifically validated as a psychological assessment, which was important to us as therapists.[2] But we respected Jane and our friends, so we began our own careful research and learning, testing everything against the truths of Scripture and through prayer. It didn't take us long to realize this was indeed a powerful tool for repentance and growth in Christ.

As I learned about the Enneagram type One, I immediately felt like I was reading about Bill. It was as if someone knew my husband better than I did, even better than he knew himself. It gave me so much insight into his unconscious emotions, behaviors, habits, and needs. I grew significantly in my empathy for him and in my ability to pray for him and love him.

But as I read about the Enneagram Two, I thought, *Ugh! I don't like this personality. How awful to be a Two!* I was irritated by what I read. I began to think of people I knew who were insecure Helpers like I was reading about and how much I wanted to avoid them. Later, one of my friends in the school where Bill and I were earning certificates in spiritual direction told me that she thought I might be an Enneagram Two, and she read to me some descriptions that exposed me. It was painful, and I felt naked and horrified at my root sin of pride. Thankfully, she was empathetic, and I came to feel hopeful that the Holy Spirit was leading me on a path for me to change and grow in my freedom and maturity in Christ.

We cannot repent of sin we are not conscious of. We cannot be healed of brokenness we refuse to feel. As the prophet Jeremiah pointed out, "You can't heal a wound by saying it's not there!" (Jer. 6:14 TLB). The Enneagram provided understanding and invitation for me to see my sin, feel my deep shame, and bring my defended false self into relationship with Jesus and his people for the help I needed to be truly secure in God's love and better able to joyfully love others well.

The foundation of the Enneagram theory and system of personality goes back to Evagrius Ponticus, a Christian from the fourth century who was one of the Desert Fathers. Evagrius identified a list of eight sins that later were referred to as "deadly sins"[3] and more recently became the nine root sins of the Enneagram.[4] He and the other Desert Fathers and Mothers used the deadly sins for spiritual counseling. Over the years, there have been contributions by spiritual teachers from different cultures and religions. Then in the 1970s insights from modern psychology started being added as well. Today the Enneagram is a highly developed assessment tool. The foundation of the theory is compatible with the Bible, but many Enneagram teachers do not come from that perspective. Our view is that *all truth is God's truth* and that the Enneagram teaches us helpful truths about human personality. Of course, the theory and its teachers are not perfect, so we chew the meat and spit out the bones.

In our Soul Shepherding Institute and in spiritual direction for our clients, we use the Enneagram as a spiritual psychology tool. We have added to the theory our own insights on emotions and spiritual growth. In our use of the Enneagram, we put our confidence in Jesus Christ, *the One* in whom are hidden all the treasures of wisdom and knowledge (Col. 2:3). We look to his perfect life, his loving Father, his ever-present Spirit, his true Word, and his servants. We are thankful for how the Lord has used the insights of Christian psychologists and spiritual directors to contribute to the wisdom of the Enneagram.

Four Hurts in Your Personality

All of us are like Eustace from C. S. Lewis' story *The Voyage of the Dawn Treader*: we have a false self like dragon skin, and we need to let Aslan tear it off.[5] This is quite painful! But it's the only way we can be free from the destructive effects of our root sin to become our best self that's more like Jesus—more authentic, free, intimate with God, lively, and loving.

I (Bill) first became aware that I had dragon skin when I was a senior in college and in a group therapy class led by my favorite psychology professor, Cara. She was also a therapist, and her class included weekly group therapy sessions. Each week different students got on "the hot seat" and shared their emotional struggles, and Cara provided counseling while also drawing out the reactions of others. I have to admit that after each group I thought, *I'm sure glad I don't have problems like these other students do.* Then during one group a student looked at me with icy eyes. "What about you, Bill? You just sit up there on your pedestal, analyzing and judging us who share. Why don't you ever share? What are you struggling with?"

I was quite affronted but also tongue-tied. Later that week, I slunk into Cara's office. She asked me the same question she always asked: "How are you feeling?" The first time she had asked, I almost looked over my shoulder to see who she was talking to! *Feelings? Me?* I was dumbfounded. I had no idea what I felt, and it seemed irrelevant. I wanted to study counseling to help others. I was fine—or so I thought. When I felt emotional stress or pain, I just got busy with work, school, sports, and giving advice to other people. But now *I was hurting*, and I knew that Cara would listen to me, so I took the risk to be real and raw.

My counselor helped me put feeling words to my inner swirl of anger, shame, and anxiety from being called out in group. I learned that my experience was much less about what the student said to me and a lot more about the brokenness in my personality. As a general rule you can go to the bank with the idea that what you experience in your life is mostly determined by your personality—not other people or your circumstances. In my conversation with Cara, the Lord started tearing off my dragon-skinned false self and setting me free to be loved and to love as a real person, but it was quite painful emotionally.

Underneath my emotional reactions, I was hurting—I felt sad and had unmet personal needs. As the late Christian psychiatrist Gerald May wrote, "The joy and beauty of freedom and love *must* be bought with pain."[6]

In the years after that, I continued to learn more about my personality as a hero child and a perfectionist, a One on the Enneagram. I always felt I had to be right, capable, ultra responsible, and strong for others. Inside my soul was a pressure cooker of unconscious distress, including resentment from all the heavy, unfair expectations I felt, mostly from myself.

One day Dallas Willard shared with me, "We work with words and people." That's been a helpful distillation for Kristi and me in our counseling, writing, and teaching. To help you communicate clearly and lovingly in your relationships, work, and ministry, we teach you a vocabulary of emotions that increases your self-awareness and enables you to receive the empathy that is oxygen for your soul. Of the many emotions that we name, we focus on four main hurts that can damage your identity: anger, shame, anxiety, and sadness.

The Four Hurts

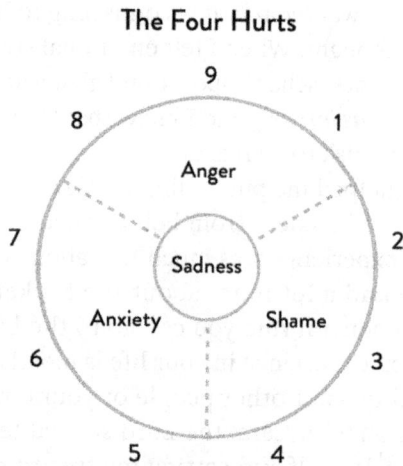

Anger is a feeling of protest, reacting to being wronged or
  intruded on. It drives you to take a stand or fight back in
  order to feel in control or respected. It can malform your
  identity on the lie "I am what I do."

Shame is feeling bad about yourself and can lead to depression. It compels you to impress or please other people to
  feel better about yourself. It can malform your identity on
  the lie "I am what others feel about me."

Anxiety is feeling overwhelmed, worried, or scared about
  problems or dangers. It pressures you to gather resources
  to feel secure. It can malform your identity on the lie "I
  am what I have."

Sadness is feeling loss, hurt, unmet need, or longing for
  love. Usually, it's hidden underneath anger, shame, and
  anxiety. Even though it's painful, it's also a positive emotion that can readily move you to pray or ask for empathy.

Your hurt shapes your personality and becomes your dragon-
skinned false self. Yet most of the time, instead of seeing your
false self as a dragon, you see it as an angel that helps you! We get
charmed by our false self and its defense mechanisms because they
make for us a "psychological anesthetic"[7] that denies our emotional pain, especially our sadness over hurts and losses. But, as
Christian psychologist John Townsend teaches, it's foolish to hide
from the truths and loving relationships that we need.[8] Instead,
we can learn how to understand and care for the emotional hurts
and needs that are embedded in our personalities.

Here's a quick overview of the four hurts and how they relate to
the felt needs of the nine Enneagram types that we'll be unpack-
ing in this book.

Anger (Gut Types)

Eight (Challenger): Act with power
Nine (Peacemaker): Act to avoid conflict
One (Reformer): Act to be perfect

Shame (Heart Types)

Two (Helper): Feel wanted
Three (Achiever): Feel successful
Four (Individualist): Feel special

Anxiety (Head Types)

Five (Observer): Think to have resources
Six (Loyalist): Think to have security
Seven (Enthusiast): Think to have pleasure

Sadness

All types: Need empathy, forgiveness, and grace

Those felt needs may seem pretty nice, but actually they are ways of denying anger, shame, anxiety, and sadness. In the early stages of growth, we don't see that our personality is bent away from God and resisting the grace we need by hiding our emotional pain, sin, and deeper needs in our unconscious shadow self.[9] Eventually, we run into reality in the form of painful consequences to our defended personality, and that's when we can finally realize that our personality has been charming us to keep us from seeing what's broken inside. That's what happened to me (Bill) when I got confronted in group therapy for sitting atop my perch, thinking I didn't have any significant problems or hurts.

To wake up to reality and change, we need to feel our hurt emotions, ultimately getting to the deepest hurt of sadness. This includes verbalizing sadness, grieving losses and injuries, praying from your heart, forgiving sins, asking for what you need, learning to trust someone's empathy, and receiving grace. As we'll explore in the pages to come, this is how you can move through anger, shame, anxiety, and sadness into the blessings and positive emotions of freedom, joy, peace, and love.

How to Read This Book

In Psalm 139 (NCV), David marvels that Yahweh has created him so that his thoughts and feelings can "rise with the sun in the east and settle in the west beyond the sea" and even there his Spirit guides him and holds him in love (vv. 8–10). He praises the Lord for creating his personality "in an amazing and wonderful way" (v. 14). He concludes his prayer by pleading with the Lord to search his heart to find whatever is not good and lead him on "the road to everlasting life" (vv. 23–24). The Enneagram is a tool that God can use to answer this prayer for you. But it's like a scalpel that can heal or harm, so here are some guiding principles on how this book can help you and the people you care for become more like Jesus.

Emotions are central to personality, so each type is grouped by its primary hurt (or core emotion) of anger, shame, or anxiety. These emotions, along with sadness, often hide under each other. When you care for your distressed emotions, it opens the way for you to feel positive emotions like freedom, joy, peace, and love.

Your felt need is the deep desire of your type that God created, but it's easily taken over and corrupted by your root sin (sometimes called "sinful passion"). Your personality is deeply formed by good and bad motivations that are mostly unconscious.

It's helpful to learn the map for your type (number), which includes your wing (the number next to yours that you relate to), stress line (in stress you take on unhealthy traits of this number), and growth line (in growth you take on healthy traits of this number). Developing the strengths of the other numbers in your map gives your personality more options and helps you to be healthier and more loving.

You'll relate to more than one type, so in addition to reading the chapter on your type, read the chapters on your wings, stress type, and growth type. (You'll find help in the chapters about the other types also.) Settling on your best-fitting type is a deep work of reflection that takes time.

Let people find their own type. It's important to respect people's dignity by not putting them in a type box or joking about their type.

Stopping your root sin is like catching a rat in the cellar, to use an illustration from C. S. Lewis.[10] Listening for your type's "emotional alarm" will help you sneak in to stop the destructive rat in your personality.

Observe your unhealthy personality in a relaxed way. Recognize your stress emotion and smile. *Oh, there I go again!*

Self-awareness helps you ask for what you need, confess your sins, experience God's love, and love others. It's essential for your well-being and becoming more like Jesus.

We all need empathy for the four hurts of anger, shame, anxiety, and sadness and other personality struggles. Learning about someone's personality can help you love them well.

Sadness opens a path of healing, so we give special focus on helping with grief in each of the nine type chapters and the last two chapters on sadness.

Seeing Jesus in your type from his life in the Gospels gives you insight and encouragement to be healthy in your emotions and personality. It does not change your type—*it helps you be more like Jesus within your type.*

Your virtue is your type's compass for depending on God's grace to be your best self. It's your sweet spot that supports your experience of the freedom, joy, peace, and love that flow from Jesus in his Kingdom of Light.

Soul care practices for your type and emotions help you be healthy and loving in your type. (You can also benefit from the recommended practices for other types.)

Jesus in Your Type!

Whatever you are feeling in your life and personality, Jesus of Nazareth has felt it and was tempted to react by securing himself but chose to trust God. In fact, the New Testament specifically names thirty-nine different emotions that Jesus felt.[11] Our Savior felt deeply and *intelligently*. When the Son of God took on human flesh, he stepped into human personality to empathize with us (Heb. 4:15). At different times, he embodied each of the nine Enneagram types at their best. He feels your damaged emotions and the temptations of your personality, and he mirrors back your type with God's grace and glory. He is the model for your type and, better yet, he *mediates* your type's virtue to you, shaping your personality to be more like his. He shows us that healthy feelings go with a thriving faith.

In the pages to come, for each of the four hurts and the nine types, we help you find words to pray and share with friends, and we draw you to Jesus, the Wonderful Counselor (Isa. 9:6). Through Scripture, real-life examples of broken personalities being restored, and practical soul care tips, we help you to discover *Jesus in you*. You will feel his empathy, join his intimacy with the God he knows as "Papa" (Mark 14:36 MSG), and learn from him how to become a more loved and loving expression of your personality type.

In some way, each of us is like the man with a deformed hand whom Jesus encountered at the synagogue one Sabbath (Mark 3:1–6). The man probably felt ashamed as he hid in the shadows, anxious about how to provide for his family, and angry for being judged and boxed out by the high-nosed priests. Jesus felt his emotions. On another occasion, we're told that when Jesus encountered a certain rich man, "Jesus looked at him and loved him" (Mark 10:21). That's what's happening here with this poor man. Both the rich man and the poor man felt sad. The rich man walked away depressed and clinging to his wealth, while the poor man was hopeful. *He kept his eyes on Jesus*, took him at his word, reached out his deformed hand, and was made whole! Your opportunity is to stretch out your hurting personality to Jesus and be made whole in God's love. It's an ongoing process of becoming more like Jesus.

To help you get the most benefit from this book, take our free online "Enneagram and Emotions Assessment." You'll receive your results and personalized guidance right away. Just scan the QR code or visit SoulShepherding.org/Enneagram.

PART 1

ANGER

A GUT REACTION

Enneagram Types: Eight (Challenger) • Nine (Peacemaker) • One (Reformer)

2

Anger as Broken Boundaries

> **GUT TRAITS**: anger-based; react on gut instinct; want control; action-oriented

Rest in the LORD, and wait patiently for Him; . . .
Cease from anger.
Psalm 37:7–8 NKJV

(Bill; One)[1] played football as a boy and was nicknamed "Thunder Thighs." I was one of the smallest players on the field, but my legs were big and strong, and I crashed into the line of defenders, driving my legs, spinning my body, and powering across the goal line. I would not let myself be tackled until I scored. So whenever our team got near the goal line, our coach yelled out, "Give the ball to Billy! He'll get us a touchdown!"

That's what men were like in my family. We're from Chicago, the Windy City with broad shoulders and a face set like flint. We're square-jawed, intense, and aggressive. Both of my grandfathers worked in the steel mill, and my dad started off there too. He was an all-city football player on offense *and* defense, which became his ticket out of the steel mill. He went to college and graduate school and went on to become the top salesman at IBM, selling computer systems to cigar-smoking company executives who had never even seen a computer. He was also the lead elder at our church. I wanted to be just like my dad. So I scored touchdowns, got As in school, started earning money for college at age twelve, and tried to be a model Christian.

I had no idea that underneath my determined, achieving personality was boiling anger. Back then I didn't have words to describe my feelings, but in hindsight I see my anger problem. My parents didn't know it, but I cussed around my friends, got in fights after school, talked trash on the basketball court, threw snowballs at cars driving by, and shot spit wads through a straw to make them stick on the ceiling above the teacher's head. When I got my driver's license I drove fast, cranked up the rock music, and didn't let anyone cut in front of me.

Gut Types

Anger

Anger is the first of four big hurts that affect your personality, with the others being shame, anxiety, and sadness. It's also the main emotion and energy that forms the Enneagram Gut types—Eights, Nines, and Ones. Whatever your personality type, you deal with anger issues through your wing, stress line, or growth line, or in another way. It's especially in the Gut (or Body) center that we suffer from the cycle of anger (see figure 2.1).

Anger is a gut reaction to stress, sin (our own or that of others), or personal weakness. It hurts people, even ourselves, so we defend against it by taking control. It can foster an unhealthy identity of "I am what I do." Angry words, attitudes, and actions are often sinful. Sin is very misunderstood. It's commonly thought to be

Figure 2.1

Cycle of Anger

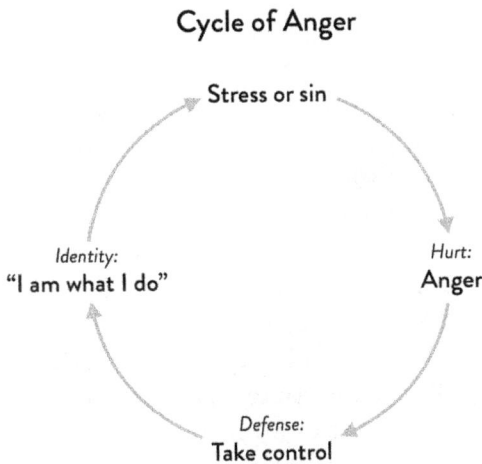

bad things people do, but the real problem of sin is *not trusting God's loving presence.* "For whatever does not proceed from faith is sin" (Rom. 14:23 ESV). At times, probably we all get influenced by anger to distrust God but don't realize it because of our defense mechanisms that operate unconsciously.

Gut anger is expressed by asserting boundaries outwardly or inwardly in order to be free, not controlled by anyone or anything. Enneagram experts Don Riso and Russ Hudson describe the attitude of strong-willed Gut types as, "Stay away from me so I can have my own space! I want and need to be independent."[2] Each of the three Gut types that we'll unpack over the next three chapters gets trapped in their own personality pattern that's shaped by anger:

Eights deny and act out anger by challenging and leading people.

Nines numb anger with peacemaking to harmonize with others.

Ones replace anger with improving things to try to do what is right.

Gut Intelligence

God designed our Gut as an intelligence center that complements our Heart and Head intelligence centers. To be healthy and holy we need to learn to draw on each of these three ways of knowing and interacting with reality.

In most situations Gut types have an uncanny instinct. In their bones they know what needs to be done, and in their adrenal glands and muscles they are determined to make it happen *now*. They shoot from the hip. As a Gut type, I (Bill) tell our staff, "We learn by doing." Prayer and strategy get us started, but then we start the work, collaborate as we go, analyze our results, adapt our approach, and try again. But if your gut instincts are fueled by anger, then acting quickly will be reckless and unloving (Prov. 29:11; Eph. 4:26–31). Gut intelligence is undermined by unhealthy anger that's denied or acted out.

Understanding Anger

In Jesus' Sermon on the Mount (Matt. 5–7), 28 percent of the verses deal with anger and related struggles with contempt, verbal degradation, conflicts in relationship, unforgiveness, and judging people.[3] Jesus, our Savior, is a master psychologist who understands the dynamics and dangers of anger. If you reflect on your personal history with conflict, sin, and pain, you'll see that more often than not anger was involved, whether it was your own anger or another person's. That's why Jesus taught so much on how to deal with anger.

What is anger? You likely know how anger feels, but you may be murky on its definition. Dallas Willard explains, "Anger is a spontaneous response that has a vital function in life. . . . It is a *feeling* that seizes us in our body and immediately impels us toward interfering with, and possibly even harming, those who have thwarted our will and interfered with our life."[4] It's natural to feel angry when your will is crossed, you get hurt by someone, or you're afraid that you won't get what you want. Anger is a *feeling* of being wronged and it's an *energy* that moves you to assert your will to right the wrong or get what you want.

Jesus emphasized the danger of anger leading to contempt, which is extremely harmful. Contempt is "a kind of studied degradation of another. . . . It is never justifiable or good."[5] Common expressions of contempt toward people include name-calling, disgust, judging, exclusion, and pushing away. Contempt dehumanizes people, marginalizes them, and disdains the image of God that they are created in.

Denying anger and related emotions will limit your success in life, and it will eventually cause pain for you and your loved ones. Daniel Goleman's groundbreaking research identified emotional intelligence (EQ) as a crucial factor in healthy relationships and work effectiveness. Increasing EQ begins with self-awareness of our emotions.[6] Most of us need a lot of help with learning the language of emotions. In a large research study, Brené Brown (One) found that out of eighty-seven human emotions, most people could identify feeling only *three* of them—happy, sad, and angry.[7] That's a crippling lack of self-awareness.

In an analysis of other studies on emotion, Brené concluded that anger is often a secondary emotion that hides behind deeper emotions—*nineteen* of them! Underneath anger may lurk emotions like shame, guilt, depression, fear, anxiety, hurt, grief, isolation, rejection, helplessness, jealousy, confusion, and sadness.[8] That's a flood of emotions that rise in conflict, disappointment, or stress.

To be healthier and more like Jesus requires understanding and caring for your angry emotions, which have many nuanced variations. Learning the language of stormy emotions is essential to giving and receiving empathy, which promotes effective self-control, conflict resolution, intimate relationships, emotional health, and compassion. The following list names feeling words (or idioms) for anger.[9]

Feeling Words for Anger

Emotions: offended, irritated, frustrated, annoyed, irked, cranky, grumpy, crabby, disgusted, envious, resentful, bitter, rancor, provoked, mad, indignant, riled, heated, seething, fuming, furious, ferocious, enraged, infuriated, irate, livid, mean, contemptful, hateful

Idioms: chip on the shoulder, having a short fuse, doing a slow burn, driven up a wall, bent out of shape, boiling, steaming, storming, have a bone to pick, up in arms, ticked off, pissed off, blustery, fit to be tied, raving mad, going ape, mad as a hornet, flying off the handle, blowing a gasket, throwing a fit, screaming bloody murder, going ballistic

Hebrew idioms: having a red-hot neck,[10] snorting like a bull,[11] a mama bear protecting her cubs,[12] raging fire,[13] a river overflowing its banks[14]

Idioms are word pictures that are especially effective to use in your self-expression and empathy for others. This is because they more clearly depict the physical, concrete nature of emotions like anger. The ancient Hebrews knew that anger and other emotions are not just feelings with related thoughts—they're *embodied*. Before you have a conscious feeling or thought that you're angry, it'll be in your body in some way, maybe as a frown, red face, narrowed eyes, clenched teeth, fisted hands, heat in your neck, rapid heartbeat, churning stomach, surge in blood pressure, bulging veins, tightened muscles, raised voice, or aggressive physical movements.

Paul knew this too. He located anger, and all our emotions and desires, in our *bellies* (Phil. 3:19). Surprisingly, Jesus insisted that Holy Spirit resides in the bellies of his followers and surges up like a geyser of living water (see John 7:38–39 KJV). It's amazing to realize that God has created us so that the Spirit of Jesus flows in and out from our soft, vulnerable, and emotional belly. This signifies a much closer connection between our emotions and spirituality than most Christians think. That's why we've themed our Soul

Shepherding Instagram account as "Following Jesus with feelings and faith." We list feelings first, not because they're most important but because developmentally they come first in human experience.

Is It Good to Get Angry?

It's often taught that we need to distinguish between "righteous anger" and "unrighteous anger." How would you define the difference? Are you able to recognize unrighteous anger in yourself and stop it?

The danger with human anger is that most of the time when people get angry, they feel convinced that their anger is righteous, not unrighteous. This emboldens them to escalate their anger and act on it to right the wrong that was done to them or others—*and they even put God on their side against others.* That faulty, prideful logic is a main reason for the atrocities of murder and war, as well as common disrespect like judging or excluding people. For instance, when James and John felt that some Samaritans were persecuting them because they were Jews, they wanted to call down thunder from heaven on them, but Jesus corrected the two brothers for their unloving anger (Luke 9:54–55). Later, in a playful way, he would nickname them the "Sons of Thunder" (Mark 3:17).

James (the half brother of Jesus) explicitly warns us, "Everyone should be quick to listen, slow to speak and slow to become angry, because human anger does not produce the righteousness that God desires" (James 1:19–20). Paul cuts to the chase: "But now, set them all aside—anger, rage, malice, slander, and foul language out of your mouth" (Col. 3:8 TLV). He warns that if we feel righteous about our anger, hold on to it, and stir it up, then we "give the devil a foothold" to harm ourselves and the people we're angry at (Eph. 4:26–27). Anger readily dishonors God and harms others because "our motives for anger are seldom pure and untainted by selfishness."[15] This is why Evagrius identified anger as one of the deadly sins and urged us not to feed this barking dog that is ready to attack people.[16]

The problem of anger is illustrated by a bitter, vengeful dispute between an auto shop employee and his boss (one or both are likely Eights, the type most prone to meting out revenge). When the employee suddenly quit his job and requested his final paycheck of $915 in wages owed, the boss dragged his feet on payment because he was mad at him for leaving him in the lurch. The former employee kept demanding payment, so finally the boss got revenge by dumping 91,500 greasy pennies on his driveway! The former employee then upped the ante to get his own revenge by posting the company's injustice on Instagram. Finally, the US Department of Labor got involved, determined that the fault lay with the employer, and filed a lawsuit against his company for retaliation.[17] That's a crazy case of "Ego-Venge"![18]

Human anger by itself is unrighteous anger that harms people. However, if our anger is governed by God's love and wisdom, then it becomes righteous (see chapter 6). That means slowing down to feel your angry emotions, trusting the mercy and compassion of Christ for you and the person(s) you're angry at, and then setting healthy boundaries.

Anger and Healthy Boundaries

The emotion of anger best serves us and others when we treat it like a headache alerting us to a personal problem needing attention. When your alarm of anger sounds, it often means your boundaries have been crossed and you need to establish personal limits. For instance, you're likely to feel angry when your will has been thwarted or you feel there's been an injustice that hurt you or someone you care about.[19] We all need clear boundaries that define our self-identity, which includes our needs, feelings, beliefs, morals, values, opinions, and abilities. When you own these aspects of your personality and verbalize them to others, it can help you to be known, loved, and respected.

Christian psychologists Henry Cloud and John Townsend teach that personal boundaries are what enable you to say yes to what is good and no to what is bad (Matt. 5:37). When your boundaries are healthy, they are like doors, not walls. You open the door to let in good things like nurture and truth, and you close the door to keep out bad things like disrespect and deceit. When sin or pain gets through the door to your soul, you don't let it stay there but confess the truth to God and others in order to heal (James 5:16; 1 John 1:9).[20] When your anger alarm goes off in a relationship, often the healthy response is to speak the truth in love (Eph. 4:15). To respond to your anger wisely and lovingly, it's important to *think and feel about your anger before you act.*

As therapists we have worked with hundreds of people who were impaired in their ability to feel their anger and respond to it. Many were in enmeshed, codependent relationships. Their boundaries were weak, diffuse, unclear, or insecure, and they were unable to consistently speak the truth in love or act with wisdom and courage. Perhaps as children they were judged, reprimanded, punished, moralized, rejected, or simply ignored when they expressed anger. For a child to express anger and not receive empathy sends them careening into a black hole, empty of the loving attachment they need. That child quickly learns to habitually and unconsciously divert from anger into shame, fear, people-pleasing, sarcastic humor, attention-getting rebellion, passive-aggressive behavior, provoking others, drinking alcohol, or zoning out in media. (Later chapters will explore how anger can contribute to shame, anxiety, and sadness.)

In cases like child abuse, trauma, or getting stuck in a toxic relationship, you may not be able to immediately implement the Bible's teaching, "Do not let the sun go down while you are still angry" (Eph. 4:26). Perhaps by the time you learn about the sundown warning, the sun has already gone down on your anger for months or years. Denying anger and other negative emotions is a common coping mechanism to get through pain or stress overload. It's easy to see that God's grace extends to children, the abused, trauma survivors, and others who were vulnerable and emotionally mistreated. If that's you, the initial treatment is *not* to set aside anger. Instead, you need to receive the permission that comes right before the sundown warning: "Be angry and do not sin" (Eph. 4:26 ESV). You need to feel your anger, pray about it, and confess it to a spiritual director or friend so it doesn't damage you or someone else. Then you can learn what to do with your anger (see the next four chapters).

Scriptures for Anger

"ADONAI is gracious and compassionate, slow to anger and great in lovingkindness." (Ps. 145:8 TLV)[21]

"But I tell you that anyone who is angry with a brother or sister will be subject to judgment." (Matt. 5:22)

"Understand this, my dear brothers and sisters: You must all be quick to listen, slow to speak, and slow to get angry. Human anger does not produce the righteousness God desires." (James 1:19–20 NLT)

"Complain if you must, but don't lash out. Keep your mouth shut, and let your heart do the talking. Build your case before God and wait for his verdict." (Ps. 4:4–5 MSG)

"A gentle response defuses anger, but a sharp tongue kindles a temper-fire." (Prov. 15:1 MSG)

· · · · · · · · · · · · · · · · SOUL TALK · · · · · · · · · · · · · ·

1. What did you learn about Gut types and anger?
2. Which feeling words for anger do you relate to personally (or for a loved one)?
3. How would you describe the difference between righteous anger and unrighteous anger?
4. What has your experience of anger been like—either your own anger or that of others?
5. Which Scripture for anger is especially helpful for you? Why?

Keys to Healthy Boundaries

1. Be clear and direct with your limits by saying yes or no (Matt. 5:37).

2. Ask for what you want and need (Matt. 7:7–8).

3. Serve Christ rather than pleasing or rescuing people (Gal. 1:10; 6:4).

4. Forgive so you don't get bitter and miss God's grace (Heb. 12:15).

5. Speak the truth in a loving way, including with anger (Eph. 4:15, 25–27).

Type Eight: Challenger

	FELT NEED: Act with power
	KEY TRAITS: powerful, self-confident, action-oriented, truth-telling, confrontational, control-seeking

I strenuously contend with all the energy Christ so powerfully works in me.

Colossians 1:29

Fritz Perls was a psychiatrist-therapist who was an Eight, which is an uncommon Enneagram type for a therapist. In the 1940s, he and his wife, Laura, pioneered Gestalt therapy, which has helped countless people to this day. This school of therapy force-fully challenges clients to become aware of their bodily emotions and behaviors in order to improve their psychological health. Perls did this with relentless confrontation and rigorous accountability. Sometimes he even did role-plays with clients, where he was the opposition and goaded them into fighting back.

Perls' signature technique was to point-blank demand that clients stay in the here and now rather than escaping into the past or future. He treated their "unfinished business" of being stuck in emotions such as repressed grief by intensely observing their body language and confronting how this contradicted their verbal statements. His resolute, directive techniques were designed to get them to listen to their unconscious body and be accountable to speak its truth. For instance, Perls would draw attention to a client's frown, tapping foot, wringing hands, or slumped shoulders, and he would challenge them to exaggerate their bodily gesture and give it a voice. For example, "I'm a rapidly tapping foot because I want to hurry and be done with talking about my mother." Similarly, he pushed his clients to locate the emotion in their body and use physical language to describe how they felt. For example, "My heart hurts," "My stomach feels sick," or "My chest is tight."[1]

Taking Charge

One survey found that only 6 percent of people are Eights.[2] If you are not an Eight, you may still relate through having an Eight wing, stress line, or growth line. Or you may be a One-to-One subtype that has some Eight characteristics.[3] The focus of the Eight personality is on having power and control. They're the type that's most likely to take charge and lead others. They're driven for big influence and bottom-line results, which they achieve through passionate vision, strategic thinking, and delegating responsibilities to others. They act boldly, work hard, bend rules, and strong-arm to get their way.

An Eight Christian leader who met with me (Bill) for therapy wanted me to be more like Fritz Perls. "You remind me of Mr. Rogers in his cardigan sweater," he challenged. "You're too nice and deferential. I don't need your empathy—just shoot straight and give me your advice." Eights want the truth and are ready to spar over it. But therapy is not war; you can't use General Patton's (Eight) approach that says a violent execution is acceptable as long as it's a good plan.[4] I've found that Eights and others who tell me they just want my advice, not my empathy, especially need empathy, but they also need direct feedback.

An Eight CEO who was known for high turnover in his staff quipped, "The one who creates the chaos is in control." Until I challenged his leadership style, he didn't realize how much his brokenness and disruptive anger were hurting people. Thankfully, he humbled himself, grew in self-awareness, and became more considerate and caring for his staff, which made his company more successful.

Eights get a bad rap that's often unfair. An Eight's truth-telling, loud voice, big presence, slaps on the back, power moves, and angry challenges are usually not mean. That's their *energy*. Eights are truth tellers and deal with problems head-on, and that's what they want from other people. An Eight megachurch pastor told me, "I'm a nice Eight." I found that to be true. Even when he came across as critical or controlling, that was not his intention. The wife of an Eight commented, "My husband is not a jerk. *Really.* He's actually compassionate if you get to know him."

One day a friend of mine who is an Eight told me, "When I was praying for you, the Lord impressed on me that I need to listen to you like a spiritual director." He's been exceptionally empathetic and supportive to me. (He's the social subtype of the Eight, which is the countertype and can get mistyped with the Three.) People who trust the loving leadership of an Eight can experience tremendous advocacy, protection, encouragement, generosity, and compassion. Martin Luther King Jr. (Eight) is a great example. He led the Civil Rights Movement in America by using Jesus' teachings on confronting racial injustice with nonviolent love.

When I was seeking to get licensed as a psychologist almost thirty years ago, I hired an Eight psychologist who was cut from the same cloth as Fritz Perls to coach me, which is what I needed. His nickname was "Grizzly," and with his huge size, gray beard, and deep voice, he looked the part. I paid him a pretty penny to conduct eight mock oral interviews with me in which he asked probing questions and offered critical feedback. Each meeting felt like being emotionally beat up—*twice*: once in his office and again when I watched the video at home. But his direct feedback toughened my skin, sharpened my skills, and enabled me to pass the exam.

Personality Development of Eights

Family Formation: Fighter

In their families of origin, Eights tend to take on the role of a *fighter*. According to Beatrice Chestnut, a psychologist and Enneagram specialist, "Many Eights report having grown up in combative or conflict-heavy environments in which they had to grow up fast to survive. Most were unable to maintain a sense of childlike innocence because they were either deprived or not sufficiently protected as children."[5] It was not safe for them to be a child with needs, emotions, or weakness, so they deny any vulnerability. There may be a scared child on the inside, but they put out a bold front, making themselves big with confidence or aggression—even if they're physically small. When asked how she felt, one Eight retorted, "Don't ask me what I feel! Ask me what I think." When Eights are rejected, betrayed, or violated, they steel themselves: "I don't need them anyway. I'm not going to let anyone tell me what to do. I can take care of myself!"

Fritz Perls' story from his diaries illustrates how an Eight becomes a fighter. For most of Fritz's childhood, his father was absent, and when he was present, he bullied and ridiculed Fritz. Fritz carried his anger into school, where he got in fights and was expelled. As an adult, he viewed his father as a hypocrite and would not even attend his funeral.[6] His aggressive manner was imported into his approach to therapy. Although many clients were helped, others reported that he was disrespectful or lost his temper with them.[7]

Root Sin: Lust for Power

Eights get malformed by their lust for power and control. A summary of Enneagram research studies found that in every study Eights were negatively correlated with agreeableness.[8] Their shadow self keeps stoking an inner fire of intensity to give them power over others. Eights incite themselves to feel alive through adrenaline, anger, challenges, debates, fights, overworking, risk-taking, hurrying, sex, physical contact, stress, loud music, sports, or spicy foods. But their unconscious lust to be the top dog can shut down their deep soul needs. Unwittingly, they may set a trap for themselves. If they choose power over others rather than vulnerability with others (the Eight's virtue), it causes them to miss out on the care and grace they need to be truly alive.

Defense Mechanism: Denial

Eights don't want to let anyone hurt or control them, so they take charge and call the shots. They power up with boldness or angry reactions to protect themselves from being exposed. But under the surface they are unconsciously denying their vulnerable emotions, needs, and weaknesses. That denied emotion can erupt later in angry words and behaviors. Additionally, as Fritz Perls did in his role as a therapist, Eights may unconsciously project their own denied needs onto other people so they can be in the powerful position of helping or protecting someone who is weak.

Emotions of Eights

Core Emotion: Anger

Blair, an Eight, had a personality like a bull in a china shop that nearly wrecked her career as a CEO.[9] She told me (Kristi) that her board chair took her through the hallways of their company and told her, "I want to show you the damage you've caused." Blair was shocked, "What do you mean? Look at all the money I've made you." The board chair explained, "Yes, but your operations manager had panic attacks whenever he saw a phone call coming in from you. Your VP of sales got divorced because she was working seventy hours a week to meet your expectations. The chair for your IT director is empty because you burned him out."

In a room, Eights make their presence prominent so others have to deal with them. Just being in a room with an Eight you can often feel the force field of intense energy that radiates from their bodies. People are often intimidated by their loud opinions, strong boundaries, and high expectations that can be like a bulldozer. To be great leaders, Eights like Blair need to restrain their snorting-bull anger that can intimidate and bulldoze people. To not act out anger requires not letting it boil in their body but feeling it, owning it, confessing it to a friend, and getting help to manage it. When the anger energy of an Eight is governed by compassion (integrating at the healthy Two), Eights can be a great force for good.

Stress Emotion: Anxiety

A survey of 19,000 Enneagram test-takers found that, while most people's performance is hindered by stress, Eights become *more* active and productive under stress (which is also the case for Ones and Threes). The same survey found that Eights under stress identify with fewer emotions than any other type.[10] Somebody has to lead the group, and Eights believe it should be them, so they gut-act with decisiveness. They push their agendas, overwork, and fight endless battles with people till they've exhausted themselves. At some point they may slide into the gutter of their stress line to an unhealthy Five. That's the chink in their armor of self-confidence.

To understand an Eight you need to see the anxious, fearful Five that's hidden inside their personality. They especially fear anyone having power or control over them in any way—social, organizational, financial, sexual, or emotional. When Eights are overstressed, feel threatened, or experience a big setback, they may go into their Five stealth mode of retreating into "a bunker where they take shelter . . . to protect themselves through withdrawal in a remote place of safety where they can regroup."[11] In their bunker they gather more data to win at their work, day-trade stocks to get more money, binge on movies to escape, or get lost in a book.

Additional Emotion: Shame

Red-blooded Eights who are dominated by lust for power or sex can be *shameless* in their readiness to get what they want, even if it happens to disrespect someone's dignity.[12] Normally, if they react in anger or do something hurtful, they unconsciously convert their feelings of guilt or shame into more anger directed at either someone else or their circumstance. However, when they've harmed someone who depended on them or failed in a big way, they may feel guilt and shame. As Eights expand their personality by integrating with a healthy Two that's considerate and caring toward others, they learn to feel healthy conviction or sadness when they've hurt someone or not fulfilled a responsibility.

Underlying Sadness

Of all types, it's the hardest for Eights to accept that they have soft emotions like sadness. (This is also true of the One-to-One subtypes.) They need to do the inner work of incorporating the Heart-type feeling and compassion of a healthy Two, which is their growth line. Increased self-awareness and softness are especially important for Eights to learn how to handle their aggressive energy wisely and kindly. In Blair's case, she got help from an executive coach and a friend at church. She slowed down and learned to get underneath her anger and anxiety to feel sad about the pain she'd caused others and herself. This opened her to deeper relational engagements and becoming more considerate of her staff.

Emotional Alarm: Toughening Up

To grow in health and character, Eights need to learn to catch themselves in the act of getting tough when challenged. That may look like denying their needs and emotions, going into fight mode, or retreating to gather more resources. When their "be tough" alarm sounds, they instead need to feel their anger or fear and admit this to God and a true friend. True courage includes being vulnerable to ask a trusted and capable friend for empathy. If you're an Eight, that's how you can know that you are a "beloved Eight."[13]

Empathy for Beloved Eights

You want people to be direct and speak the truth with you.

Injustice makes you angry, especially when it affects someone you care for.

You feel you have to be strong to protect yourself and others.

You feel you have to hide any weakness, fear, or self-doubt.

You don't want to be controlled or allow others to have power over you.

Sometimes you feel the heavy weight of so many people depending on you.

It's frustrating when people keep talking about what to do rather than doing it.

Jesus as the Model Eight

Jesus Is Valiant and Vulnerable

Jesus was valiant and fiercely loving, like the ultimate Eight. Mother Teresa (Eight) remarked, "[Jesus] can be very demanding."[14] That view flies in the face of a common misconception of Jesus being like Caspar Milquetoast, the nice, wispy man from H. T. Webster's classic comic strip, who spoke softly and kept getting hit with a big stick.[15] King Jesus had the most power, and he used it to be tender with the weak and protect them from religious abuse. That's the true portrayal of him as "gentle and lowly in heart" (Matt. 11:29 NKJV). The tenderness from strength that he provides for us is what his Abba provided for him when he was weak and in need (Mark 1:12–13; 14:36; Luke 22:41–43).

Father Robert Nogosek wrote, "We will never understand the prophetic stance of Jesus unless we see his willingness to be *vulnerable*."[16] As a case in point, look at Jesus when a group of Pharisee legalists grabbed an adulterous woman and threw her to the ground at his feet (John 8:1–11 TLB). With rocks raised, they

45

railed, "Moses' law says to kill her. What about it?" (v. 5). She lay in the dirt, trembling, weeping, and clinging to a bedsheet covering her nakedness. Jesus knew they were using her to bait him into contradicting the law. Immediately, he stepped between her and the religious bullies, kneeled down, and remained quiet. They kept demanding an answer. Finally, Jesus straightened up and shot back, "All right, hurl the stones at her until she dies. But only he who never sinned may throw the first!" (v. 7). Then he kneeled beside her again, shielding her from the thugs. One by one, they dropped their stones and walked away. Then Jesus gave her mercy and urged her to live a pure life.[17]

▶ **PRAYER:** *Jesus, soften my heart to be vulnerable to trustworthy people, as unto you.*

Virtue to Cultivate: Mercy

Mother Teresa (Eight) illustrates for us the virtue of mercy, which is the key for Eights (and helpful for all of us) to become more like Jesus. Merciful Eights use their power to give compassion, kindness, protection, and empowerment to others. One day, Mother Teresa found a man near death from cancer on the streets of Calcutta, India. In her home for the dying, she washed him tenderly and the man muttered, "How can you stand my body's stench?" Her kindness continued. After several minutes he looked into her eyes and said, "Glory to you, woman." Mother Teresa looked back and replied, "No. Glory to you who suffer with Christ." Then they smiled at each other. He died with love and dignity in the arms of Jesus.[18]

All Mother Teresa wanted to do was to love the poorest of the poor, one at a time, in Jesus' name. She and her team of social workers, teachers, nurses, and doctors were serving Jesus among the "the least" (Matt. 25:37–40). In her words, "We are not here for the work, we are here for Jesus. All we do is for Him. We nurse Him, feed Him, clothe Him, visit Him, comfort Him in the poor, the abandoned, the sick, the orphans, the dying. But all we do, our prayer, our work, our suffering is for Jesus."[19] She called herself "a

Jesus as a Healthy Eight

The Son of God set aside his divine privileges to become human for us (Phil. 2:6–7).

A mob was pushing Jesus off a cliff, but he cut right through them (Luke 4:28–30).

He spoke with authority from living the truths he taught (Matt. 7:28–29 MSG).

Jesus "shot back" to defend the need of an arthritic woman for healing (Luke 13:15 MSG).

The Lord of all gladly stooped low to wash his disciples' feet (John 13:1–17).

Attacked by a band of soldiers, Jesus trusted God, not Peter's sword (Matt. 26:52–56).

Struck in the face by a temple guard, Jesus spoke the truth in love (John 18:22–23).

pencil in God's hands"[20] so he could write love notes for the poor. Her mission was to keep spreading smiles and kindness for Jesus and his poor and do it in secret, without any attention on her.

We might never have known about Mother Teresa if it weren't for Malcolm Muggeridge's 1971 biography and film that introduced her to the world. Then the Holy Spirit exploded her mission to over five thousand sisters and thousands more lay workers, serving millions of people every year in centers located in over one hundred countries. She was just five feet tall, but her large Eight personality was expressed in her feisty leadership, raising the bar on social justice, tireless ministry, and irrepressible positivity. She overcame the Eight's root sin of lust for power through spiritual practices like silent prayer, obedience to God, and being emotionally vulnerable with her spiritual directors. In her little acts of care and kindness (like a healthy Two), she shows us the Eight's virtue of mercy.

In 2007 her private letters to her spiritual directors were published as *Mother Teresa: Come Be My Light.*[21] In letter after letter, she cries out to Jesus because she can't feel from him the smile and touch of God's love. Yet, she accepts her spiritual darkness as an opportunity to smile with love for her Lord and his poor.

Key Soul Care Practice: Spiritual Friendship

The key personal discipline for Eights to grow in Christlikeness is being emotionally honest with a spiritual friend or guide. This includes confessing stressors, struggles, and sins and asking for prayer. Being vulnerable is the last thing an Eight wants to do, but it's what they need to root out lust for power from their soul. Mother Teresa's vulnerable, gut-honest sharing facilitated her becoming a healthy, holy Eight marked by Jesus' virtue of tenderhearted mercy.

Deborah, the Old Testament judge, is another Eight who has inspired me (Kristi). At a time when people were doing whatever they wanted, she sat under a solitary palm tree in the hill country and served as a spiritual mother and counselor for her people. Then she roused her nation to fight for freedom from oppression. Her motto for her army was, "March on, my soul; be strong!" (Judg. 5:21). Against all odds, Deborah led a revolt with 10,000 men to stand against an enemy army numbering 100,000 men and 900 iron chariots. She encouraged Israel's army to put their faith in the Lord, and the Lord poured down rain from heaven (Judges 4)! She wrote a poetic praise song of victory that she and Barak sang as a duet for the nation. Then the Lord ushered in forty years of peace for Israel (Judg. 4–5).[22]

Eights who are healthy and truly powerful develop gentle and tender feelings for Jesus, others, and their own self.

Soul Care Practices for Eights

Regularly meet with a friend to give and receive listening and encouragement.

Shout Deborah's (Eight) motto to yourself: "March on, my soul; be strong!" (Judg. 5:21).

Dare to be vulnerable with a friend. Take courage from Mother Teresa's exhortation: "We should not be ashamed of loving Jesus with our emotions."[23]

Today extend mercy to someone who is hurting by offering forgiveness, a secret prayer of blessing, or a kind note.

Read *Scenes in the Life of Harriet Tubman* or watch the movie *Harriet*. By listening to God, Harriet Tubman (Eight) escaped slavery and freed hundreds of other slaves.

Let go of control. In a stressful situation, pray, "Father, into your hands I commit _____" (Luke 23:46).[24]

SOUL TALK

1. What did you learn about Eights and how they deal with anger?
2. What is an example of a situation that tempts you to lust for power?
3. What do you admire about Jesus as the model Eight? What can you do to be more like him?
4. What can you do to apply Deborah's story of leadership in your life today?
5. Which of the soul care practices for Eights seem most helpful for you personally? Why?

How Eights Become Like Jesus

CHALLENGER

1. Meditate on Jesus using his power to be tender to the weak (like a healthy Two).

2. Repent of lusting for power (root sin). Rely on Jesus to be governed by love, not anger.

3. Pray to not react to stress with greed for resources (like an unhealthy Five).

4. Ask for empathy from a friend when you feel angry or controlled by someone.

5. Rely on Jesus to help you give mercy (virtue) to others.

Type Nine: Peacemaker

FELT NEED: Act to avoid conflict

KEY TRAITS: inclusive, optimistic, reassuring, slow to start, go with the flow, merging, acquiescing

> Let the peace of Christ keep you in tune with each other, in step with each other.
>
> Colossians 3:15 MSG

The Russian novel *Oblomov* gives a poignant caricature of a Nine. The story centers on Ilya Ilyich Oblomov (meaning "sloth"), a young nobleman who sleeps the day away, rarely leaves his room, and avoids making decisions. *More than two hundred pages go by and Oblomov hardly even gets out of bed!* He will not leave his bedroom, even when he receives a letter from the manager of his estate pleading with him to come home and deal with financial problems. Instead, he goes to sleep and has a happy dream about going on vacation with his family and not needing to work. When he awakes, he conducts all his daily business right from his bed by communicating with his site manager. Later, his friend Stoltz is finally able to pull Oblomov into the social life of the town, and he has to learn to assert his personal boundaries with people. In the end, Oblomov marries his motherly landlady, they have a son, and their family enjoys the routines of life in their village, which center on the church.[1]

Getting on a Roll

In a large survey, Nines were the most common Enneagram type, tied with Sixes.[2] They are the pure Gut type on the Enneagram, in the center of the triad, so they are most defined by unconscious anger and a felt need for control and autonomy. But Nines appear to be the opposite of controlling.

As Oblomov's story illustrates, it's difficult for Nines to initiate, disagree, or be assertive. One research study on the Enneagram showed that Nines are the most agreeable type.[3] For instance, ask a Nine, "Where do you want to go for lunch?" The Nine might reply with a shrug, "Meh." That's an old Yiddish word that has become a colloquial expression of indifference or going along to get along.[4] *Meh* is like saying, "I can be happy with whatever you want."

Nines like to "swim with the current."[5] They don't want to rock the boat—they avoid conflicts and expressing anger because *they are afraid to lose connection with people they care about.* Nines want an easy, pleasant time with people who are happy to be together. When they have something hard they have to do, they may need extra support and encouragement to get up their gumption. Other people may feel that Nines need prodding, but that can mobilize their resistance because Nines want to be in charge of their own life. They get their energy from collaborating with people who are supportive and affirming.

Nines like Oblomov may need more sleep than most people. (The Social subtype, which is the countertype Nine, is more energetic, like a Three.) Maybe that's why Ryan O'Neal (Nine) named his Christian band Sleeping at Last. Similarly, a pastor smiled at his Nine wife (many pastors' wives are Nines) and joked that she was like Winnie the Pooh—except the rumbling in her tummy was not for "hunny," it was for a nap! He was being sweet and playful, but we need to be careful not to judge Nines for sleeping or having lower energy—that can be hurtful to them.

I (Bill) *never* took naps and thought they were a sign of laziness, till I learned how to really rest when Kristi and I took our first sabbatical in our early fifties. Now we like to say, "Jesus took naps!" (see Mark 4:38). Nines appreciate the need for sleep that we all have. Christian psychologist Archibald Hart recommends we all get eight or nine hours of sleep in order to not overuse our adrenal glands and suffer from stress disease.[6] Many studies have reported the health benefits of getting enough sleep and taking naps, something farmers have known by experience for thousands of years. To this day in Spain, many people take a break early in the afternoon, enjoy a leisurely meal with loved ones, and take a nap (siesta) so they can return to work fresh.[7] That's perfect for Nines. They also like to relax and hang out at home with family or friends, get cozy and comfy, and even fall asleep on the couch!

Some people mistakenly think Nines are lazy, but that's usually not true. While Nines can be slow to get their gears going, once they get on a roll they are very industrious and competent. In fact, many of the best leaders in the world, including a high percentage of US presidents, have been Nines. Healthy peacemaker types tune in to people's needs, listen with empathy, smooth out tensions in relationships, bring deep insight, see the good in everyone, work hard, care deeply about doing excellent work, champion the needs of others, minister God's love and peace, and unite people around a common good. Read over that long list of loving traits again and consider how much energy Nines put out, which is why they need their rest!

At the heart of the Nine's strengths is the biblical ideal to "live in harmony with one another" (Rom. 12:16). We've found that Nines are the ideal type to serve as spiritual directors, which is surely why we have more Nines than any other type earning a certificate in spiritual direction from our Soul Shepherding Institute.[8]

Personality Development of Nines

Family Formation: Lost Child or Peacemaker

In their families growing up, Nines often found themselves in the role of the *lost child*. Feeling bonded in their primary relationships is so important to them that they may discount (or even forget) their own needs and desires as they continually accommodate to their parent(s) and others. They have a pleasant, easygoing nature and don't want to cause anyone stress. Their positive views of their loved ones and happy memories help them to draw strength from those relationships. However, their agreeable and reassuring nature can leave them sitting on the sidelines or feeling forgotten in the background.

Family dynamics and other relationships may also have played a part in Nines becoming a lost child. They may have acquiesced to a controlling parent or sibling, shut down to endure trauma or conflict, felt overlooked in a large or busy family, or held back their own needs because of a family member's problems, illness, or special needs. A common way the lost child role plays out is to be a *peacemaker* for others who are stressed or to mediate in conflicts.

Root Sin: Lethargy

The Achilles' heel for Nines is lethargy. Like Oblomov in his immature years, Nines are prone to *fall asleep to themselves*. In their shadow self they avoid difficult things or go on autopilot. It's like they're driving with their right blinker on for a long time before they finally turn. Their difficulty is with self-activation, which is a spiritual and psychological inertia in which they don't know what they feel or want so they hold themselves back.

When the Lord called the prophet Jonah (Nine) to preach salvation to the Ninevites, Israel's enemies, he avoided it. In fact, he boarded a ship going in the opposite direction. He was angry, but he denied it. A terrible storm arose, and Jonah was so depressed that he told the captain to throw him overboard. When the captain tossed Jonah into the raging sea, the storm calmed and God sent a huge fish to swallow Jonah, swim to Nineveh, and spit him out on dry ground!

Finally, the reluctant prophet obeyed God and walked through the city streets preaching the need for everyone to confess their sins and ask the sovereign God for mercy. But when his enemies did this and received God's forgiveness and blessing, Jonah again became depressed and lethargic. He lay down under a plant in the desert and waited to die. Then God showed Jonah his problems with repressed anger and lethargy (Jon. 4). Psychologist Abraham Maslow identified a "Jonah syndrome" in all of us, in which we fear our own greatness and evade a full life.[9]

Defense Mechanism: Emotional Numbing

Nines numb their disquieting emotions like the lotus-eaters in Homer's *Odyssey* who keep eating the flowering lotus plant that makes them pleasant and calm, but the price they pay is increasingly *deadened feelings and desires*.[10] Eventually, they may fall asleep to their true self and to the opportunities for good that lie before them. Yet, Nines can be like the duck that looks to be peacefully swimming along the water while under the surface its legs are paddling furiously! To dissipate their stress and anger, Nines rely on the psychological defense mechanism of dissociation or emotional numbing. They can just turn off the lights on their distress. They zone out or escape into sleep, TV shows and movies, social media, alcohol, or comfort foods. They retreat to their "Inner Sanctum."[11]

Emotions of Nines

Core Emotion: Anger

Nines are typically pleasant, positive, and easygoing, so it may be hard to believe that their primary emotion is anger. Their assertive energy is buried in their bodies and shows as stubbornness. That somaticized anger is what creates their Oblomov-like sloth in which it's very difficult for them to self-activate. Jungian analyst

Margaret Keyes points out that Nines "want to control as much of their lives as possible. They prefer to stay hidden because what others expect of them is unclear."[12] They are the opposite of Eights in that they underexpress their anger. They avoid asserting their desires, disagreeing, saying no, or upsetting people because they don't want to disrupt their relational connections. But rather than letting the sun go down on their anger, which lets the devil stick his foot in the door to their soul (Eph. 4:26–27), healthy Nines verbalize their angry feelings respectfully by speaking the truth in love (Eph. 4:15), clearly saying no when they need to set a limit (Matt. 5:37), and proactively asking for what they need (Matt. 7:7–11).

Stress Emotion: Anxiety

Nines often present as easygoing and even-keeled. But when their problems mount, their defense mechanisms of internalizing conflict and numbing anger break down. They may start tumbling down their stress line to an unhealthy Six, facing a hornets' nest of worry, anxiety, and fear. As a Two, I (Kristi) relate to the Nine's pattern of repressing anger and pleasing others. The difference is that Twos avoid anger with a heart orientation of seeking acceptance and esteem from people, whereas Nines have a body orientation of merging with others to get energy. Another difference is that the main stress reaction for Twos is to get confrontational (like an unhealthy Eight), whereas Nines get anxious and fearful (like an unhealthy Six).

A church counselor named Jeremy (Nine) who attended our Soul Shepherding Institute shared his story:

> I really appreciate the way you drew me out. As a child I suffered with selective mutism and was anxious and scared to talk. There were only a few people in my life that I felt safe enough to talk to—I couldn't break through the wall of silence. Even after I overcame that, I still found myself getting shut down by intimidating personalities. The authentic and affirming community this week helped me feel safe to really open up. It was healing and empowering for me.

Jeremy's muzzled anger over being mistreated made him mute. His energy was like a dammed-up river. His repressed anger was causing a secondary emotion of anxiety (the Nine's stress line to an unhealthy Six). When Nines own their anger and process it with a spiritual director or friend who gives them empathy, this calms their anxiety and strengthens them so they can return to their peaceful self.

Additional Emotion: Shame

In words that have been widely attributed to spiritual psychologist Carl Jung (Nine), "Shame is a soul-eating emotion." That was the prophet Jonah's experience. His anger turned inward as self-hatred that motivated his disobedience to God and would've killed him in the raging sea if God had not sent a huge fish to swallow him. The book of Jonah ends with him finally getting emotionally honest in prayer, venting his anger at his enemies and at God for showing them mercy. Jonah sharing his story publicly shows that he probably worked through his shame and depression to act with love for God and all people.

Underlying Sadness

Placating people creates a pseudo-intimacy that leaves Nines empty of being loved for their true self. They need to admit they feel deep loss and sadness because *they want to be seen, heard, known, loved, and respected by others for the unique contributions they have to offer.* To get unlocked, they need to be emotionally honest with the Lord and with a friend. They need to take courage to bring their lost inner child into the light, asking for empathy and acceptance.

Emotional Alarm: Accommodating Others

The "wake-up call" for Nines so they don't lose their true self is catching themselves in the act of accommodating others.[13] They try to secure themselves by acquiescing to what others want, but *it's a trap.* In merging with someone else to feel connected, they

Empathy for Beloved Nines

You're feeling invisible in that group of friends.

You have some important things to say but don't feel confident to speak up.

You're tired of being nagged about this, but you don't want to fight.

You absorbed all your friend's hurt and stress and now you're exhausted.

For you it feels better not to talk about that conflict and just let it go.

Deep down you're angry about this issue.

That disagreement made you feel upset and anxious.

fall asleep to their own needs, desires, and opinions. Instead, they can set an alarm by developing a habit to notice their placating tendencies. As soon as this alarm sounds, they need to step away from other people and ask themselves, "What am I feeling? What do I want now?" This helps them to self-activate by setting a limit or asking for what they need. They especially need empathy that strengthens their true self. Then they can relate to others without getting lost or numb.

Jesus as the Model Nine

Jesus Is the Mighty Prince of Peace

The Prince of Peace (Isa. 9:6) is the perfect Nine we all need. In the garden of Gethsemane, Jesus teaches us how to be alert and activated in God's presence (Mark 14:32–42 MSG). From "a pit of suffocating darkness" he tells his friends, "I feel bad enough right now to die. Stay here and keep vigil with me" (vv. 33–34). Then he cries to his Papa for help. But when he looks back for his reinforcements, they've fallen asleep. He challenges Peter, "Stay alert, be in prayer, so you don't enter the danger zone without even knowing it. Don't be naive. Part of you is eager, ready for anything in God; but another part is as lazy as an old dog sleeping by the fire" (v. 38). But Peter and the others again fall asleep in prayer. In contrast, Jesus is vigorous in prayer because he has done his training, and his faith is in Papa God. In the garden, our mighty Prince of Peace goes to the cross spiritually, battling Satan, sweating drops of blood, and emerging victorious (Heb. 5:7).

We need to bring our lazy, old dog self to Jesus for dog training! He shapes and strengthens us to be soulfully awake and attentive to God. The way to begin is with what Richard Foster (Nine) calls "simple prayer." Jesus went to his Papa like a little child and bared his heart, and that's what he teaches us to do.[14] Simple prayer is not proper; it's real and raw. We share our needs and feelings. We complain. We confess our sins. We share whatever is going on. We say, "I love you."

> ▷ **PRAYER:** *Jesus, energize me to act with confidence in your Spirit with me.*

Jesus as a Healthy Nine

As a peacemaker in conflicts and trials, Jesus relied on God's peace (Matt. 5:9).[15]

Jesus did not acquiesce to pressure from enemies but set his limits (Mark 3:22–29).

Jesus' intimacy with the Father and listening to him kept him alert (John 8:28; 10:30).

Jesus was angry when children were mistreated and acted to protect them (Mark 10:14).

In trials, Jesus did not worry about what to say but trusted the Spirit to speak (Matt. 10:19–20).

Jesus' peace is powerful to overcome the troubles of this world (John 16:33).

Virtue to Cultivate: Self-Activation

A Nine wore a shirt with the slogan "Good energy is contagious." That expresses the virtue of self-activation, inspired by the Spirit of Jesus, that Nines most need to develop. John Woolman (Nine), a Quaker who lived in the mid-1800s, beautifully embodied this virtue, showing that we need the Holy Spirit, not our own self, to activate us. Woolman owned a retail store in New Jersey, selling items like tea, coffee, butter, chocolate, rum, linens, thread, knitting needles, and earthen dishes. He served his customers well and his business was successful and expanding. But he "grew uneasy" because running his business "felt too cumbersome" and was distracting him from being "content with a plain way of living" and from his call to minister in the churches near him. He resigned himself to the Lord's heavenly will, and soon after he wrote, "I felt a stop in my mind." He felt led to simplify so that instead of selling retail goods or hiring apprentices he began working as a tailor for a small number of customers and referring everyone else to other stores and tailors.[16]

Woolman's boundary made space for him to begin writing his spiritual journal, which over time became a book that helped millions of people. Shortly after his decision to reduce his business, he was awakened in the night and began meditating on the goodness and mercy of the Lord. In his journal he wrote, "I saw a light in my chamber . . . words were spoken to my inward ear which filled my whole inward man. They were not the effect of thought . . . but as the language of the Holy One spoken in my mind . . . 'Certain Evidence of Divine Truth,' and were again repeated." Then he was guided by "the Inner Light" of the Holy Spirit to be one of the first leaders in America to work for an end to slavery. Later he also ministered to Native American Indians.[17]

When I (Bill) first learned Woolman's story, I was in my mid-thirties and had the opportunity to expand our psychology business. Kristi and I talked and prayed about it, and we decided to keep our business small by referring potential clients to other therapists. In the following years, God filled in the spaces of time and energy we created with spiritual renewal for each of us and then led us to start the ministry of Soul Shepherding. As with Woolman, our self-activation in ministry was enabled by setting limits on our work, cultivating intimacy with Jesus, and responding to the prompting of the Holy Spirit.

When Nines are awakened and empowered by the Spirit of Jesus, it's a beautiful thing to behold. Riso and Hudson call Nines "the crown of the Enneagram" because they are the top symbol on the nine-pointed diagram. "Nines can have the strength of Eights, the sense of fun and adventure of Sevens, the dutifulness of Sixes, the intellectualism of Fives, the creativity of Fours, the attractiveness of Threes, the generosity of Twos, and the idealism of Ones."[18] At their best, Nines are activated to express the fullness of God's peace through their type, which includes incorporating the strengths from the other eight types.

Key Soul Care Practice: Spiritual Direction

The discipline of talking with a spiritual director (or another mentor) is helpful for every type, but it's especially important for Nines. Their pattern in relationships is to focus on other people's needs and lose touch with their own. When they practice receiving empathy and prayer support, it increases their self-awareness, trust in God's love, and capacity to self-activate in following God's will. In this way they come to feel lively, knowing that their presence in the world really matters.

Jonah (Nine) probably gave and received spiritual direction, though the book of Jonah is focused on his prophetic ministry to Nineveh. But the prayer Jonah prays while inside the huge fish shows that he received spiritual direction from the psalmist David, as he references eleven psalms from memory (Jon. 2:2–9).[19] This helped Jonah articulate his emotions, confess his sin, and trust the Lord. Even before the fish spit him out on the beach, Jonah's soul was reawakened and strengthened for him to carry out his mission.

Soul Care Practices for Nines

PEACEMAKER

Meet with a spiritual director to process out loud and receive empathy.

In conflict, ask for what you need, as Abigail (Nine) did when David was angry at Nabal, her husband (1 Sam. 25).

Take a walk with Jesus in a beautiful nature setting. (Nines and Ones thrive in nature!)

With a safe friend, practice verbalizing a disagreement to strengthen your identity.

Read *Celebration of Discipline* by Richard Foster (Nine).

Next time you nap, do "naptio divina" by meditating on Scripture till you fall asleep.

While seated, exclaim, "Awake, my soul!" (Ps. 57:8) and then stand up (to fight lethargy).

SOUL TALK

1. What did you learn about Nines and how they experience anger?

2. What is a situation that drains your energy? What makes you angry about this?

3. What do you especially appreciate about Jesus as the model Nine?

4. What can you do to apply Jonah's story to your life today?

5. Which of the soul care practices for Nines seem most helpful for you personally? Why?

How Nines Become Like Jesus

1. Appreciate Jesus' alert prayers in trials to release anger (like a healthy Three).

2. Turn from lethargy (root sin) and rely on Jesus to bring peace to others.

3. Pray to not react to stress with anxiety (like an unhealthy Six).

4. Ask for empathy when you feel angry or controlled by someone.

5. Rely on the Spirit of Jesus to self-activate (virtue) with compassion.

CHAPTER

5

Type One: Reformer

> **FELT NEED:** Act to be perfect
>
> **KEY TRAITS:** principled, idealistic, earnest, self-controlled, teaching others, perfectionistic

My grace is sufficient for you, for my power is made perfect in weakness.

2 Corinthians 12:9

The 2013 hit movie *Saving Mr. Banks* tells the backstory of how the book *Mary Poppins* by P. L. Travers (One) became a mega-successful Disney musical in 1964. "Miss Travers" (as she asked to be called) was so perfectionistic, critical, and combative that not even the charming and affirming Walt Disney could smooth out her prickliness. Richard Sherman, the songwriter for Disney, recalled that the first thing she said to them was, "This is not going to be a musical" and that the intensity of her scrutiny and opposition tied up his stomach in knots.[1] "She didn't care about our feelings, she chopped us apart."[2] She pummeled the

Disney creative team with caustic remarks about the silliness of songs and cartoons, insisting over and over, "I won't let you ruin Mary Poppins!"

Later, Walt Disney was surprised to learn that "P. L. Travers" was a pen name that the author had taken in honor of her father. So he decided to reframe the story of Mary Poppins, telling Miss Travers, whom he addressed as Pamela, "It's not the children she comes to save, it's their father. It's *your* father, Travers Goff."[3] That was the turning point for the making of the movie and the remaking of stuffy "Miss Travers" into the more friendly "Pamela."

Improving Everything

I (Bill) am a One. Usually Ones are known as "the Perfectionist," but that can make the One's inner grind into a negative label. In this book we use *Reformer* as the key descriptor. (Did you notice that as a One I just "improved" the moniker!) "Everything can be improved" is the motto of Ones. Whatever they do, they want to redo it, to make it better—even if it's good and other people say so. It seems they can't help but see and fix what's wrong, unloving, unhealthy, unwise, messy, or out of place. They keep thinking or saying, "It would be better if . . ." or "That's not right, it should be done this way . . ."

Ones don't realize that when they share their insights or advice with others, it's likely to make those people feel pressured, criticized, or controlled. The last thing Ones want is for people to look at them and think, "Oh no, here comes the judge!" That's because in their heart, Ones are trying to help. *Doesn't everyone want things to be better?* Ones are people of good intentions, like Twos. It's very difficult for them that their well-meaning aspirations can't be fully realized. I've learned that I need to trust Jesus' offer, "Blessed are you who pursue seemingly unattainable ideals, for you can find God" (Matt. 5:8, authors' paraphrase).[4]

When Ones lose touch with Jesus' grace, their drive to improve things turns on themselves. I have never met a One who did not struggle with being self-critical, even *ruthlessly* self-critical. That's certainly been my nemesis, especially in times of stress. Enneagram expert Beatrice Chestnut found that Ones report that their inner critic judges them 90 to 100 percent of their waking hours![5] Richard Rohr (One), a Franciscan writer and speaker, illustrates his own battle with self-judging: "Inside Ones, court is continually in session; they are their own prosecutor, defender, and judge. The conflicting voices keep nagging them; they bicker, interrupt, contradict, and correct one another . . . how exhausting it is to go through this endless inner trial."[6]

Ones (along with Eights and Nines) are in the Anger triad, meaning their personality is largely malformed by anger. They don't want to admit it, but unconscious anger is the force behind their improving and judging. A helpful descriptor to understand Ones is that they're *frustrated idealists* (like Fours and Sevens). In fact, in their Enneagram map they're frustrated idealists in their type, stress line, and even their growth line. In their One they pursue being more perfect, under stress in their Four they pursue being more special, and even when they're relaxed in their Seven they pursue being more positive. *More perfect! More special!! More positive!!!* That's a pressure cooker in the One's soul that can steam out with anger, criticism, advice, controlling behavior, envy, shame, or over-the-top enthusiasm.

It's commonly said that Ones are rule-followers. Yet, like P. L. Travers, they often do *not* follow other people's rules, just their own. A summary of research studies on the Enneagram found that Ones are the most likely type to be conscientious.[7] They live according to their own inner sense of what is right and may flout external rules to follow their own principles. As Gut types, Ones do not want anyone or anything controlling them. A young One mother and her husband took their little children to a shopping mall. She had their youngest child in a stroller and got on the escalator, wheeling right past the sign that said, "No strollers on the escalator." Her husband was following behind and asked, "Did you see that sign?" She replied, "That's for people who don't know how to use a stroller on an escalator!"

Perfectionism is not all bad. I sure enjoyed my grandma's perfectly prepared Italian food with homemade pasta, bread, multiple dishes, and desserts! One of the ways my own perfectionism shows up is in my writing and editing of this book. But is it perfectionism or excellence? I want it to be excellent so that it's helpful for readers and *draws people to Jesus*. Did you know that there are more devotional classics written by Ones than by any other Enneagram type?[8] Ones are often a great inspiration to others. They do quality work. They're disciplined, attentive to details, persevering, self-controlled, responsible, fair, and considerate to do what's good for others. Healthy Ones integrate discipline with grace, justice, and compassion. In all that I do I want to rely on the Lord who "arms me with strength, and makes my way perfect" (Ps. 18:32 NKJV).

Personality Development of Ones

Family Formation: Parentified Child

Like many Ones, I was a *parentified child* in my family growing up. Even though my parents loved me in many good ways, I grew up not feeling free and safe to have emotions, needs, or problems. As the oldest of five children, I took on many adult responsibilities like babysitting, doing extra household chores, and earning money to contribute to the family finances. I carried burdens, became very serious, overworked, and felt pressure to always do the right thing. Looking back, I wish I had enjoyed more opportunities to play, receive emotional holding, and trust I'd be well cared for when I had problems.

As a One child, I tried to parent myself, and I excelled by scoring touchdowns, getting As in school, and being a good son, which earned praises from my parents and others so that I also took on the family role of the *hero*. Ones try to surpass what their parents and others expect so that they can't be judged and won't cause anyone stress or pain. They say in effect, "I will give myself guidelines. I will become my own father-figure [or mother-figure] and be my own moral guide. I will police myself so no one will police me; I will punish myself so no one else will punish me."[9] It wasn't until my late twenties that I realized I had totally unrealistic self-expectations that were covering deep anger and hurt I needed to work through.

Root Sin: Resentment

When Kristi and I were learning the Enneagram in 2007, she suggested that I was a One, and I rebutted through gritted teeth, "That can't be me because I don't struggle with resentment!" (Can you hear the resentment in my voice?!) I thought I'd worked through my anger issues. *Hah!* The Lord will use the Enneagram to humble us if we let him. I learned that my tendencies to be perfectionistic, overearnest, tense, and critical were signs of resentment in my unconscious shadow self. Resentment is tamped-down, simmering anger and is the root sin of Ones that damages their personality. It's old anger from not forgiving sins, being overly ascetic to reach an ideal, or not accepting weaknesses in themselves or others. It can leak out in irritation, frustration, criticisms, judgments, or sarcasm.

When Charlton Heston (One) was interviewed about being the lead actor in *Ben-Hur*, it seems he had a low-grade resentment that leaked out. He reflected on his experience, "I've become convinced that a good film is not something you enjoy making. You enjoy looking at it afterwards." His earnest self-expectations and emotional constriction were pulling him into perfectionism. But what put him over the edge was when he had *two* people pressuring and criticizing him: himself *and* his director! Heston complained, "Willie [Wyler] won't quit . . . his whole concept of a working day is not quitting on the smallest shot until he's absolutely convinced that nobody on the shot can do any better, including him. . . . You feel as if you're constantly emptying grain onto an enormous bin that is always empty!"[10]

Defense Mechanism: Reaction Formation

Ones strive to know and do what is right all the time. Since they view anger as not good, they repress it and put out their ideal self that's responsible, moral, objective, wise, positive, cheerful, or caring. This is the psychological defense mechanism of *reaction formation*, which is saying or doing the opposite of what you feel. For instance, when Ones are frustrated with someone, they may unconsciously act friendly or compliment them anyway. They push down their "bad" feelings into their unconscious mind and profess "good" feelings. It's a false comfort. Over time, their denied anger festers into resentments, draining their energy, faith, and love.

Emotions of Ones

Core Emotion: Anger

Ones, like all the types, are charmed by their personality. They believe they're trying hard to do what's right and don't think they're angry, much less resentful. On the surface, their emotions appear as earnest, tense, or weighed down with burdens rather than overtly angry (the One-to-One subtype of the One, which is the countertype, is more likely to get outwardly angry). Ones especially put their expectations and criticisms on themselves, always thinking they should do better. When Ones do get angry with others, they tend to be convinced that their anger is righteous, which is why the judgment of a One can *cut right into a person's heart.*

In *Inferno*, the section about hell in his allegory *The Divine Comedy*, Dante portrays angry people as biters who are endlessly biting each other and their own selves.[11] *Ouch! I don't want to be a biter!* That's Dante's point. Jesus took a more humorous approach to wake up Ones and others who are judgmental: "Why do you look at the speck of sawdust in your [neighbor's] eye and pay no attention to the plank in your own eye?" (Matt. 7:3).

Stress Emotion: Shame

Brené Brown (One) writes from personal experience, "Where perfectionism exists, shame is always lurking."[12] When Ones see they made a mistake or could've done something better, their inner critic may knock them off their feet and send them careening

down into feeling frustrated, discouraged, inadequate, bad, useless, no-account, ashamed, self-pitying, melancholy, withdrawn,
and alienated. It feels like no one understands them or how hard
they've been working. That shame gutter is the One's stress line
to an unhealthy Four.

Additional Emotion: Anxiety

The repressed anger of Ones often manifests as anxiousness
that may include frustration, pessimism, pressure, hurry, complaining, and stress reactions. Ones are prone to be stressed about
doing what's right or fixing what's wrong. They worry about avoiding criticism or pressure from other people. They strain and scurry
to get all their ducks in a row so they pass inspection. Ones may
show anxiety in their body and behavior but not realize it. Feeling
and verbalizing anxious emotions is a start. Anxiety is always a
secondary emotion; hiding below it are emotions like fear, anger,
shame, or sadness.

Underlying Sadness

Deep inside, Ones are sad because all their earnest work, ascetic self-denial, and improving things causes them to miss out
on pleasure, adventure, creativity, and, most of all, intimate relationships with God and others. But often they don't feel their
sadness because they judge it as weak or needy, they don't want
to be distracted from their work or projects, or they're afraid to
be vulnerable and get hurt. Whatever your type, denying sadness
about losses or unmet needs separates your heart from the healing
flow of Jesus' compassion and wisdom.

In *Saving Mr. Banks*, sour-pickled P. L. Travers becomes surprisingly likable when we feel her sadness in scenes that show her as
a little girl who was a parentified child for her depressed mother
and alcoholic father. Then, much to our delight, her cranky adult
steps back and her childhood self skips forward, weeping tears of
joy as she watches on the big screen while Mary Poppins helps Mr.
Banks (aka Travers Goff) recover from his mistakes and become
the loving father that little Pamela adores. She gets underneath her

anger at the world to feel and express her grief and her desire to be loved. Then she's able to reclaim her father's affection for her.

Emotional Alarm: Personal Obligation

As a One, when I (Bill) feel an urgent obligation to fix a mess or overwork, I see it as an emotional alarm. It means I'm falling into an unhealthy personality mode of perfectionism. If I don't hear the alarm, usually the problems keep mounting, and before long I'll feel the weight of the world on my shoulders. The alarm of feeling duty-bound wakes me up to emotions like frustration, anger, or resentment, which I need to pray or talk through in order to receive cathartic relief and regain the sanity to accept my limits. A turning point for me was in 2008 when the Lord sounded this alarm loudly in my ears as Kristi and I were praying about whether or not to start a nonprofit ministry. I sensed the whisper of the Spirit say, "There are people who will help you if you let them." Collaborating with others has been the key to starting and growing Soul Shepherding. Since then, that alarm often echoes for me. When I feel like a lone ranger, I can ask for help from the Lord and other people.

Empathy for Beloved Ones

You need to be appreciated for all your hard work.

You're trying so hard to reach your ideals and it's frustrating to be thwarted.

It feels to you like what you do is never good enough.

There's always another expectation for you to measure up to— *it's exhausting*.

It's unfair when people judge you and don't appreciate your good intentions.

You are carrying the weight of the world on your shoulders and I'd like to help.

You feel angry they didn't do what they were supposed to do.

Jesus as the Model One

Jesus Is Serene and Gracious

Jesus is the perfect One, but he's not an exacting perfectionist—he's serene and gracious. It may be confusing when Jesus says, "Be perfect, therefore, as your heavenly Father is perfect" (Matt. 5:48). Perhaps Jesus was misunderstood in his day and so he adjusted his wording in his later sermon that Luke recorded, saying, "Be *compassionate*, just as your Father is compassionate" (Luke 6:36 NLT, emphasis added). The essence of the law is love. For instance, when Simon the Pharisee saw the town harlot weeping at Jesus' feet, he scorned her, but Jesus had grace for her and *he honored her* for showing Simon how to love. Simon was upset about her past sins, but Jesus was helping her to learn from her wrongs to become more loving (Luke 7:36–50).

By appreciating Jesus' grace and compassion, Ones can be softened to be less critical and less ruled by a sense of personal obligation. Jesus' love for others does not come out of personal obligation. Rather, it's the overflow of him basking in the love of his Abba, like he did on Sabbath days and in solitude (Luke 4:16; 5:16). Thomas Kelly (One) describes this as "a life of unhurried serenity and peace and power . . . where No as well as Yes can be said with confidence."[13] Choosing to set limits on their work and have more fun (like a healthy Seven) enables Ones to experience unhurried serenity and joy as they serve the Lord.

> ▶ **PRAYER:** *Jesus, thank you that we can be serene in your perfect compassion.*

Virtue to Cultivate: Serenity

The virtue that Ones most need to develop to become more like Jesus is serenity. Watchman Nee (One) was serene and content—not by nature but by discipleship to the Lord. One day when he was twenty-six years old, he was walking down the street, aided by a cane because of his poor health, when he ran into his old law professor. This man looked him up and down and with

Jesus as a Healthy One

REFORMER

Jesus studied the law and brought reform to Judaism: "You have heard that it was said . . . But I tell you . . ." (Matt. 5:21–22).

Jesus was appreciated for his integrity—he lived out what he taught (Matt. 7:28–29 MSG).

Jesus wasn't a lone ranger; he helped others work with him in his easy yoke (Matt. 11:28–30).

As he fasted, Jesus feasted on God's will to minister to the woman at the well (John 4:1–42).

Jesus challenged Pharisees who tithed mint but neglected mercy (Luke 11:42).

Jesus doesn't let the bad spoil the good; he accepts the weeds in the wheat (Matt. 13:24–30).

Instead of being picky, Jesus was patient and playful with his "little-faith" disciples.[14]

raised eyebrows told him that when Nee was in college everyone had such high hopes for him, but now everyone was disappointed because he had made *nothing* of his life. Nee almost broke down and wept right there. He recalls, "My career, my health, everything had gone. . . . But the very next moment . . . the thought of being able to pour out my life for my Lord flooded my soul with glory." Then he prayed, "Lord, I praise You! This is the best thing possible; it is the right course that I have chosen." He realized, "To my professor it seemed a total waste to serve the Lord; but that is what the gospel is for. . . . When once our eyes have been opened to the real worth of our Lord Jesus, nothing is too good for Him."[15]

Nee went on to become one of the great Christian leaders of the twentieth century. He planted over two hundred churches in China, and his devotional writings have reached untold millions around the world. In 1952 he was imprisoned by the Chinese communist government on trumped-up charges and persecuted for twenty years. He remained faithful to Jesus and exemplified the words of the apostle Paul (One): "I have learned the secret of being content in any and every situation, whether well fed or hungry, whether living in plenty or in want. I can do all this through [Christ] who gives me strength" (Phil. 4:12–13).

Key Soul Care Practice: Abandoning Outcomes to God

The apostle Paul is a One mentor for me (Bill), teaching me the ropes about apprenticeship to Jesus. A crucial lesson has been on abandoning the outcomes of situations to God, which is the path to serenity and contentment.[16] The story in Acts 16:16–34 says it all for me. In the Philippian jail, Paul is bruised and bleeding from being whipped. His hands and feet are in iron chains, he's stuck in the company of brutes, and he's breathing putrid smells. He hadn't done anything wrong. He had simply been sharing Jesus' love with people. But there in the jail he wasn't bothered about his pain or the stink, he wasn't ruminating about the injustice of it all, and he wasn't trying to get away. Instead, he was singing happy hymns of praise to God and turning the jail into a choir room!

Abandoning outcomes to God is like bowling: You send your bowling ball down the lane. You let it go and watch to see what it does. That's how you lead your family, perform your job, or preach a sermon. You do your part with Jesus. Then you watch and pray, putting out some body English as you hope for a strike! That's what Paul did in jail. He didn't know the Lord would rearrange his circumstances and use him to help save the jailer and his family. He didn't know the jailer would make him the guest of honor at a feast in his home or that God would enable them to plant a church together. While Paul was in jail, he was with Jesus in God's kingdom of righteousness, peace, and joy (Rom. 14:17). For years beforehand, Paul had trained himself to live in the world *from the heavens* and trust that in every situation the sovereign Lord was doing wonderful things that he could participate in (Rom. 8:28; Eph. 1:3). This enabled him to feel joy even in difficulty.

Imagine yourself stuck in a bad situation. Then pray Paul's words from the book of Philippians: "Be glad in God! . . . filling the air with Christ's praise" (3:1, 3 MSG). "The Master, Jesus Christ . . . [will] make us beautiful and whole" (3:20–21 MSG). "I'm glad in God. . . . I'm just as happy with little as with much" (4:10, 12 MSG).

Soul Care Practices for Ones

Submit to God's purposes in every situation.

Consider the story of Priscilla (One) in Acts 18. She wasn't a famous speaker, but God used her to lead a house church and to encourage pastors.[17]

Take a walk or go for a run and enjoy being in nature. Let God's beauty wash and renew your soul.

Try being like an enthusiastic Seven by skipping like a child until it makes you laugh!

Practice letting go of perfectionism. Do your best and trust God with a smile as you say, "Good enough."

Read *The Pursuit of God* by A. W. Tozer (One). He penned his classic book in an all-night prayer vigil, with very little editing.

Breathe in: "Jesus delights in me . . ." Then breathe out: "I delight in you, my Lord."[18]

SOUL TALK

1. What did you learn about Ones and the challenges they have with anger?
2. What is an example of a situation when you struggled with perfectionism or resentment?
3. What do you especially appreciate about Jesus as the model One?

4. What were your insights or feelings after reflecting on Paul's experience in the Philippian jail?

5. Which of the soul care practices for Ones seem most helpful for you personally? Why?

How Ones Become Like Jesus

REFORMER

1. Appreciate Jesus' grace to do your work with joy (like a healthy Seven).

2. Turn from resentment (root sin) and rely on Jesus to make helpful improvements.

3. Pray to not react to stress with self-criticism and shame (like an unhealthy Four).

4. Ask for empathy when you feel criticized or pressured.

5. Cultivate serenity (virtue) through abandoning outcomes to God.

Help for Anger

Don't be angry with each other, but forgive . . .
because the Lord forgave you.

Colossians 3:13 ERV

Many years ago, I (Kristi) used to dread riding in the car with Bill (One) driving. When rude drivers would offend him, he would react with anger and drive competitively with them. It was like he had been punched in the gut and so he was putting his fist in their face. *What happened to my loving, self-controlled husband? Who is this offended, reactive, aggressive, angry man next to me?*

Bill was a caring pastor, but you wouldn't know it if you were in the car with him at those times. Even though his angry reactions didn't happen that often, to me it felt like they happened *every time we drove somewhere.* Just sitting beside him when he was at the wheel, my body was jumpy and I felt scared. I kept trying not to be a backseat driver, but sometimes I couldn't help reacting and making comments, even if he just drove faster than I liked or got too close to the car in front of him. Then he'd get defensive and irritable with me. Thankfully, the times when he got angry and aggressive with drivers and I voiced my fear, he would calm down—until the next temptation came around the corner.

Then one day I started noticing changes in how Bill was driving. I could tell he was driving slower and more carefully, with sensitivity to me and to other cars on the road. There were a lot fewer times that I felt uncomfortable, but when I did and I told him, he listened with empathy, apologized, and went back to being cautious.

Underneath Angry Behaviors

At a seminar Kristi and I (Bill) led, Keith (Eight) and his wife heard me talk about my history of struggling with anger while driving, Kristi's fearful reactions, and how I'd learned to make my car part of Jesus' school of discipleship for me. I shared that I still needed to be careful not to rev up my internal motor because I was a strategic driver, readily finding the best routes to where I was going, and I enjoyed driving my Tesla that can go from zero to sixty in 3.1 seconds! Keith laughed and felt that I could understand his challenges with anger, so he asked to meet with me for coaching. He was a mortgage broker and led a ministry to families living in a motel in his town. He was a father of four, and between work, family, and serving he felt shackled with responsibility. Pressures, problems, expectations, goals, and people's needs all pressed in on him. He tried to hold it all together, but sometimes his anger would erupt emotionally and harm other people, especially his wife and children.

A flash point was when Keith was driving and someone cut in on him or was rude. He would get angry, cuss at the driver, and either ride right on their tail or zoom around them and cut in front. His wife felt endangered and fearful and would ask him to stop, which only fueled his anger, and he would begin criticizing her. Then the children would start crying or fighting. This type of eruption was happening more and more often. In the last month, Keith had put a hole in the wall of their bedroom when he and his wife had a disagreement, lost his temper at his son for losing his basketball, made sharp critical comments to a waiter who was too busy, and yelled at a slow driver in front of him. His wife had withdrawn from him, having lost trust and respect for him. One of his daughters was now having anger problems, and the other three kids felt anxious or embarrassed about their dad's problem. Too often family outings that were meant to be fun were ruined by Keith's anger.

Chances are you're somewhere in my story or Keith's. Most of us struggle with either our own anger or other people's anger, and often this surfaces in driving.[1] In either position, it's helpful to understand what's going on under the surface of an anger problem. As we discussed in chapter 2, it's natural to feel angry when your will is crossed, you're not setting a boundary with someone, you're overstressed, or you've been hurt or disappointed. Anger is intensified when it's stuffed or denied. Like the "leaky gut" syndrome of digestive disturbances, repressed anger seeps out with irritability, critical comments, sarcasm, passive-aggressive behavior, or stubbornness. Many people don't feel safe with their anger, so they unconsciously convert it into resentment, guilt, shame, depression, fear, anxiety, or insecurity. Then it leaks out to hurt other people and themselves.

An example of leaky gut anger is when slander lives in our tongue and so we speak an ill word about someone before we realize what we've done (James 3:5). It's easy to fall into this pattern even though you've been trying to speak only good words about others. But human willpower is actually rather weak. As Dallas Willard would often remark, "Our problem is that our habits keep eating our willpower for breakfast!"

Anger that's repressed lies in wait in the shadow (unconscious) region of our embodied self, ready to defeat our good intentions by impelling us to act impulsively before we feel and think. That's what was happening with me when I was driving aggressively—I was just reacting.

In Keith's case, he had volcanic rage that had been building up since his childhood shame of being picked on by an older brother and bullied and called "shrimp" at school. On the football field in high school, Keith learned that when he hit people hard, he got his teammates' respect, and his coach praised him and played him more. He didn't realize that he was recruiting anger and adrenaline to dominate people and feel strong and powerful. He hated feeling vulnerable, the way he had felt as a kid. Two decades later, whenever Keith was driving, it was like his body was still hitting people on the football field. He had been formed and habituated in using aggression to feel confidence instead of shame. That approach kept recycling his anger and underlying shame, and it was hurting his family and others.

Letting Go of Anger

To let go of anger, you first need to feel it, own it, and accept it. That means getting out of denial, not being too busy, not distracting yourself. Your anger is not about someone else or some situation—it's about *you*. Accepting angry emotions is not a self-help project. You need to ask for listening, empathy, and prayer support from a friend or spiritual director.

When a compassionate listener feels your emotions, it helps you to feel them and learn how to manage them. Christian psychologists Todd and Liz Hall point out that these caring relational connections can produce positive changes in the neural networks of our brains. They cite a study that when monkeys with a genetic predisposition for aggression were raised by substitute female monkeys who were nurturing, then their aggressive behavior disappeared and they learned to thrive socially.[2]

A contrasting approach to understand and work through anger issues is practicing being still and quiet before the Lord. Stillness—like solitude, silence, fasting, and other disciplines of abstinence—evokes repressed emotions or sins, which you can then pray through or share with your support person. Christopher Heuertz (Eight) wrote that contemplative prayer "helps empty out the junk that we stuff into the storehouses we call our souls. Sometimes hard scraping is required to loosen and remove the toxic mental clutter and debris."[3] In his case, which is typical of Gut types, Heuertz says he had to be *forced* to make space to get honest about his soul rubbish. He ended his twenty years of humanitarian work, in which he'd been fighting injustice around the world, and began to face the inner work of addressing his blind spots.[4]

Since Keith had a long and painful history with repressing his anger, I (Bill) had him do some *anger workouts*. This was in addition to using empathy and contemplative prayer. He started using a punching bag, aggressively shaking out rugs and doormats, and shouting in private. It's not that venting his anger made it go away so he wouldn't lose his temper anymore. Rather, his anger workouts helped him consciously experience the intense and dangerous force of the anger in his body, and it taught him the value of managing anger in a safe and healthy way that was not destructive to himself, others, or property. Similarly, after a phone conversation where Keith's father put an unfair burden of responsibility and guilt on him to care for his mother, Keith wrote his father a *poison-pen letter* to articulate and express his angry feelings, release them to the Lord, and gain insight on the boundaries he needed to set with his parents. Then he shredded the letter so no one would be hurt by his angry words that flowed as he processed his emotions.

Governing Anger with Love

When anger is governed by love (righteous anger), it's a constructive energy to set and maintain good boundaries. It's a problem-solving emotion that God has wired into human beings to help us love what is good and hate what is evil (Rom. 12:9). Loving anger can help us to fight injustice, unrighteousness, and whatever is bad. But the danger is that anger is *directional*, and it often gets poorly aimed. Obviously, abusing another person is wrongly aimed anger. But anger is also wrongly aimed when an abuse victim turns their anger inward, blaming themselves and feeling guilty and ashamed.[5] If you've been mistreated, and yet you feel guilt and shame about this, then you need help with denied anger, underlying hurt and loss, and trusting in God's redeeming love (see chapters 17 and 18). This inner work supports the process of forgiving people who harm you.

Forgiveness is often misunderstood to our detriment. To forgive someone who has violated or wounded you is not excusing the wrong, forgetting about it, or overlooking it. Nor is it just a decision—unless it's a small insult (Prov. 12:16). Forgiveness is a process that takes time. It includes feeling your hurt, anger, and other emotions, while seeking empathy (Ps. 40:11–17). You pray to forgive *as you've been forgiven by the Lord* so you can overflow with the grace you're receiving (Col. 3:13). To forgive means you refuse to play the judge yourself but entrust the matter to the Lord of grace and justice (Isa. 30:18–19). Even as you release the wrong to God, you may be reminded of it or reinjured, in which case you need to keep praying for Jesus' forgiveness to flow through you (Matt. 18:22). As part of the forgiveness process, it's important to learn from your experience and reestablish your personal boundaries for protection. Reconciliation is often a separate issue from forgiveness and normally occurs only when you feel safety and trust (Matt. 18:15–17).

Jesus taught forgiveness as an example of loving and blessing those who mistreat us and promised that when we do this it will further our healing and freedom (Matt. 5:43–48; 6:12–15; Luke 6:27–36). This is not denying the injustice or your emotions; it's participating in Jesus' sufferings to share his mercy with someone who needs it, which can become a great honor and joy (Phil. 3:10–11).

Jesus Is Your Anger Mediator

One time when Jesus had given himself to love and serve people in three cities, they rejected him and his ministry. Despite his many miracles there, the people there were not won over to become his disciples, so he was angry and spoke of their judgment (Matt. 11:20–24). He wasn't being mean or unkind with his anger; he was praying for them. It seems that Jesus realized he was stirred up with anger and needed to refocus on the people who were with him and who wanted his ministry, for in the next beat we read, "Abruptly Jesus broke into prayer: 'Thank you, Father, Lord of heaven and earth'" (Matt. 11:25 MSG). Jesus submits to his Father as he always did (John 12:49–50). It's here that he gives his inspirational teaching on the easy yoke and light burden. But before he ministers this to us, we get to see that Jesus was sustained in the easy yoke of his loving Father (Matt. 11:25–30).

Jesus saw vulnerable people being mistreated. He himself was sinned against, judged, manipulated, abused, rejected. He felt anger. He was tempted either to react out of anger or to deny it, which would've depressed him (Heb. 4:15). But he stayed obedient, and his Father helped him; Jesus governed his anger with love. You can draw on Jesus' holiness and his empathy for you. He feels your anger. He has a heart of compassion when you're mistreated or when you sin. Whatever angry situation you experience, Jesus is your Anger Mediator who brings love and justice to you and through you to others.

> Jesus was angry at the Pharisees for opposing his healing of a man on the Sabbath (Mark 3:5).
>
> Like a loving dad, he's angry to protect rejected children (Mark 10:13–14).
>
> When Peter had an ego-agenda, Jesus rebuked, "Get behind me, Satan!" (Matt. 16:23).
>
> He drove out the hucksters in the temple so the poor could be healed (Matt. 21:12–14).
>
> He was angry at the Pharisees for putting crushing burdens on people (Matt. 23:4).
>
> He confronted the guard who slapped him (John 18:22–23).

Stillness for a Relaxed Body

Trusting that the Lord Jesus is the judge and mediator who makes all things right helps us to wait for his justice to be manifested, release our anger, and relax. The discipline of stillness or waiting is crucial for Gut types because it forces them to stop overidentifying with their drive for doing and learn to relax.[6] To be still in God's presence helps them to give up their program of getting power and control over people or projects. It gets them in touch with their hidden anger or resentment so they can truly pray. When body-centered personalities heed the Word, "Be still, and know that I am God" (Ps. 46:10), they grow in the virtue for their type.

Eights renounce their lust for power and develop a heart to serve others.

Nines stop accommodating others to feel in control and contribute their unique gifts.

Ones abandon their resentment and their need to fix things and instead are at peace in trials and give grace to people.

Being still before the Lord is a bodily posture of submission to God and is essential to releasing anger. For instance, when Moses and Aaron were upset about God's pending judgment of Israel, they fell facedown to the ground in prayer (Num. 16:22). Jesus himself prayed facedown as he battled Satan and submitted to his Father's will in the garden of Gethsemane (Matt. 26:39; Heb. 5:7). There are twenty instances in the Bible of prophets, disciples, and others falling on their faces to pray to the Holy Lord.[7]

An inspiring example of facedown prayer is when an anonymous woman fell at Jesus' feet, crying over her sins and hurts (Luke 7:36–50). She wet Jesus' feet with her tears, wiped them with her hair, kissed them, and poured perfume on them. She adored Jesus with great affection and honored him as her Lord and Savior, which greatly refreshed him. But in the background lurked Simon the legalist (One). He had rigorously studied his Bible, made rules to live by, and taught others how they should live. Yet he showed no appreciation for Jesus and expressed contempt for "the sinful woman." She received forgiveness and peace, but Simon walked away shaking his head with anger and judgment (Luke 7:36–50). Her shame (anger turned inward) melted in the heat of Jesus' intense mercy and compassion for her.

To practice a bodily posture of stillness and submission, try praying facedown on the floor before the Lord. As you do, imagine yourself pouring out your heart to Jesus and then hear his words of affirmation: "Your faith has saved you; go in peace" (Luke 7:50).

Bodily Prayers for Anger

Praying with your body engages your thoughts and feelings and will help you submit totally to the Lord. Here are some bodily prayer practices to help with anger:

Lie prostrate on your face before the Holy One.

Speak, journal, or *shout* a "Cursing Psalm."[8]

Take a prayer walk (e.g., in nature or a labyrinth).

Breathe a prayer in and out: "Father . . . into your hands I commit my anger . . ."[9]

In prayer, stand straight with your arms stretched out like a cross.[10]

Tighten and relax each body part as you submit it to God.

Kneel in prayer to forgive someone, as the Lord forgives you (Col. 3:13).

Steps to Help with Anger

The action steps below describe the process for being released from anger:

1. *Identify anger.* Remember that anger is an emotional alarm. Whenever you feel angry at others or yourself, it's wise to pause to explore your emotions. Often anger relates to other emotions like fear, anxiety, shame, depression, or sadness.

2. *Ask for empathy.* Repressed anger lives in your body, draining energy and causing stress illnesses. Asking for empathy from the Lord and a friend can bring peace and strength. The feeling words list in chapter 2 will help you get started.

3. *Set boundaries.* When you are angry, your will has been crossed and probably there is a boundary that you need

to set, like establishing a personal limit or speaking the truth in love. Processing your emotions in prayer or with a friend provides new insight and helps you communicate with love and effectiveness.

4. *Practice stillness.* Gut types and active doers especially need to learn to be still in God's presence. Limiting your work and busyness surfaces your deeper emotions, needs, or desires that you need to release to God. Submitting your work, activities, and relationships to God guards against gut-acting on your own in ways that can be unwise or hurtful.

5. *Be empowered in Christ.* Being still and relinquished to the Lord enables you to affirm the identity-building truth "In Christ I am empowered." Other soul care practices that focus on the body—including exercise, bodily prayers, being in nature, and meeting with a friend for prayer or accountability—can also strengthen your soul.

SOUL TALK

1. What is your experience with aggressive driving, either as a driver or a passenger?

2. What did you learn about anger or trusting Jesus as your Anger Mediator?

3. Which bodily prayer for anger might you try? What do you hope to experience?

4. What was your experience reflecting on the woman who prayed and wept at Jesus' feet?

5. Which of the steps for dealing with anger seem most helpful for you personally? Why?

Check out our free bonus resources for more help with anger. You can also talk with one of the spiritual directors or coaches who have earned a certificate in our Soul Shepherding Institute. Just scan the QR code or go to SoulShepherding.org/enneagram.

PART 2

SHAME
A HIDDEN HEART

Enneagram Types: Two (Helper) • Three (Achiever) • Four (Individualist)

Shame as Self-Rejection

HEART TRAITS: shame-based, tune in to others' feelings, want approval, image-oriented

> Be content with what you have, because God has said, "Never will I leave you; never will I forsake you."
>
> Hebrews 13:5

When I (Kristi; Two) was four years old, my parents took my older sisters and me out to a new, festive restaurant in town called Farrell's Ice Cream Parlor. It had an early 1900s theme with a carnival atmosphere, a player piano, and waiters wearing straw boater hats and brightly colored costumes. We were having fun when all of a sudden there was commotion, an ambulance siren began to blare, and all the waiters started running and shouting as they carried a punch bowl filled with thirty scoops of ice cream on a stretcher.

It was meant to be fun, but I was flooded with fear and burst out crying. My mom tried to reassure me that it was just an ice-cream parade, but I was terrified. My dad kept repeating, "Stop crying!

Everything is okay. There's nothing to be frightened about." My mom blurted, "Kristi, snap out of it!" But all that just made me cry even more hysterically. Finally, my dad whisked me out and shut me alone in the car, telling me he would let me out when I stopped crying. *I felt abandoned and ashamed.*

My parents and sisters were loving to me in so many ways, but I was the only Heart type in my family. They were Head and Gut types and didn't understand my emotions. I have always been sensitive to feeling rejected when people who are important to me are in a bad mood, say unkind words, or ignore me. When my parents punished my crying as disobedient, irrational, and lacking self-control, I internalized their anger and felt shame.

As an adult I continued to judge myself as "too sensitive," "too needy," "weak," and "stupid." I did not want to be sensitive and emotional. I viewed my hurt feelings like a whining, spoiled child that needed to be ignored or punished. To protect myself from being judged or rejected by others, I hid my emotions from everyone—even God. I believed the common teaching that if I'd just think more rationally and positively, I'd feel better. My emotions seemed to control my thoughts, so I failed at that. But even when I was able to change my thinking, it did not go nearly deep enough to heal my shame wounds.

Heart Types

Shame

Shame is the second of the four big hurts in life and the core emotion in the Heart triad of the Enneagram (Twos, Threes, and Fours). The other types also experience shame in different ways, especially through their lines or wings. The cycle of shame in figure 7.1 illustrates the dynamics of this painful emotion.

Shame is a heart reaction to stress, sin (your own or someone else's sin against you), or personal weakness. Recall that sin is separating from God's loving presence (Rom. 14:23). Like a bad virus, shame secretly infiltrates your personality with hurtful condemna-

Figure 7.1

Cycle of Shame

tion, disconnecting you from the grace of Christ. Your unconscious defense mechanisms minimize the pain of shame. Like a peacock, you may display your colorful feathers to impress people in order to feel better about yourself. Your personality charms you into believing the identity-damaging lie "I am what people feel about me." But creating an ideal self to impress or please other people hides your real self, separates you from intimacy, and traps you in shame (Gen. 3:7–10). It's a self-defeating, vicious cycle: *shame begets more shame.*

The three Heart types, which we'll discuss in the next three chapters, are especially vulnerable to engage in image management that traps them in a web of shame.

Twos repress shame by helping others in order to feel wanted.

Threes deny shame by achieving a feeling of being admired by others.

Fours swallow shame by being unique in the eyes of others in order to feel special.

Remember that even if you are not a Heart type in the Shame triad, you probably fall into one or more of these shame modes at times. For instance, even though I (Bill) am a One and in the Anger triad, I also relate to the Shame triad because my Two wing and Four stress line both put me in the Shame triad at times.

Emotional Intelligence

When I (Kristi) was earning my doctorate in psychology, I was surprised to learn that in my heart where I felt shame, I had a repressed emotional intelligence center. *I felt stupid, but actually I was emotionally smart.* God had created me with the capacity for emotional awareness, motivation, empathy, and relational skills, the traits that make up emotional intelligence (EQ). I was encouraged because research has shown that EQ has even more influence on success in relationships, life, and work than IQ and that, unlike IQ, it can be significantly increased.[1]

The Bible teaches the value of our feeling-heart. It's with the heart that we do our deepest thinking (Prov. 23:7 NKJV), discern God's wisdom (Ps. 16:7; Prov. 3:5–6), serve Jesus with affection and reverence (Eph. 6:6–7), love God and people well (Mark 12:30–31), enjoy the wellspring of life (Prov. 4:23), and thrive in all we do (Prov. 13:19 MSG).

If you deny feelings of shame or accept them as true indicators of your identity then your heart intelligence will be diminished. Becoming healthier, smarter, and more like Christ Jesus in your feeling-heart requires learning the language of emotions related to shame.

Understanding Shame

When Jesus opened his Sermon on the Mount, he began with comforting words of blessing for the people who felt ashamed (Matt. 5:3–16). Always a master psychologist, the Lord knew that he had to free people of shame so that they could benefit from his teaching. He was talking with people who had been judged and rejected by others: the poor, the lame, those who were sick or oppressed by demons, women, children, fishermen, tax collectors, minority races, and others who were marginalized in the culture of that time (Matt. 4:24–5:1). As Dallas Willard pointed out, "Those poor in spirit are called 'blessed' by Jesus, not because they are in a meritorious condition, but because, *precisely in spite of and in the midst of their ever so deplorable condition*, the rule of the heavens has moved redemptively upon and through them by the grace of Christ."[2] Jesus' blessings are also for the perfectionists,[3] which includes all classes of people, like the scribes and Pharisees who were in the crowd listening to Jesus. Shame afflicts those who are earnestly seeking to do right and be good.[4]

If Jesus were giving his sermon today, people like Antwone Fisher (Three) would receive Jesus' blessing. Antwone was born to a single mother in prison, then was shuffled between foster homes. He was abused as a child, was violent with his temper, and lived as a homeless man till he joined the US Navy. He described the shame and humiliation he endured: "I hated the internal wounds, the words that said I was worthless and unwanted, the teasing, the ridicule that echoed in my ears and shattered my insides into dust. If given the choice, I'd have picked a beating over being shamed."[5]

Research studies have shown that shame is so debilitating that it is significantly correlated with addiction, violence, bullying, eating disorders, and depression.[6] But Antwone was able to beat the odds and become a responsible, loving citizen, husband, and father. At the age of forty-two, after writing *forty* drafts of his autobiography, he finally got it published, and it became a bestseller. *Finding Fish* became a hit movie that he wrote and directed.[7] Through therapy and writing his story, he came to understand and care for his broken emotions and beaten-down self.

Probably you've experienced the feeling of shame, but let's define it. *Shame is a soul-killing feeling and attitude that you are bad, unworthy, and unlovable.* "In shame we are self-condemned for being the person we are."[8] It attacks your identity as a person created in God's image. You'll feel shame if someone important misunderstands you, judges you, mistreats you, or dismisses your needs—*and you accept that.* In other words, an essential aspect of shame is putting yourself down because of your weakness, emotions, needs, mistakes, failures, or sin. Also, don't miss the often overlooked point that you're vulnerable to feel shame if you're emotionally vulnerable with someone and don't experience empathy and acceptance. (That's how much we need care and belonging from others.) Once shame gets in your soul, it can take over, making you feel terribly nauseous but unable to vomit.

Other emotions cluster around shame. You feel *guilty* when you fall short of your standards or expectations. A guilty conscience declares, "I did something wrong or unloving." But shame cuts much deeper than your behavior by denigrating your character: "*I am wrong. I* am a bad person." Shame is also related to *embarrassment*, which is a temporary discomfort of feeling self-conscious or not liking how you appear in front of other people. *Humiliation* is an intensely painful experience of public shaming in which you feel unfairly degraded, devalued, and demeaned in your identity by someone or, worse, a whole group of people.

Learning the language of shame emotions can help you to stop accepting shame messages, feel sad about what hurts instead of shaming yourself, and receive the empathy that heals shame. The table below lists feeling words and idioms for shame.

Feeling Words for Shame

Emotions: guilty, inadequate, insufficient, undeserving, insignificant, unworthy, self-reproach, bad, embarrassed, blushing, flawed, abashed, judged, chagrined, blamed, condemned, demeaned, debased, humiliated, mocked, defamed, scorned, derided, disgraced, dishonored, cursed, stigmatized, estranged, alienated, ostracized, self-rejection, self-hatred, useless, ugly, despicable, wretched, revolting

Idioms: sheepish, red-faced, fell short, small, beaten down, downgraded, bad-mouthed, caved-in, given a bad mark, slapped in the face, lost face, laughingstock, branded with a scarlet letter A, stripped, tarred and feathered, no-account

Hebrew idioms: dropping your head,[9] licking the dust,[10] made lightweight[11]

As with anger, notice all the physical expressions of shame. Before you consciously feel shame, it's probably in your body with a closed mouth (or talking softly), closed eyes (or avoiding eye contact), dropped head, and shoulders slouched, as your body curves in on itself to be made small and hide from others. Additionally, notice that shame (like other emotions) is social—it's experienced in our relationships with people and with God. The Psalms help us pray out our shame to the Lord. In one instance, the psalmist strings together seven different words for social shame covering the face:

> You have made us the *taunt* of our neighbors,
>   the *derision* and *scorn* of those around us.
> You have made us a *byword* among the nations,
>   a *laughingstock* among the peoples.
> All day long my *disgrace* is before me,
>   and *shame* has covered my face. (Ps. 44:13–15 ESV,
>   emphasis added)

As this psalm shows, the experience of shame often has nothing to do with sin; rather, it is connected to *feeling rejected*, in this case by God. Being ostracized stabs our heart because our most fundamental need as human beings is to be wanted, accepted, and loved. "It is not good that man should be alone," our Creator declared (Gen. 2:18 NKJV). Shame isolates us from God and one another, which is why shame intensifies in secrecy. Conversely, the way to get free of shame is to receive empathy, and if our shame is connected to sin, then we also need forgiveness and reconciliation through the mediation of Christ (1 Tim. 2:5–6).

Shame as Self-Rejection

When I (Kristi) was in the throes of shame related to my abandonment wound, I received healing of memory prayer from Jane Willard. After one of our sessions, she directed me to read *Restoring the Christian Soul* by Leanne Payne (Two). Leanne spoke my language of feelings and got right to the heart of my problem, naming my shame as self-rejection rooted in an unconscious sin of *self-hatred*:

> I can be a Christian filled with the Spirit of God, but if I hate myself ... I will not be seeing myself through the eyes of God; I will not be listening for the affirming as well as the corrective words He is always speaking to me, His beloved child. I will be dependent upon others ... even [for] their permission for my every move. Failing to accept myself, I will have no solid center.[12]

That's what I was like as a child and in my twenties. Secretly, I hated myself, especially my emotional self, which made it impossible for me to deeply experience love from God or anyone. Instead, I lived in a people-pleasing mode, insecure and feeling bad about myself if someone was unhappy with me. But with Jane and Leanne's help, instead of staying engulfed in shame, I took courage to feel the deep pain of my brokenness, receive healing prayer, and trust God's forgiveness for me. You might wonder why I needed forgiveness when I was hurting. Embedded in my self-hatred was *pride*. I was constantly trying to be good enough to appease my distorted image of God rejecting my emotional self. Confessing my sin of self-hatred was essential for my inner healing and the reconstruction of my self-image.

A woman in her thirties named Lucia (Two) had a similar dynamic of freezing up in red-faced shame in conflict. Especially with her father, she was like a sitting duck. He was a very large man, and he was often angry, insulting, and manipulative. But she loved him and was praying he'd become a Christian. Her small group was going through Bill's book *Your Best Life in Jesus' Easy Yoke*, and each week they did the spiritual experiment for that chapter. In their next meeting when they shared their experience, Lucia shared that when she visited her father, she decided to practice what she'd learned from the chapter on boundaries. She had started using the Breath Prayer, "In Christ I'm strong ... In conflict or harmony."[13] She prayed this before her visit with her father as a way of asking

God to strengthen her boundaries, give her peace, and show her how to be independent and kind at the same time.

During Lucia's conversation with her father, he started yelling at her. But as he did, she took refuge in God's presence. Instead of flooding with fear and trying to please him, she did her Breath Prayer, breathing in, "In Christ I'm strong . . ." then breathing out, "In conflict or harmony . . ." She kept doing this and said she felt Jesus standing between her and her father. She was buoyant when she told her group, "When my father got all angry, I quietly did the breathing prayer. It was like the Spirit of God was a shield around me, and I stayed calm and confident. It even helped him pipe down!"

Healthy Self-Image

If Lucia had stayed in her usual personality mode of self-rejecting shame, she would not have been able to pray from her deep heart, trust God, and hold her boundaries. She was constructing a new self-image that secured her in God's love and strengthened her to be loving to someone who was angry and unkind. Her self-image, united to Christ by faith and practice, erected the Christ shield that protected her and strengthened her to be loving to her father even when he got unruly. A healthy self-image is important for all nine Enneagram types, but the Heart types (Two, Three, and Four) have a special need for help with their self-image because that's where they're most wounded and dysfunctional.

To understand self-image and heal from shame, it's important to start with a good psychological understanding of what the "self" is, while staying true to the Bible. There's a lot of confusing advice today about self-care and self-esteem. What the Bible teaches about the new self and old self is closely related to the psychological terms "true self" and "false self." Your true self was created wonderfully by God but is damaged by stress and sin (your own and that of others). Then your unconscious defense mechanisms create a false self to cope with the pain that stress and sin bring. Psychiatrist and author Carl Jung referred to the false self as a "persona," which is a kind of social mask to make a positive impression on others while concealing disliked aspects of your true nature in your shadow self.[14] In the Heart-Shame mode we live in our persona.

The way to set aside your false self persona and live into your true self as God created you to be is through trusting Jesus Christ's forgiveness and grace. This includes receiving the ministry of his cross and all the other ways that God's word of life comes to us through the Bible, nature, and people the Lord uses. As children and as adults with an inner child, we all need grace-filled relationships with parents, teachers, and friends who minister God's friendship to us (John 13:34; 2 Cor. 5:20). This is how your true self is loved into being a person who is increasingly healthy, valued, productive, and loving toward God and neighbors. Our Lord Jesus, as seen in the Gospels, is the perfect picture of the *fully alive* human being that God created each one of us to be like.

In the mid-1900s, D. W. Winnicott, an accomplished pediatrician and psychoanalyst, did extensive studies on how children are loved into being their true self through their relationships with their mothers and other caregivers, which he then applied to healthy adult functioning. Winnicott taught that the true self comes into flourishing through the care of a "good-enough mother" who orients and adapts herself to care for her child's developing physical and emotional needs. This involves providing "emotional holding," which is empathy and nurture. In this state the child becomes increasingly real, lively, spontaneous, creative, and original. In contrast, the false self defends against stress and pain and hides the inner reality of their true self. In the false self mode the child is an actor playing a role, restless, rigid, overly compliant, and unable to concentrate.[15]

For your true self to become more like Jesus, Paul explains that you need to "put off" your old self (false self and sin habits) and "put on" your new self (true self created by God, cleansed of sin, and recreated by God in Christ). He gives a simple illustration for this, saying it's like putting off dirty clothes and putting on fresh and clean clothes (Eph. 4:22–24; Col. 3:9–10). Let's define Paul's contrasting terms for the self and then apply his teaching:

Your old self is unattached to Christ, deceitful, selfish, and corrupted.

Your new self is attached to Christ, honest, loving, and renewed in divine life.

To put off your old self relates to the repeated teaching of Jesus and his apostles to "deny yourself" and to "lose your life" so you can find it, experiencing real and abundant life that continues forever.[16] To put off your old self is to resist temptations to the nine root sins of the Enneagram types. When your heart is attached to your old self, it's "deceitful" and "desperately wicked" (Jer. 17:9 KJV). You are wise to deny and even hate that self.[17] In contrast, to put on your new self is to pursue attachment to Christ, which enables you to develop the nine virtues of the types. The Lord would not want you to deny or hate your new self, but rather to nurture and develop it.

Be careful not to misinterpret self-denial to mean *self-negation*, which erases or invalidates your natural feelings, desires, needs, gifts, and other aspects of your self. Self-denial means not acting on temptations to sin—it does not mean *rejecting* your self. To reject your real self that Christ has redeemed leads to depression, lapses in self-control, and emotionally distant relationships with people and God. The Bible is on the side of self-awareness (becoming conscious of what had been unconscious), because when you know something about your inner self, then you can choose to respond to that with prayer and wisdom.[18] This is even true with sin. To wisely deny acting on a sinful desire begins with being aware that you're feeling it and then confessing it to our God of mercy. This even includes loving your *sinning self* (not the sin) as God does. Our only hope in life is for our great Savior to come to us while we are in our sin and extend God's mercy and compassion to make us new (Rom. 5:8).

Scriptures for Shame

"Oh, guard my soul, and deliver me! Let me not be put to shame, for I take refuge in you." (Ps. 25:20 ESV)

"The LORD is close to the brokenhearted and saves those who are crushed in spirit." (Ps. 34:18)

"Therefore, there is now no condemnation for those who are in Christ Jesus." (Rom. 8:1)

"For we are God's masterpiece. He has created us anew in Christ Jesus, so we can do the good things he planned for us long ago." (Eph. 2:10 NLT)

SOUL TALK

1. What did you learn about Heart types and shame?
2. Which feeling words for shame do you relate to personally (or for a loved one)?
3. What is an example of a time you struggled with self-rejection, self-hatred, or self-negation?
4. What helps you to appreciate your new self in Christ?
5. Which Scripture for shame especially encouraged you? Why?

Keys to a Healthy Self-Image

1. Share your feelings of shame with God and others (Ps. 139:23–24).

2. In stress and conflict make the Lord your refuge and strength (Ps. 46:1).

3. Trust Jesus' forgiveness of sins and share it with others (Col. 3:13).

4. Meditate on Scriptures that affirm your new self or identity in Christ.[19]

5. Rely on the Holy Spirit to use your gifts to love others (1 Cor. 12:4–11).

Type Two: Helper

> **FELT NEED:** Feel wanted
>
> **KEY TRAITS:** caring, romantic, sensitive, pleasing others, indirect, give to receive

Nothing in all creation will ever be able to separate us from the love of God that is revealed in Christ Jesus our Lord.

Romans 8:39 NLT

*T*he *Angel That Troubled the Waters* is a one-act play by Thornton Wilder that recalls the ancient pool of Bethesda where Jesus healed an invalid (John 5:1–9). The sick, the blind, and others who are suffering are scattered about, groaning. A burdened, weary doctor (Two) arrives seeking healing. In a flash, an angel appears at the edge of the pool and the waters start to tremble. The doctor calls out, "Come, long-expected love. Come, long-expected love. Let the sacred finger and the sacred breath stir up the pool. . . . Free me, long-expected love, from this old burden.

Since I cannot stay, since I must return into the city, come now, renewal, come, release."[1]

An invalid recognizes the doctor as the one who cared for his son and daughter, but still he asks him to go back to his work and leave the miracles for the disabled. The tired doctor keeps praying, "Heal me, long-expected love. . . . Come, long-expected love." But the angel tells him to draw back from the pool, explaining, "Without your wound where would your power be? It is your very remorse that makes your low voice tremble into the hearts of [people]. . . . In Love's service only the wounded soldiers can serve."[2]

Finally, the angel draws a finger through the water, stirring up ripples, and a divine wind strikes, making waves splash onto the steps. The invalid casts his body into the pool, followed by a whole company of the sick who lurch, roll, or hobble in. The invalid leaps joyfully up the steps, shouting that he is healed and freed, like a child! Then he looks back at the doctor and asks him to help his son who has dark thoughts and his daughter who is grieving. He does not understand them and is not able to help them. He begs the doctor, "Only you have ever lifted [their] mood[s]."[3]

Being Needed by Others

In Wilder's play, the doctor's compassion for others seems to trap him in a life of taking care of others' needs but *not his own*. That's the pain point for Twos (and for Sixes and Nines, who often mistype as Twos). The Enneagram can put a spotlight on the faults of all the types. Twos "are limited by their shadow side—pride, self-deception, the tendency to become overinvolved in the lives of others, and manipulate others to get their own emotional needs met."[4] They're so proficient at attending to what their loved ones want that it's like they get them to hang on an "invisible leash."[5] It's because Twos "are so ashamed of their own neediness that they have to make others dependent on them in order to develop a little feeling of worth."[6] "Any message, however small, that indicates someone dislikes them can feel crushing because their well-being is based on how others feel about them."[7]

Fifteen years ago, when I (Kristi) was learning the Enneagram, I attended an all-day seminar, and the speaker honed in on the negative traits of Twos as detailed in the previous paragraph. I respected the teacher and thought it must all be true, but I felt like I was being given a bad mark. A friend was at this same workshop, and afterwards she pulled me aside. "I hope you're not feeling bad about yourself after the seminar. I felt the speaker was extremely harsh on Twos. I don't experience you at all like she described." Immediately, the shame slid off of me! I felt deep empathy and affirmation.

Twos are my (Bill's) favorite personality, which I'm sure is mostly because Kristi is a Two! Usually, they are cheerful, friendly, considerate, kind, empathetic, generous, and eager to serve. An Enneagram research study found Twos to be the most likely type to be extroverted (tied with Sevens), the second most likely type to be feeling (after Fours), and the second most likely type to be agreeable (after Nines).[8] Best of all, Twos know that what's most important in life is *compassion*. The warmth from their deep feeling hearts glows with love for God and people. They're affectionate like teddy bears, appreciative, and in any situation they're eager to squeeze more life out of it. Additionally, it's often not appreciated that in their work and management of family and daily life Twos are emotionally intelligent and competent.

As we'll discuss, I think it's easy to see Jesus showing us a healthy Two because his perfection is best seen in his compassion for all people (Matt. 9:36; Luke 6:36).

Personality Development of Twos

Family Formation: Enabler

Twos often take on a role in their family and elsewhere of being an *enabler* or rescuer who tries to make others feel better or fix their problems. They may become codependent in taking care of an addict, unwittingly enabling the person's irresponsible behavior. They are prone to *overfunction* in their relationships, which enables others to *underfunction*. Sadly, they come to believe that they are only loved when they care for others and defer their own needs. This belief tends to become a self-fulfilling prophecy that generates conditional love from others.

As I (Kristi) illustrated in the last chapter, when I was a little girl I felt my emotions and needs were "too much" for my parents. Many Twos experienced something like this. Often rejecting or shaming experiences happen at school. One time a teacher saw that I'd written on my hand and told me that was a sin and I'd go to hell if I kept doing that! I caved in and cried, and then she got even more angry at me. Being emotional was humiliating for me, yet I couldn't help it. In a research study Brené Brown found that 85 percent of people could recall a school incident that was so shaming it negatively affected their self-image as a learner or creative person.[9] Young Twos felt rejected as too needy from being in a large family, having a special needs sibling, having a caregiver who was overwhelmed with their own problems, being a very sensitive child, or their own pride.

Root Sin: Pride

Pride is relying on yourself rather than trusting God. The puffed up self of Twos is seen when they secure themselves, garnering affection and esteem from people by being exceptionally sensitive, caring, and helpful for them. Unhealthy Twos can develop an unconscious messiah complex of making themselves indispensable to their loved ones. It's a trap that leaves them stuck in shame. It's just their helper self that is wanted and appreciated; their real self is hidden, so they feel unwanted and insignificant.

When I (Kristi) act in pride as a Two, it's unconscious for me; it's hidden in my shadow self. At the time, I just feel that I am loving well, like Jesus taught. I'm not aware of the kickback for me that I'm securing myself to feel loved and valuable, that I'm earning my keep instead of depending on God's grace. I get trapped in my personality, and then the terror of abandonment rushes in on me: *I will never get the love I want. I will be left all alone!* This can send me plummeting into depression and shame. But when I'm in my healthier self (my new self), I feel sad that I did not trust and rely on God's unconditional love to be enough for me and others. Then, instead of continuing to rely on myself, I get emotionally real with God and rely on Christ's mercy through journaling a prayer or asking for empathy from a friend or my spiritual director.

Defense Mechanism: Repression

Twos defend against possible rejection and feelings of shame by repressing their needs and tuning in to the needs of others in order to be helpful and feel appreciated. But their unconscious needs aren't eradicated—they get expressed *indirectly* with hinting, flattery, or giving to others with unconscious expectations of receiving something back. Most Twos repress their anger, especially if it could lead to disapproval or disconnection from loved ones, but eventually a volcano of anger erupts when they act out their stress line to an unhealthy Eight. (The One-to-One subtype of the Two is more direct with anger.)

Emotions of Twos

Core Emotion: Shame

Twos feel shame if they're unappreciated, criticized, or dismissed by loved ones. They are especially susceptible to these hurts because unconsciously they're already shaming themselves.

Henri Nouwen (Two) often wrote about the pain of shame in his own life and became the patron saint for all of us who give care but feel unworthy to ask for it. In his late fifties he hit a wall in his work as a famous professor of spiritual psychology at Harvard. He confessed in a secret journal (made public eight years later), "I experienced myself as a useless, unloved, and despicable person."[10] He took a sabbatical from his work and met with two spiritual counselors to unpack his raw, dark emotions and faith struggles. One day he sensed the Spirit say, "You are inclined to blame yourself for the difficulties you experience in relationships. But self-blame is not a form of humility. It is a form of self-rejection in which you ignore or deny your own goodness and beauty."[11]

Instead of feeling ashamed of their needs and emotions, Twos can learn how to *befriend their emotions* by trusting someone to give them empathy and guidance.[12]

Stress Emotion: Anger

When I (Kristi) get angry, I'm not a cuddly teddy bear—I show my claws! The most common way Twos like me get big with anger is to defend a loved one. But it's often a reactive anger on our stress line to an unhealthy Eight. I feel justified and powerful, like, *Hey! I've been sacrificing for you, and you don't even appreciate it. It's my turn. I need some help and care too!* But my self-righteous anger is short-lived. It's not long before I start beating up on myself for hurting someone I love, and then I feel a horrible whiplash of shame. That self-condemnation is also a hidden cause of the anger—I get angry because I've been rejecting or repressing my needs. That's why we say that anger is usually a secondary emotion for Twos. I've learned to reduce and minimize these angry reactions by paying much closer attention to my feelings of disappointment, hurt, and frustration. This requires that I not judge my emotions and needs as selfish but accept them as *human*. Then I can acknowledge my limits, set boundaries, and ask for what I need.

Additional Emotion: Anxiety

Twos fear rejection more than any other type (Nines and Fives also have a high fear of rejection). They live with an insecure, anxious hypersensitivity that's born out of low self-worth. So they shrink back from taking initiative with people and constantly read how people feel about them. If a loved one is grumpy, frowns, or does not express warmth, they may interpret it as rejection. Their anxiety shows in their continual, unconscious efforts to stabilize their self-esteem by pleasing, helping, and caring for their family, friends, and coworkers. Additionally, making decisions that affect other people can evoke an anxious obsession to reach an impossible standard of doing what is most loving for everyone—except their own self!

Underlying Sadness

In *The Angel That Troubled the Waters*, the Two doctor at the healing pool woke up to the pain of how much he'd sacrificed to bear the burdens of his patients—he'd lost his heart, his joy, his true self. He did what is so hard for Twos to do: be vulnerable to share his own emotions and ask for help. But the angel turned him away! That feeling of being cast aside is the Two's worst fear. The play ends on a sad note for the doctor because he went back to his medical practice without receiving a miraculous healing. But therein was his hope. As the angel indicated, what the doctor needed was not a physical healing but a *personal healing* through accepting his wound, grieving, and receiving empathy. Then he could joyfully fulfill his call as a wounded healer who gives empathy to others.

Expressing sadness and receiving empathy are the deepest emotional needs for all of us, whatever our type. It's important to differentiate between tears of *self-pity*, which add to shame, and tears of *self-knowledge*, which facilitate emotional healing and absorption of God's grace (see chapter 17).

Emotional Alarm: People-Pleasing

I (Kristi) led a group for women church leaders that was hosted by a pastor's wife named Suzie (Two). For lunch she ordered everyone else's meal but forgot her own! I can relate, as can most Twos. Later she shared with me that she was burned out from helping. It's tiring to be continually caring for others, all the while holding up an imaginary thermometer in the air to take the temperature of people: "Do you like me?"[13]

Like most Twos, Suzie was trying to fill the hole in her heart with warm feelings from others. Instead, I taught her to watch for her people-pleasing habit and treat it as an emotional alarm. By catching herself in the act of being overly helpful, flattering people, or shutting down her desires, she could ask herself, "Suzie, what are *you* feeling? What do *you* want right now?" Receiving empathy helped her feel loved and to give cheerfully rather than out of duty or emptiness (2 Cor. 9:7).

Empathy for Beloved Twos

In your heart you really want people to feel your care for them.

Your intentions were so loving, and you wish your friend would appreciate you.

You're feeling bad about yourself and unworthy of respect.

You're not sure what you need personally, and that's creating tension in your relationship.

In your stress, you have anger brewing in you because you have unmet needs.

You really want your loved one to reciprocate by considering your feelings.

It hurts so much when you feel unwanted (or rejected) by a loved one.

Jesus as the Model Two

Jesus' Little Way Is Big

With Jesus, it's truly like Father, like Son. He's "the exact likeness of the unseen God" (Col. 1:15 TLB). He continually enjoyed intimacy with his Father (Matt. 11:27; John 8:29). But we might forget that, in a personal way, he's also like his mother Mary (Two). From her he gleaned humility, compassion, and relational-spiritual wisdom. This does not disrespect the divinity of the Son of God. Quite the contrary. Jesus' humility is a standout virtue.

We see Jesus as the loving Two at the wedding in Cana (John 2:1–12). When Mary asks Jesus to help because her friend hosting the celebration has run out of wine, he tells her no because it was not yet time for his public ministry. Yet, she winsomely says to the servants, "Do whatever Jesus tells you to do" (v. 5 CEV). Then Jesus changes his mind and turns the water into wine! Why? Was it his compassion? His mother's wisdom? A new word from his Father? Perhaps each of those factors played a part. In any case,

Jesus' bond with his mother and their shared compassion for others are beautifully on display.

In the nineteenth century, Thérèse of Lisieux (Two) called acts of compassion the "little way."[14] Jesus of Nazareth's life gives great honor to Twos and others whose kindness often goes unnoticed. Of the four Gospel writers, Dr. Luke especially emphasizes Jesus' kindness. With love he fixed broken chairs (4:22; see also Matt. 13:55), affectionately touched lepers (5:13), blessed the poor (6:20–21), comforted grieving widows (7:11–17), affirmed unsure students (7:40–50), cared for the homeless (9:58), received rejected women as his disciples (10:38–42), played with children (18:15–17), blessed those who cursed him (6:28; 23:39–43), forgave his enemies (23:34), and offered paradise to a thief on a cross (23:43). At the same time, Jesus shows all of us who are helpers how to care for our own souls so that our joyful lovingkindness does not falter (5:16; 6:1; 8:2–3).

▶ **PRAYER:** *Jesus, help me to trust the help that good people offer to me and others.*

Jesus as a Healthy Two

Jesus cared for his family without resenting their lack of appreciation (Mark 3:31–34).

He did not act on his own but only did what he saw the Father doing (John 5:19).

He expected people to do their part to receive from his ministry (John 5:8; 8:11; 9:7).

He practiced solitary prayer for soul care and intimacy with his Father (Luke 5:16).

He did not heal everyone and sometimes said no to people (Matt. 13:58; 16:23).

He asked for emotional support and prayer from close friends (Matt. 26:36–38).

Virtue to Cultivate: Humility

It's been said that humility is the mother of all virtues. I (Kristi) have found that to be true for me as a Two who struggles with the root sin of proud self-sufficiency. As a mother, I spend a lot of time in the kitchen and shopping. It feels mundane and tedious compared to counseling a leader or speaking to a crowd of thousands. But the humble, heartfelt spirituality of Brother Lawrence (Two) corrects my thinking. He was a monk in France during the seventeenth century who learned to practice God's presence within his ordinary, everyday duties. But at first he felt trapped working in the kitchen and shopping, which were jobs he hated. He struggled with feelings of insecurity, guilt, and shame that made it hard for him to pray. He tried to be like Christian teachers who were more intellectual and studious, but he couldn't. Finally, he concluded, "I have read many accounts in different books on how to go to God and how to practice the spiritual life. It seems these methods serve more to puzzle me than to help, for what I sought after was simply how to become wholly God's."[15]

The turning point for Brother Lawrence was when he started talking to God from his heart "in an exchange of love, simply by an act of praise, or adoration, or just by desire . . . an attitude of simple waiting, or by thanksgiving."[16] Through experimentation, he found that he could feel as close to God in the noise and clatter of the kitchen as he did in the daily prayer services at the monastery. It was the same with shopping. He had to buy wine on a wobbly ship, and the only way he could get around was to roll his body over the casks, but he did this in God's loving presence. He found that developing a habit of doing his work for the love of God caused labor that had been hard to become *easy*.

Brother Lawrence's spirituality inspires me. He also felt shame and limitations. He talks my language of feelings and relationships, and he does it in a down-to-earth way. Humility is the most important virtue for Twos because it undercuts our pride and also our shame, which is the underside of pride. Genuine humility is not judging or rejecting yourself; it's knowing and accepting your real self. "Humble yourselves, therefore, under God's mighty hand," Peter says, "that he may lift you up in due time" (1 Pet. 5:6). For Twos to receive from heaven's mighty hand of grace, we need to disbelieve our feelings of shame and not let our fear of rejection hold us back from asking the Lord (and other people) for what we need.

Key Soul Care Practice: Solitude

As a Two, the spiritual discipline I (Kristi) need the most is solitude. It's something I used to fear and avoid because it felt like punishment. I was sent to my room and left alone when I was a problem for my parents, and I felt unloved and abandoned. As an adult, I learned to practice time alone with Jesus and saw how helpful it was. When I take time away from other people, I am relieved of being tuned in to their feelings and needs and wanting to care for them in order to secure myself. I get in touch with my own needs and emotions so I can share with Jesus and appreciate his loving presence. This helps me to feel esteem for myself.

Recall the story of John (Two) at the Last Supper with Jesus and the other eleven disciples (Matt. 26:17–30; John 13). As a Two, John was probably tempted to be up serving and helping everyone else. There would be other times to care for the needs of others. At this time, instead of being the one who has to give, he's receiving, and it's as if he and Jesus are alone in solitude. He leans into Jesus and lays his head on his chest where he can hear his heartbeat and they can talk intimately. He's letting himself receive Jesus' love and enjoy the closeness and affection. You wouldn't do that if you didn't believe you were wanted. We all want to be wanted, especially Twos. John dared to believe that he was Jesus' special friend—and he was! At that moment John decided that forever he wanted to be known not as a leader of the church but simply as "the disciple Jesus loved" (John 13:23 NLT).

Soul Care Practices for Twos

HELPER

Set aside time in solitude to receive from the Lord.

Ask Jesus and others for what you need, that your joy may be full (John 16:24).

Practice your boundaries. Before you respond to a need, pray, *Is it for me to help?* Listen before you act.

Do some good deeds for others in secret to please your heavenly Father (Matt. 6:1).

Read *The Way of the Heart* by Henri Nouwen (Two). It's a short read that will inspire you to put your intimacy with God first so that serving others is a joy.

Pray, "Jesus is enough for me to keep my soul tranquil and quiet, like a child in its mother's arms."[17]

SOUL TALK

1. What did you learn about Twos and their struggle with shame?

2. What is a time or situation in which you've struggled with people-pleasing?

3. What do you appreciate about Jesus as the model Two? How do you feel about this?

4. How do you feel about the story of Jesus turning water into wine at the wedding? How does this miracle express his compassion?

5. Which soul care practice for Twos seems most helpful for you personally? Why?

How Twos Become Like Jesus

HELPER

1. Practice solitude to let go of people-pleasing and shame (like a healthy Four).

2. Turn from pride (root sin) and rely on Jesus for compassion to others.

3. In stress, pray not to react with anger (like an unhealthy Eight).

4. Ask for empathy, especially when you feel shame or rejection.

5. Cultivate the virtue of humility through verbalizing emotions and needs.

Type Three: Achiever

> **FELT NEED:** Feel successful
>
> **KEY TRAITS:** adaptable, optimistic, productive, pragmatic, driven to succeed, show ideal self

> You are God's special treasure . . . so that you can give him praise. God brought you out of darkness into his wonderful light.
>
> 1 Peter 2:9 NIRV

There's an old Hasidic story about a Russian rabbi named Zusia (Three). One day he came out of prayer red-faced and distressed. His students saw him and asked what he was upset about. He explained that he'd had a vision about the question God would ask him at the end of his life, and it did not go well for him. His students were puzzled. "But Zusia, you have accomplished so much for God. You have helped us so much and you are so holy, wise, humble, and compassionate. Why would God's question upset you?"

Looking up to heaven, Zusia was quiet for a few moments. Then he reflected, "God will not ask me, 'Why were you not like Moses, leading people out of slavery?'"

His students questioned, "So what will he ask you?"

"God will not ask me, 'Why were you not like Joshua leading people into the promised land?'"

His disciples eagerly pressed, "Tell us, what question will God ask you?"

"God will say, 'Zusia, why were you not Zusia?'"[1]

High Achievers

America likes winners, so their favorite personality is the Three. Threes are the pure Heart type on the Enneagram, in the center of the Shame triad, so they are most defined by unconscious shame and a felt need to be appreciated by people. The story of Zusia illustrates the Three's core temptation of striving to achieve an image of success that ends up betraying their true self. They keep performing, producing, and building like machines, without realizing that their striving to achieve more and feel worthwhile is compensating for deep, hidden feelings of inadequacy, inferiority, and shame. That's why every mountain peak they climb ends up being a false peak with still higher ground to take. This quest for success is never satisfied.

Ironically, the worst day for a Three might be when they achieve a big success or retire. Years ago, I heard about some greyhound dogs on a racetrack that caught the mechanical rabbit when it broke, and that ruined them as racing dogs. They lost their purpose and became disoriented and lethargic. If Threes don't have projects to accomplish, they are likely to feel bored, empty, and depressed. To cope, they're likely to busy themselves with donkey work, doing endless mundane jobs in the house or yard or running errands (on their stress line to an unhealthy Nine).

Being a high achiever is a good thing when our motivation is to love God and other people. So Paul asserts that "to aspire to leadership is an honourable ambition" (1 Tim. 3:1 NEB). Threes are assertive in their work and relationships, doing whatever it takes to reach their goal of success (which is also true of Sevens and Eights). As leaders they delegate to staff or volunteers and partner with colleagues to promote teamwork and shared success (Threes, Sixes, and Nines are collaborators). Threes are also pragmatic (another trait they share with Sixes and Nines), industrious, energetic, and efficient. They love to keep checking items off their to-do list.

In addition to being doers, Threes are the central Heart type (a Two or Four wing is also in the Heart triad). Healthy Threes use their emotional intelligence and relational influence to provide others with warmth, friendliness, and encouragement. They're socially responsible people who sacrifice their personal needs to support and strengthen others. Threes are also great at communicating insightful and inspiring emotional word pictures, making complex truths engaging and practical. When they have a great story or insight, they will repeat it often. The family of a Three who was a seminary professor teased him for being "Dr. Repeato."

Personality Development of Threes

Family Formation: Hero

It seems like Threes pop out of the womb ready to perform. In their family of origin, they often take on the role of the *hero* that excels in academics, sports, music, art, or church. They're the golden child who can do no wrong. They learn to thrive on being lauded and celebrated for their special achievements. But the flip side is that often they do not feel loved for their own sake. Even well-intentioned parents may overpraise their children and neglect to provide them the emotional presence, affection, empathy, and comfort they need in order to develop a secure attachment and healthy personality. As adults, many a Three has become a human *doing*, addicted to achievement and success.

Root Sin: Vainglory

Deceit is often identified as the root sin of Threes, but actually that's embedded in what Evagrius identified as the deadly sin of *vainglory*, which is striving to be admired by others and loving the show.[2] Threes are prone to craft a glowing image of themselves that's exaggerated or even untrue, and they display this to others for attention and applause. Carl Jung identified this as a "persona," which is a social mask we wear to hide what's lacking in our self.[3] Trying to win the approval of others is a *deadly trance* in which self-deceived Threes walk right into the trap of hiding their true self in their unconscious shadow, isolated from the love of God and others. That's why Jesus warns us, "Watch out! Don't do your good deeds publicly, to be admired by others, for you will lose the reward from your Father in heaven" (Matt. 6:1 NLT).

Defense Mechanism: Identification

Threes defend against shame and the fear of being taken down a peg by identifying with important people they admire. They construct an ideal self from the values of those people and identify with that. Then they engross themselves in their goals, work relationships, and projects to ward off the feelings of failure that nip at their heels. As one Three bragged, "Feelings are like speed bumps—they just slow me down."[4] But this go-go-go coping strategy diverts their attention and energy from their true self that needs to be known, accepted, affirmed, and unconditionally loved.

Emotions of Threes

Core Emotion: Shame

A Christian musician (Three) who met with me (Kristi) for spiritual direction described herself as "Avatar" because she identified herself with her popular media icon. She shared, "Sometimes I like my Avatar better than the real me, but other times I feel trapped in it, and I wish I could be free to be myself." Underneath her spirited and successful public image she felt insecure, insufficient, and ashamed. Today it's easy for all kinds of people to lose their real self to their social media profiles. For the watching public we readily "shape-shift to match an image of competence, attractiveness, and high status."[5]

Of the nine types, Threes most believe in their own abilities, so it's surprising that they tend to be plagued with feeling they are not good enough. For them, failure is not an option. For instance, a wife told her busy Three husband that she missed connecting with him, but he heard her through the lens of his personality and interpreted that to mean he was not performing up to snuff. For most Threes, self-esteem goes up and down based on their perception of how important people view their accomplishments. That's the imaginary thermometer they hold up in the air to take the temperature of how other people feel about them. Recall that Twos do this to feel appreciated. For Threes it's about being admired. They use their emotional thermometer to read a room, size up people's influence, or build a collaborative partnership in order to reach their goals for success. But, like chameleons, they may change their color to fit their environment and not be their authentic self, which reinforces their hidden shame.

Stress Emotion: Anger

Threes feel frustrated when their goal is thwarted. But they try not to show anger because they are image-conscious and want to appear like everything is going well for them. In stress, overworked Threes tend to take on the characteristics of an unhealthy Nine that internalizes anger. They go into a shutdown mode of disengaging from their relentless achieving. They may become tired, testy, resentful, stubborn, or passive-aggressive. When Threes get mad, it's often best understood as a defensive reaction to inner shame. Healthy Threes can be direct with their anger, speaking the truth in love and being assertive to reach a goal.

Additional Emotion: Anxiety

The anxiety of Threes is likely from a fear of failure or feelings of inadequacy, and it manifests in overworking and overperforming. An anxious, workaholic Three church leader admitted, half boasting and half exasperated, "I just gun it internally to get to the ideal Christian!" Their headlong rush into accomplishing more and more can cause them to crash and burn in a health crisis, depression, moral problem, or stress overload.

Underlying Sadness

Underneath the Three's ideal self and hidden emotions of shame, anger, and anxiety lies a deep sadness because what they really desire is to be recognized and valued for their true self apart from their performance. Adrenalized Threes need to learn to slow down, rest, and spend time in solitude, which will likely evoke a depressive withdrawal. Then they can grieve and seek comfort, and their genuine self will begin to blossom. If they don't do this inner work, then it's probably just a matter of time before they burn out or have a big fail. Ironically, that can be their saving grace, as happened with Moses (Three). Because he acted in anger and distrusted the Lord, he did not get to go to the promised land (Num. 20:8–12; Deut. 3:23–28). But he penned Psalm 90, which records his inner grief work that helped him to be satisfied in God's unfailing love and be glad day by day (v. 14). Expressions of sadness over our sins, failures, hurts, and losses are essential for all of us to receive God's comfort and strength.

Emotional Alarm: Conditions of Worth

The wake-up call for Threes is to catch themselves in the act of their habitual response of thinking, "If I could just achieve _____, then I would know that I am worthwhile."[6] In other words, they place conditions of worth on themselves that undermine their experience of the grace they need. A Three in our Soul Shepherding Institute spent five hours in solitude, practicing her intimacy with Jesus apart from works. She confessed, "Even when I stop doing and just be, I end up trying to *be the best at being!*" She realized her personality had snared her soul. Through further solitude and processing with her spiritual director, she learned that instead of wearing her ideal-self persona as a cloak to hide her

Empathy for Beloved Threes

You're doing such a good job in your work, and it's making a huge difference.

It's natural that you feel tired from working so hard.

It's frustrating for you to have to put up with people who are not doing good work.

You like people looking up to you, yet the weight of responsibility is heavy.

Underneath your achieving self you feel inadequate.

You really want to be known and loved for your true self apart from your performance.

feelings of insufficiency, she could keep clothing herself in Christ's compassion, kindness, humility, gentleness, and patience, which nourished her true self (Col. 3:12).

Jesus as the Model Three

Jesus Is Huge-Hearted and Hard-Working

Jesus is the preeminent Three. One of my (Bill's) favorite scenes in *The Chosen* film series shows Jesus working a fourteen-hour day of preaching and healing people. Afterwards, he drags his body back to his tent with his shirt bloodied, like an ER doctor's scrubs, and collapses to the ground. Then his mother, Mary, washes his feet as he mumbles his nightly prayers and drifts off to sleep.[7] Probably there were days like that where Jesus totally poured out every ounce of love he had for people.

Mark's run-through of Jesus' early ministry in Galilee portrays him as a huge-hearted, hard-working Three. Often so many people were lining up to meet with Jesus that he worked late into the night. To get some rest and pray he had to sneak off into the wilderness, but even there people found him, and he cared for their needs (1:32–37). Crowds overflowed houses to listen to him teach (2:1–2). Sometimes he and his disciples were so busy with ministry that they did not even have time to eat (3:20; 6:31). Wherever Jesus traveled, large multitudes followed and he ministered to them. A woman touched him to be healed and he felt power go out of him (5:24–30). People were *running* from faraway places to wherever they heard Jesus was, and he provided healing and teaching (6:55–56). He cut short a spiritual retreat to minister to a crowd that interrupted him (6:31–34). He had to climb a mountain to get alone and find space to be quiet and commune with his Father (6:46).

Threes can relate to Jesus' work ethic and unflagging love. (As a One, I can too.) In your type, you may be a hard worker also. George Müller (Three) had a practice that helps us see the key for Threes. He worked industriously leading his sprawling ministry to orphans in nineteenth-century England, and in all his needs for money and volunteers and the many challenges that came up, his attitude was, "I encourage myself with faith in God's ability."[8]

Jesus as a Healthy Three

As a carpenter, Jesus dignified common labor and hidden service (Mark 6:3).

Appreciating his Father's unconditional love came before his work (Mark 1:9–14).

He joined his Father's works of love and they worked as a team (Matt. 11:27 MSG).

He did not try to do it all but delegated his mission to twelve apostles (Mark 3:13–15).

He embraced "failure" for the success of his mission (Mark 14:50; John 6:60–70).

Jesus was authentic and emotionally honest about his needs (Mark 14:32–42).

That's how Jesus worked with his Father all the time. Yet, with all the important demands on our Savior's time, Mark shows us that Jesus' first priority was his love relationship with his Father, which he then brought into his work. May we do the same.

▶ **PRAYER**: *Jesus, help me trust that you love the real me apart from how well I perform.*

Virtue to Cultivate: Authenticity

Becoming authentic by living from your true self is the virtue that Threes especially need to work on. Jarena Lee (Three) is an inspiring example of someone who overcame racism, lack of opportunity, and fear of failure to achieve true greatness. In the early 1800s, when slavery was legal in America, she became the first black woman preacher and the first black woman to publish a spiritual autobiography.[9] In one year alone she traveled 2,300 miles on foot and on horseback to preach 178 sermons. (As a Three she counted her achievements!) She ministered in large and small churches, one-room schoolhouses, open fields, barns, and homes throughout the northeast. People of all colors and creeds—even atheists—were spellbound by her inspiring preaching and writing.

As Jarena writes, she was not "going to heaven as in golden slippers."[10] When she was seven years old, her parents were scraping to get by and hired her out to work as a maid sixty miles away. She was not educated or allowed to read the Bible. Yet, at age twenty-one, when she heard a missionary speak, a ray of sunlight darted into her soul and she fell in love with Jesus, "the second person in the adorable Trinity," and she knew that she would "forever enjoy the smiles of the Creator."[11]

After Jarena received a dramatic call from God to preach, her African Methodist Episcopal pastor put the brakes on, telling her that women could not be preachers. Eight years later, she was in church one day when a lay brother was preaching about Jonah being stuck inside a whale for not heeding God's call to preach. Suddenly, she sprang to her feet and *interrupted the sermon* to exclaim that she was like Jonah and had "a fire shut up in her bones"[12] for eight long years! Then she let out some of that spiritual fire, giving an exhortation to the congregation. When she sat down, she felt embarrassed. But this time her pastor stood up for her and endorsed her ministry. The next Sunday she began preaching, and her ministry took off.

Like many Threes, Jarena communicated in fresh idioms and poignant word pictures that penetrated people's hearts. Her abandonment wound and struggle with depression deepened her dependence on the Holy Spirit and her compassion for people. God spoke through her sincere passion with holy lightning that went right into people's hearts. When she preached, people cried, shouted with praise to God, fell to the ground in prayer and repentance, "caught the Hallowed Flame,"[13] and rose up to serve God. Jarena Lee's story encourages us that God does extraordinary things with ordinary people who are authentic, courageous, compassionate, and, most of all, devoted to Jesus.

Key Soul Care Practice: Emotional Honesty

For years, Hannah (Three) had suffered from deep shame and anguish because she had not been able to have a child, and she was often taunted and made a laughingstock. One day she traveled to God's house and poured out her raw emotions of embarrassment and grief to God. She prayed fervently for a son, vowing to dedicate him to the Lord's service. The priest Eli saw Hannah weeping. At first, he mistakenly accused her of being drunk, but then he blessed her with God's peace and assured her that her prayer would be answered. Sure enough, the Lord gave her a son—Samuel! Hannah cared for him till he was five and then brought him to serve in the Lord's house as she had vowed (1 Sam. 1:1–20).

Baring her heart to Yahweh and Eli and experiencing divine provision inspired Hannah to compose a psalm that became the basis for Mary's Magnificat (1 Sam. 2:1–10; Luke 1:46–55). Hannah is an example for Threes, and all of us, on being emotionally honest with God and others. Even in giving vent to her feelings, she "retained her serenity of soul and was a veritable lily among thorns."[14] Authentic sharing of their emotions helps Threes to feel accepted and loved apart from their performance.

Soul Care Practices for Threes

Practice confessing your sins, struggles, and hurts with a confidant.

Pray to emulate Moses (Three) in working to achieve for God's glory and to help others.

Follow a Bible reading plan or other devotional program to offer your heart to Jesus.

Participate in a small group to be emotionally honest and to give and receive grace.

Sometimes bless others secretly to stay out of image management (Matt. 6:1-4).

Read *Answers to Prayer* by George Müller (Three) and ask God to help you learn to be led by the Spirit of Jesus in your work and to be grateful for his provisions.

Breathe in God's word: "Be still and know that I am God . . ." Breathe out: "*Selah*" (Ps. 46:10-11).[15]

SOUL TALK

1. What did you learn about Threes and their struggle with shame?

2. What is an example of a situation when you struggled with performing to impress someone or trying to live up to an ideal self?

3. What do you appreciate about Jesus as the model Three? How do you feel about this?

4. What were your feelings after reflecting on Hannah's story of trusting God when she felt ashamed and then experiencing true success?

5. Which of the soul care practices for Threes seem most helpful for you personally? Why?

How Threes Become Like Jesus

1. Confess your sins and weaknesses and trust Jesus' grace (like a healthy Six).

2. Turn from vainglory (root sin) and rely on Jesus to be genuine with God and others.

3. Pray to not react to stress by zoning out in robotic work (like an unhealthy Nine).

4. Ask for empathy when you struggle to succeed or when people don't do what they say.

5. Cultivate authenticity (virtue) through emotional reflection and honesty.

10

Type Four: Individualist

FELT NEED: Feel special

KEY TRAITS: dramatic, self-focused, creative, romantic, emotional, melancholy

Those who look to [the Lord] are radiant;
their faces are never covered with shame.

Psalm 34:5

I n *The Great Divorce* by C. S. Lewis, the ghosts of people who have died take a bus trip from the Gray Town at the outskirts of hell to the threshold of heaven. Each person is given the freedom to choose either heaven or hell, but surprisingly many do not want to live in God's presence because their personality has trapped them in their sinful passion.

In one scene, the ghost of a famous artist (Four) arrives and keeps complaining that he can't paint the beautiful scenery of paradise because he doesn't have any paints or brushes. A celestial spirit shows him that in the artist's best paintings on earth he had caught glimpses of heaven that blessed other people. He explains that for the first time the artist has heaven right in front of him, and if he were to try painting it, then he'd miss out on experiencing its wonder and delight.[1]

But the ghost is impatient to show off his artistic talents and sell his paintings to the world. He is not able to enter the moment and enjoy God's blessings. The shining spirit cautions him not to make the mistake that many poets, musicians, and artists make by being drawn away from the love of the thing to the love of the telling. That's sinking into a self-absorbed personality that's obsessed with being admired. The ghost talks on and on about wanting to meet interesting people in heaven and distinguish himself as an artist. But the spirit insists that in heaven *everyone* is special and the glory of God flows into and through everyone like light and mirrors. The artist-ghost becomes melancholy at the prospect of being an ordinary mirror of light like everyone else, and he kicks up a fuss, insisting that he be released to go back to earth so he can paint, write, and publicize his work. Then his specter vanishes.[2]

Being Unique

If you relate to the Four—as I (Bill) do, since I have a line to the Four—you don't want the artist from the Gray Town to be your doppelgänger! You don't want to be a show-off who needs more publicity. In fact, for a Four to be like *anyone* is a disgrace! Fours want to be one of a kind—that's what makes them feel special. The Four is the most complex of the nine types because they have the deepest feelings and are the most private, which is why they can be so creative. The innovation of a Four may be expressed through music, art, drama, writing, fashion, cars, technology, or other ways. For all of us who are creatives, the character of the artist-ghost haunts us with the helpful reminder that we are prone to idolize what we craft.

Fours want to draw attention to the unique gift they bring to the table, and if they can't be the main event, they may get gloomy, touchy, emotional, or feel sorry for themselves. Whatever Fours feel, it's very significant to them, and they're in danger of falling into a victim mode where they parade their emotions to seek sympathy. Fours are sure the grass is always greener on the other side of the fence, and in that netherworld is the idyllic home they're looking for. (They're frustrated idealists, like Ones and Sevens.) If they're not careful, they keep spoiling what's good because it's not ideal, and they paint themselves into the corner of melancholy.

The great blessing of Fours is that they are "the deep-sea divers of the psyche: they delve into the inner world of the human soul and return to the surface," sharing their treasures of emotional insight and creativity birthed out of pain.[3] Fours are the type that most correlates with the Myers-Briggs preferences of feeling and introversion.[4] They help people feel emotionally alive, make things beautiful, cultivate realness and intimacy, and offer deep wisdom. We all need those qualities, but Twos like me (Kristi) especially need the traits of a healthy Four.

As I shared in chapters 7 and 8, feeling my emotions, desires, and needs tempts me to shame. So my personality avoids asking for what I need and helps other people instead. In contrast, Fours know their emotions, desires, and needs are important and seek to gratify them (which is why the healthy Four is the growth line for a Two). Instinctively, as a girl, I knew I needed this. I remember singing over and over the words of a Christian song, "I'm something special, I'm the only one of my kind," which helped me appreciate that *I am one of a kind and deeply loved by God.*[5]

Personality Development of Fours

Family Formation: Victim or Special

Brennan Manning (Four) writes, "It requires heroic courage to trust in the love of God no matter what happens to us."[6] He was often besieged with feelings of inferiority and low self-esteem and needed to take courage from Jesus. It started for him as a child:

> I have no memory of being held, hugged, or kissed by my mother as a little boy. I was called a nuisance and a pest and told to shut up and sit still. My mother had been orphaned at age three. . . . Having

received little attention or affection . . . she was incapable of giving any. . . . [My father] was never there. Burdened with the limitations of an eighth grade education, he would look for work futilely and frantically during the Great Depression. I could not understand why he was never around (except to speak a word of correction or impose physical discipline). When I saw kids my own age enjoying a great relationship with their moms and dads, I concluded that there must be something missing in me. It was *my* fault.[7]

Like Brennan, many Fours have suffered from painful losses from feeling unwanted or rejected or experiencing the death of a family member, their parents' divorce, or moving away from friends. Seeing how they've been mistreated or what's lacking in their family and life, they may identify as a *victim*. Unconsciously, they may become adept at enticing people to come to their rescue and treat them as special. Some Fours in childhood *were* victimized by abuse or mistreatment. Being a victim feels so painful and powerless, it's hard not to carry that as their identity: "I am a victim."

For some Fours their identity centers on being *special*. Maybe in their family they were an only child or had a doting parent. Or they had extraordinary gifts that brought them extra attention in their family, school, or activities. Or they had special needs that required extra care. These Fours feel they are uniquely attractive or gifted and other people should appreciate them. As with all the types, the Four's own biological makeup and choices play a role in the formation of their personality.

Root Sin: Envy

Envy is resenting another person's good gifts because they seem better than your own and this makes you chafe on your own personal lack or inferiority.[8] Envy makes us feel like *have-nots*, and it's the Four's major trip wire. Other people have more uniqueness, more talents, more acclaim, more style, more beauty, more creativity, more romance, more fresh ideas, more of something special. Often Fours do not realize they're envious because it's denied in their shadow. Their focus is on being more special.

Alice Fryling (Four), a spiritual director and author, has learned to keep her shadow envy in view and to vigilantly guard against the lies of envy: "I must be extraordinarily special in all that I do. I believe that I am uniquely burdened by being sensitive and that others always have something I am missing."[9] Thomas Aquinas pointed out that envy is a deadly sin because it opposes the love of God and neighbor, which condemns us to a hell of our own making.[10] That's why the artist-ghost turned away from heaven; he preferred his green-eyed desires to God's glorious presence.

Defense Mechanisms: Introjection and Artistic Sublimation

Fours introject (swallow) their painful experiences with people as a psychological defense mechanism. That way they don't have to deal with a hurtful person, just a hurtful *feeling*, which gives them an illusion of control.[11] They are then prone to regurgitate "woe is me" emotions. They may also employ the unconscious defense of sublimating their pain through their art or creativity, as Brennan Manning did with writing and the artist-ghost did with painting. For recipients of these gifts, the resulting beauty, compassion, or wisdom can be extraordinary. But for Fours their sublimation can get them stuck in feelings of despondency, self-pity, and shame so that they're unable to open their heart to the love they need.

Crystal (Four), a spiritual direction student in our institute, exemplified how to use art to work through emotional pain in a healthy way. She did the Journey Map exercise in *Journey of the Soul*, which had her reflect on her experiences of consolation and desolation in the stages of faith. Related to this, she made a collage to describe her current experience of being stuck at The Wall.[12] She drew a picture of a wall and wrote on it words like *COVID, church division, faith deconstruction, depression,* and *spiritual dryness*. Before this, at her wall she felt depressed, bad about herself, and envious of others who were enjoying God. But through the support of her community, retreat experiences, and art, her emotions and faith were moving in a hopeful direction. So on her collage, she drew a sun peeking out from dark clouds and beautiful flowers growing at the base of the wall. Lastly, she added the words *empathy* and *waiting for Jesus.* She was not like the artist-ghost, denying her pain and creating art for other people—she was doing "art therapy" to receive support from her spiritual director on retreat. By the next institute retreat six months later, she felt like she was through The Wall and beginning to experience a spiritual renewal of intimacy with Jesus!

Emotions of Fours

Core Emotion: Shame

Fours are plagued with shame and embarrassment more than any other type. In social situations, many Fours feel like *misfits* and hide in the background. In relationships their shame may unconsciously motivate them to pull people close with vulnerability and then push them away by withholding their feelings or going AWOL. In the discussion below you'll see some of the ways that shame swamps Fours.

Stress Emotion: Shame

Fours under stress report having the most emotions of the nine types.[13] In stress they tend to sheepishly hold back their gifts and their best self and distract themselves by serving as a sidekick helper for others (on their stress line to an unhealthy Two). They feel for others and get lost in others' emotions, perhaps in a co-dependent way of trying to live through others. Fours and Twos share a line, and since both are shame types, going from one to the other can *recycle shame.*

Christian psychiatrist Curt Thompson empathizes, "When we are in the middle of a shame storm, it feels virtually impossible to turn again to see the face of someone, even someone we might otherwise feel safe with. It is as if our only refuge is in our isolation."[14] It's a battle between voices of love and self-hatred, light and dark. The cry of shame, whether spoken, acted out, or muffled, is urgent. Isolated in a shame storm, Fours are vulnerable to depression, addiction, self-destructive behavior, or suicidal feelings.

Additional Emotion: Anger

Often shame is anger turned inward against oneself. Brennan Manning's story illustrates this. Before his book *Abba's Child* became a bestseller, it was his *sinkhole of shame*. "During a writing session," he recalled, "for no apparent reason a pervasive sense of gloom settled in my soul. I stopped writing and sat down to read the early chapters of the manuscript. I got so discouraged I considered abandoning the whole project." Then he got a call from his wife, and his anger at himself turned on her. "My feelings were running rampant—frustration, anger, resentment, fear, self-pity, depression."[15] Notice how his anger whiplashed back onto himself in self-pity and depression and he spent the whole day swamped by waves of melancholy. Later, Brennan mustered up the resolve to act in positive ways (integrating at a healthy One). He repeated to himself, "I am not my feelings." Then he cried the Jesus Prayer over and over: "Lord Jesus Christ, have mercy on me a sinner." In faith he clung to Jesus' nail-scarred hand.[16]

Additional Emotion: Anxiety

When Fours isolate, they tend to make up emotional stories in their minds about people's negative reactions to them. Their repressed shame can foment into fear and anxiety as they project their disappointment with themselves onto others and anticipate frowning faces, thumbs down, critical words, turned backs, or closing doors.

Underlying Sadness

"True love hurts like knives, but the pain is worth it." That's something a Four might say. The wisdom in this adage is that loving people includes experiencing hurt and loss, but authentic love is worth the pain. The reverse is also true: to develop real love and real character requires being emotionally vulnerable to share sad feelings. The inability to grieve prevents loving relationships and healthy personality. It may seem that Fours grieve easily because they don't hide disconsolate moods. But that's not healthy grieving—it's getting self-absorbed in depression, self-pity, and shame. Natural feelings of grief from a hurt or loss may fall into shame (see chapter 17).

Emotional Alarm: Stirring Up Emotions

To feel authentic and alive, Fours may stir up emotional states that they identify with. Unconsciously, they form their personality around the unhealthy identity that says, "I am special if other people feel I am." They may ruminate on upsetting conversations and events to feel blue. Or they may fantasize about their dreams being realized to feel happy, but then they feel depressed that their experience does not match their ideals. Or they sing praise songs for an immersive emotional experience rather than to love and worship God. Relishing emotions can lead to *idolatry*. Fours need to disrupt this imagination-based brewing of emotions and incorporate a healthy One's objectivity, strategic wisdom, and self-discipline to act on what is good and loving. For instance, when they listen to their favorite music, instead of using it to manipulate their mood, they can give thanks to God, journal an insight, or share the experience with a friend.

Empathy for Beloved Fours

You feel torn between wanting privacy and friends who appreciate you.

You see your colleague's success and it makes you feel inferior.

There's a deep longing in you to be appreciated as unique and authentic.

In your self-talk you're cutting yourself down and shaming yourself for having needs.

You're sinking in a vortex of negative feelings.

Your energy is going to emotional fantasies and not your goals.

It's hard for you to take action and move your project forward.

Jesus as the Model Four

Jesus' Emotions Are Loving

Yeshua is the Four maestro. Appreciating Jesus' emotional health guides Fours, and all of us, to release feelings of distress and shame and be strengthened to bring beauty and love into the world.

Consider Jesus' emotions in the story of Mary anointing him. This was shortly before he was arrested and crucified, and he was in the midst of nerve-racking days of persecution. He felt the stress and sorrow. Then a banquet was held in his honor, and Mary poured fragrant oil on his feet and massaged them with tender affection and empathy (John 12:1–11). "She knew that Jesus needed something more than a party to lift his spirits. She wanted him to know that she understood the pressure and sadness in his life. He needed to feel cared for."[17] But his apostles sneered about this being a terrible waste (see Matt. 26:8–9; Mark 14:4). Surely "Jesus felt very misunderstood. Could they not sense how heavy his heart was? They were begrudging him this gesture of love from his woman friend!"[18] Even though his own emotional needs were dismissed, Jesus did not react with insecurity, shame, or self-absorption because he was securely attached to his Father (John 12:49–50). Instead, he felt empathy for Mary being scoffed at and spoke up to protect her and affirm her beautiful act of devotion.

In his famous *Confessions*, Augustine (Four) is in Mary's position at Jesus' feet. He prays to the "physician of my intimate self,"[19] making a clean breast of his sins, pouring out all his emotional distress, crying out with deep longings to feel God's loving presence, and giving thanks continually for the Lord's mercy.

> ▶ **PRAYER:** *Jesus, help me to celebrate that you love me and others just as we are.*

Virtue to Cultivate: Emotional Balance

Sundar Singh (Four) illustrates how to rely on Jesus to be emotionally balanced in difficulties, which is the virtue that Fours es-

Jesus as a Healthy Four

Jesus' dramatic ministry was done in love, not ego, so people praised God (Mark 2:12).

His sensitivity was channeled into compassion, not being touchy or reactive (Matt. 9:36).

When he was disappointed by his friends, he did not fall into self-pity; he was caring.[20]

In emotional distress Jesus acted with love for God and others (John 12:27–28).

The "man of sorrows" avoided depression and gave empathy to others (Luke 19:41–44).

He was humiliated at the cross, but he overcame shame to love his enemies (Heb. 12:2).

pecially need. He developed global influence in the early 1900s as an Indian who became a Christian missionary yet dressed in the yellow turban and yellow robe of a sadhu (a Hindu sage and ascetic). When Sundar was fourteen years old, his mother tragically died, and he was overcome by grief. He felt his training in the Sikh and Christian religions failed him. One night, in despair, he burned his Bible page by page and planned to throw himself in front of the next train early in the morning. He stayed up all night and prayed, "O God, if there is a God, reveal yourself to me tonight." Shortly before the train was to arrive, he saw a bright, glowing light with a man in the center who spoke out loud: "How long will you deny me? I died for you; I have given my life for you." Then he showed his nail-pierced hands. Immediately, Sundar dropped to his knees and put faith in Jesus as his Savior. But his father, brother, and friends ostracized him. Still, he went on to become a nomadic teacher for Jesus, traveling barefoot from village to village in India and beyond, carrying nothing but a New Testament. He became known as "the apostle with bleeding feet."[21]

Very much a loner Four who had been dramatic, emotional, and melancholy, Sundar integrated healthy One objectivity and self-discipline to increase in emotional health and stability. Instead of indulging selfish feelings and desires in fantasy and rumination, he observed and thought about his emotions, developing what psychologists call an "observing ego." He became a godly Four by training his emotions through disciplines like talking with a spiritual director, studying and meditating on the New Testament, solitude, prayer, and fasting. His intimacy with God supported his ministry of healing for the sick and discipling people in the way of Master Jesus. He used Jesus' method of telling parables and engaging people in conversations. Through his union with Christ, he had healthy Four capacity to feel pain and yet love others.[22]

Key Soul Care Practice: Thankfulness

Fours especially need the discipline of gratitude to counteract their tendencies to get down in the dumps or wish they could be in a greener pasture somewhere else. Being thankful strengthens our emotional balance, the key virtue for Fours. It's healthy for all of us to enjoy the moment at hand by giving thanks to God (and to others) for whatever is beautiful, helpful, wise, and loving (Phil. 4:6, 8–9). It's also important to give thanks to God in response to what is hurtful or wrong, which opens us to participate in the Kingdom of God where "all things work together for good to those who love God" (Rom. 8:28 NKJV). Research studies have found that people who write down things they are thankful for are happier, healthier, and more optimistic, and they exercise more.[23] Another way to practice thankfulness is to take a "gratitude shower" by giving thanks for dozens of small blessings. It's easy to do this while taking a shower, going for a walk, or going to sleep. Thankfulness balances melancholy Fours and helps them to feel and enjoy God's many blessings.

Brennan Manning often shared that meditating on the response of the bride (Four) to Solomon's courtship in the Song of Songs helped him appreciate the passionate love of Jesus as the

Bridegroom of his soul. Romantic, deep-feeling Fours resonate. For all of us, it can awaken our *positive* emotions that go with true love and intimacy with God and help us not to slide down into shame or envy. "The drumbeats of doom in your head will be replaced by a song in your heart, which could lead to a twinkle in your eye."[24]

> Jesus calls to you, "Get up, my dear friend, fair and beautiful lover—come to me!" (2:10 MSG).
>
> You reply, "I am my lover's. I'm all he wants. I'm all the world to him!" (7:10 MSG).

Soul Care Practices for Fours

Celebrate God's goodness and blessings, even when you're disappointed.

Pray, "The LORD is my shepherd; I shall not want" (Ps. 23:1 NKJV).

Review the story of Joseph (Four) in Genesis 37–50 and journal insights for your life.

Pray to detach your emotions from people's reactions to you and your creativity so that praise does not exalt you and criticism does not plummet you.

Read the allegory *Hinds' Feet on High Places* by Hannah Hurnard (Four) for emotional balance and encouragement in your spiritual journey.

Enjoy Brennan Manning's Breath Prayer, "Abba, I belong to you."[25]

SOUL TALK

1. What did you learn about Fours and how they experience shame?

2. What is an example of a time that you wanted to be special but felt overlooked?

3. What do you appreciate about Jesus as the consummate Four? How do you feel about this?

4. How does it feel for you to appreciate Jesus as the Bride-groom of your soul?

5. Which of the soul care practices for Fours seem most helpful for you personally? Why?

How Fours Become Like Jesus

1. Appreciate Jesus' emotional stability to relieve shame (like a healthy One).

2. Watch and pray to not compare yourself to others (root sin) or fall into shame.

3. Pray to not react to stress with shame and overhelping (like an unhealthy Two).

4. Ask for empathy when you feel low or bad about yourself.

5. Rely on Jesus' emotional balance (virtue) to be creative and loving.

INDIVIDUALIST

Help for Shame

The LORD GOD helps me,
so I will not be ashamed.

Isaiah 50:7 NCV

W hen we started Soul Shepherding, I (Kristi) gravitated to a serving role, supporting Bill in his ministry of speaking, writing, and pastoring. I didn't see myself as a minister or a leader.

Growing up as the youngest of three girls, I tried to keep up with my sisters, but they out-achieved me. My parents were Christian leaders and ministers who were in the spotlight, and I was used to being in their shadow. My mom was on the board of an international Christian ministry, and she traveled around the world, training pastors and leaders out of her experience as an accomplished speaker and author. After church I would hear her talk about how the speaker's delivery could have been more effective. My sister also is a gifted speaker and Bible study leader who was the executive director of an international ministry and led four hundred women in a Bible study ministry. I compared myself to my mom and sister and felt shame.

In college I began dating Bill, who was a respected leader on campus. When he ministered, I prayed and supported him. Afterwards, people wanted to talk to him, not me. I waited in the background and felt left out. It was the same after college. He was invited to leaders' retreats and gatherings, but I was not. He had endless energy and ministry ideas, but I did not. I did have my doctorate in psychology and experience in ministry at Bill's side, but mostly I felt like a servant. My work as a therapist was in private; no one except my clients saw or knew what I had to offer.

After all, wasn't I created to just be a helper? I wasn't the one with the superpowers—I was the *sidekick*.

Hiding from Love

One day, after I had shared in my small group, a woman challenged me on the way to my car: "Are you teaching? You need to share what God has taught you. I need to learn from you, and so do others." I was surprised. I heard her but still felt doubt. A month later, as I was cleaning up after a seminar that Bill taught, a friend came up to me and declared, "God wants you to know he sees you." Did she know I felt unseen, invisible, and unwanted? *God knew.*

This is what shame does. It bullies you into hiding your gifts and making yourself small. You idealize others and devalue what God has given you to do. Most people feel shame in some way at some times. *Heart types live in shame.*

I became convicted by the Holy Spirit that I was like the man in Jesus' parable who buried his talent because he was afraid (Matt. 25:18). I felt that what I had to offer as a speaker was not valuable or needed, so I buried my gift to protect myself from the risk of failure and criticism. My fear came from feeling unworthy and inadequate. I couldn't bear the prospect of someone judging me when I already felt bad about myself. I was stuck in the defense part of the cycle of shame (see chapter 6). As our friend John Townsend explains, it's self-defeating "to keep the 'unloved' parts of ourselves forever under wraps, with the hope that in time, they will go away and not cause us more pain."[1] *That's hiding from love.*

I have noticed that when people don't feel understood they tend to feel shame—even though they have not done anything wrong. I have found this to be true in my own life. When I share an emotion or experience and am not received with personal support and validation, I'm prone to fall into shame and start hiding my inner self. Shame becomes like a dark cloud that hovers over me, but I don't realize how my perceptions and experiences are being darkened. Often someone who knows me well, like Bill or a close friend, will gently point out that I'm lost in a shame cloud. This gives me the opportunity to step into the light of God's love and grace. When I take courage to be emotionally honest with myself, God, and a trustworthy ambassador of Christ, then I can receive the grace I need.

When Adam and Eve disobeyed God's instructions, they felt shame and went into hiding. God came for them in love and grace (Gen. 3:7-10, 21). In his incarnation, Jesus came for us as the light of the world to free us from the darkness of sin and shame. He released the woman caught in adultery from shame (John 8:1–11). Jesus wants to free you from shame too. Will you come out of hiding, pretending, and performing? Will you dare to believe that God loves all of you as you are?

Agreeing with God's Grace

I (Bill) shared in chapter 5 how, as a One with a stress line to Four, I also have struggled with shame. When you feel shame, the thing you most need is to not be alone but to be with someone who says "me too" and listens. Verbalizing shame feelings to a friend or spiritual director who gives you empathy ushers in God's healing grace. Brennan Manning (Four) did that for many people as a Christian writer and retreat leader. Brennan struggled with alcoholism, and after a relapse and recovery he confessed:

> Wallowing in shame . . . self-hatred, and guilt over real or imagined failings . . . emotions churning in self-destructive ways, closes us within the mighty citadel of self, and preempts the presence of a compassionate God. From personal experience I can testify that the

language of low self-esteem is harsh and demanding; it abuses, accuses, criticizes, rejects, finds fault, blames, condemns, reproaches, and scolds in a monologue of impatience and chastisement. . . . We would never judge any of God's other children with the savage condemnation with which we crush ourselves. . . .

We hide our true selves from God. . . . We withhold from Jesus what is most in need of his healing touch. In order to grow in trust, we must allow God to see us and love us precisely as we are.[2]

We're all "ragamuffins" loved by God just as we are, not as we should be.[3] Grace is the antidote to shame, but we miss it if we follow the pernicious philosophy of our world to replace God's love with self-love and self-help. God is taken out of the picture or put in the back seat. The partial truth in self-love is that it is the responsibility of each person to participate in the care they need. Jesus taught, "Love your neighbor *as yourself*" (Mark 12:31, emphasis added). But self-love is only truly loving when it remains linked to loving God and neighbor, as it is in Jesus' greatest commandment. Better wording for our need is *agreeing with God's grace.* That keeps love's initiative, power, and glory with God. To agree with grace is to ask for it, wait for it, absorb it, and give thanks to God for it. It's soaking in God's favor that brings joy and power.

Whatever challenges you and your family and friends are feeling, Jesus beams God's smile into your hearts: "Blessed are you. I see you. I feel your pain. I want you to be with me."[4]

Feeling Sad, Not Bad

Often sin—either my own sin or someone else's sin against me—is related to shame. But there's a lot of confusion today about "sin." Many people view sin as bad things we do to make God angry. Here's our definition: *Sin is the heart choice to reject God's loving care and wise governance; it's failing to love God and people.* In the Bible the Greek word for sin simply means "to miss the mark." Like an archer misses the bull's-eye when their sight is off track, so we miss the mark of love when our heart is off track. Adam and Eve sinned when they disobeyed God, wanting to be their own god and run their own lives independent of God (Gen. 3:1–7). Sin may be exciting or pleasurable at first, but sin is *slop*, as the prodigal son found out when he landed in a pigsty (Luke 15:15–16). To reject God's lovingkindness leaves us empty, splits our souls, and wounds other people.

Many people are also confused by the belief that when someone sins, they *should* feel guilty and ashamed, as if these are healthy feelings or helpful motivations. That's not true. In the Bible, Paul calls guilt and shame "worldly sorrow" that draws us away from God and into death (2 Cor. 7:10). That's an unhealthy response to sin. In contrast, "godly sorrow" is sadness or conviction that draws us near to God and leads to life, freedom, and no regrets. Paul elaborates, "And now, isn't it wonderful all the ways in which this distress has goaded you closer to God? You're more alive, more concerned, more sensitive, more reverent, more human, more passionate, more responsible" (2 Cor. 7:11 MSG). Godly sorrow is the healthy, holy, and helpful response to sin. (See chapter 17 for further discussion on worldly and godly sorrow.)

Shame taunts you with judgment to isolate you: "I'm not a good friend—I'm not kind. I should have been more loving. What's the matter with me? I'm screwing up another friendship! That's why I work all the time and keep to myself."

Sadness with empathy woos you to restore relationship: "I'm disappointed I hurt her with unkind words. I missed an opportunity to be a blessing. Jesus, have mercy on me and strengthen me to be the kind of person who is gracious with others as you are to me."

This is why we teach the maxim "Don't feel *bad* about your sin, feel *sad*." It's the same with your mistakes, hurts, struggles, and weaknesses. Feeling *bad* will depress and isolate you, giving the accuser power to beat you down (Rev. 12:10). Feeling *sad* helps you seek empathy and grace from Christ Jesus or a friend (2 Cor. 5:2, 20). It's the difference between life and death! (In chapter 17 we unpack this further.)

I (Kristi) took the risk of sharing my feelings of shame with my spiritual director and others who cared for me. I realized that underneath feeling bad about myself I was sad that I was missing out on my dream to minister with Bill. I felt sad for people like me who needed to hear my story and insights and receive from the grace that God had given me. So I started putting myself out there in talks, blogs, podcasts, conferences, and whatever doors the Lord opened. I chose to trust that God and others would appreciate my heart. When I fell into shame, I would process my experience with my spiritual director or a friend and practice trusting Jesus to be enough for me as I stepped onto the stage as a speaker or leader. As I began to step out with faith in God and speak up, I was amazed at how God worked through me and people responded.

From Shame to True Confidence

Sean (Three) shared his story with me (Kristi). He was a successful lead pastor of a large church and had a devoted wife and talented son, but secretly he struggled with shame. He felt pressure to grow the church, meet the congregation's expectations for Sunday services, lead a successful fundraising campaign for the new building, and keep the staff morale high. He overworked because he was afraid of the shame of failing, and anything less than higher achievement than before felt like failure. He couldn't let God or his congregants, elders, and family down. The harder he worked the more depressed he became. He stopped coming into the office every day and instead worked from home, distracting himself with house projects that he could achieve.

As the church suffered declines in attendance, the expectations on Sean mounted and some people became critical of his leadership. Finally, he'd had enough and resigned, hoping to breathe and push reset. But he sunk deeper into shame. He'd disappointed the people he loved. He'd lost income just when his son had been accepted at his dream college.

To ward off shame, Sean enrolled in seminary, believing that more training and knowledge would give him the confidence he lacked. This is a temptation for those of us in the Shame triad. We think achieving, being admired, pleasing people, or creating something special will free us from shame. It may for a short time, but it doesn't address our problem of looking to secure ourselves by boosting our reputation and controlling what others think of us and hiding behind a false image.

Thankfully, Sean got help when he responded to his wife's plea to go to counseling. He needed a safe place where his income did not depend on his performance or what others thought of him. A place where he could step out of hiding and into the light by being emotionally honest. A place where his shame didn't bully him and he could meet the gracious hand of God removing from him that dark shroud of shame.

As he grew in receiving and agreeing with God's grace and empathy from his counselor and a colleague, he started to breathe again. He decided to pull out of seminary and invest in his personal spiritual formation. In time he was able to recalibrate and received a call to a new church that was a great fit for him and his family.

Jesus Is Your Shame Taker!

With love for you, Jesus carried your shame to the cross along with your sin.[5] In the Gospels, he was beaten down by people and may have felt bad, embarrassed, sheepish, or ostracized—even though he knew he did nothing wrong and kept trusting in his Father's love. When you feel mistreated or bad about yourself, Jesus is with you and feels for you. Here are some examples:

Jesus was judged for being tenderhearted and compassionate (Mark 3:1–6; 14:3–10).

He was written off because he was from the hick town of Nazareth (John 1:46).

He was derided by his family as crazy and by the priests as demon-possessed (Mark 3:21–22).

He was laughed at by a crowd when he wanted to heal a girl who had died (Mark 5:39–40).

He was slandered as the friend of sinners, a drunkard, and a glutton (Matt. 9:9–13; 11:19).

He was brushed off as a blue-collar worker (Matt. 13:55).

He was bullied by wealthy religious authorities (John 18:22; 19:6–16).

He was stripped, abused, and tortured by soldiers as a crowd mocked him (Mark 15:15–24).

When you feel shame, you can look to Jesus as your Shame Taker. You'll find that he is feeling with you and for you. In shame-inducing situations, our Savior and Friend shows us how to relish the favor of his Abba, who always cherishes and never abandons us (John 8:29; 10:29). In other words, Jesus brought his shaming circumstances and ours into his Father's world so that together we could experience sustaining security and invigorating joy in the ever-present heavenly kingdom of light and love (Col. 1:13–14).

To deepen your trust in Jesus' shining face of grace, it's especially helpful to spend some time in solitude appreciating the Gospel stories that show him as your Shame Taker (see the list above). Then, whenever you are tempted with shame, pray that you'd receive Jesus' ministry of grace to you. Through Jesus Christ, you and your loved ones are totally accepted, wanted, and cherished forever!

Solitude for a Loved Heart

Heart types and feelers especially need solitude because it corrects their dependency on seeking affection and approval from other people and helps them discover who they are apart from others.[6] Their feelings of inadequacy move them to put out an ideal self that other people will admire but that keeps them trapped in shame. Solitary prayer surfaces their real self that needs to be loved and helps them develop the virtue for their type.

Twos stop people-pleasing, humbly ask for what they need, and love freely.

Threes quit overperforming, become authentic, and promote others' success.

Fours abandon being special, discipline their emotions, and
do good work.

Henri Nouwen (Two) defined prayer as listening to the voice of
God that calls you the beloved. He writes that in solitary prayer "you
will discover within yourself a desire to hear that voice longer and
more deeply. It is like discovering a well in the desert. Once you have
touched fertile ground, you want to dig deeper. This digging and
searching for an underground stream is the discipline of prayer."[7]

At Jesus' baptism, before he had accomplished anything in his
public ministry, his Abba showered him with unconditional love
and grace: "This is my beloved Son, and I am wonderfully pleased
with him" (Matt. 3:17 TLB). This experience was so life-defining
for Jesus that about two years later, after being persecuted and
threatened by a mob, he went back to the site of his baptism at

Heart Prayers for Shame

Being emotionally honest with Jesus and trusting God's grace through
him alleviates shame. Here are some heart prayers to help with shame:

Hold your heart as you thank the Holy Spirit for filling you with
God's love (Rom. 5:5).

Smile! "Dear child, Abba's love for you is wonderful!" (1 John
3:1, authors' paraphrase).

"Christ lives in you, and he is your hope of sharing in God's glory"
(Col. 1:27 CEV).

Pray Psalm 31 or another psalm that gives feeling words to comfort shame.[8]

Write down anything you feel bad about and then draw a cross
over the list (Col. 2:14).

Listen to the birds and recall that the Lord sings with love over
you (Zeph. 3:17)!

the Jordan River and reimmersed himself in his experience as the beloved of the Father (John 10:40).

Let's contemplate Jesus' baptism now (Matt. 3:13–17). Imagine yourself with Jesus at his baptism in the Jordan River . . . See yourself step into the waters . . . Look into Jesus' eyes and see him smiling at you . . . See the heavens open . . . Watch the dove of the Holy Spirit descend onto Jesus . . . Hear the Father's affirmation of Jesus as his beloved . . .

Now, identify yourself as being *in Christ*. Then slowly pray and repeat each line of the Beloved Prayer to praise Jesus, receive the Father's affirmation, and intercede for friends:

"Jesus, you are the Beloved . . ."

"Jesus, I am the Beloved . . ."

"Jesus, [*my friend*] is the Beloved . . ."[9]

Steps to Help with Shame

The action steps below describe the process to relieve shame.

1. *Identify shame.* If you are judging yourself or putting demanding expectations on yourself, then probably shame is lurking and you need care.

2. *Ask for empathy.* You are not meant to suffer alone with shame, guilt, or depression. Opening your heart to God and a caring listener can provide the grace you need. The feeling words list in chapter 7 will help you get started.

3. *Agree with grace.* If you agree with the voices of condemnation, it will damage your heart. Instead, agree with Jesus' empathy, comfort, truth, and power to help you trust that God's favor is for you now.

4. *Practice solitude.* Being alone with Jesus is difficult for Heart types or anyone who is a feeler or an extrovert. When you're alone on retreat, it separates you from people's affirmations and work you want to accomplish, which

may make you feel antsy, inadequate, or empty. But this enables you to open your heart deeper to receive empathy, grace, and insight from God and people you trust.

5. *Be esteemed in Christ.* As God the Father loves Jesus, so he loves you! You can affirm the truth, "In Christ I am esteemed." Deepening your identity in Christ is supported by engaging your Heart center in solitude and other soul care practices like praying Scripture, emotional honesty, and thankfulness.

SOUL TALK

1. What is something you learned about shame or Jesus as your Shame Taker?
2. How do you relate to Kristi's story of hiding and feeling insignificant (personally or for a loved one)?
3. How might it help you to respond to your sins and struggles by feeling sad, not bad?
4. What was your experience with the Beloved Prayer? How did you feel?
5. Which of the "Heart Prayers for Shame" seem most helpful for you personally? Why?

Check out our free bonus resources for more help with shame. You can also talk with one of the spiritual directors or coaches who have earned a certificate in our Soul Shepherding Institute. Just scan the QR code or go to SoulShepherding.org/enneagram.

PART 3

ANXIETY

A BUSY BRAIN

Enneagram Types: Five (Observer) • Six (Loyalist) • Seven (Enthusiast)

Anxiety as Repressed Emotion

Jesus promises, "I give you peace, the kind of peace only I can give. . . . So don't be worried or afraid."

John 14:27 CEV

onna (Six) came to talk with me (Kristi) after having her first panic attack at age seventy-seven. A few years earlier she had been diagnosed with colon cancer and went through chemotherapy, but it didn't work and her health had taken a nosedive. She was stubbornly resisting giving up her driver's license and accepting end-of-life care. Donna had been strong and independent all of her adult life. As a child who suffered physical abuse, she learned to survive by never being vulnerable. Instead, she was the responsible one who was loyal to others and resourceful to solve their problems and meet their needs. She had internalized the stress overload of her health crisis, which created a backlog of repressed fear, anger, and grief. Because she had always been so capable outwardly, she did not see that she was anxious and insecure on the inside.

By the end of our conversation, some tears came out. This continued the next time as she admitted how vulnerable and scared she felt. Processing her emotions and receiving empathy took down her anxiety levels, which had prompted her panic attack. This, in turn, enabled her to access her normally strong abilities to think logically and solve problems. It's like her cognitive piping got unclogged so her thinking could flow. Her love for her sons also flowed, and she was able to make the hard decisions about her needs for physical care.

Head Types

Anxiety

Anxiety disorders are the most common mental health disorder. One study showed that 31 percent of US adults will experience an anxiety disorder at some point in their life.[1] Anxiety is the third of the four big hurts in life and the core emotion in the Head triad of the Enneagram (Fives, Sixes, and Sevens). All of the other types except for Twos have a line or potential wing that puts them in the Head mode at times, but Twos can choose to develop this intelligence center. It's especially as we function in the Head mode that we suffer from the cycle of anxiety (see figure 12.1).

Anxiety like Donna's is a secondary emotion from repressed fear, anger, shame, or grief. To get anxious is a reaction to stress, sin (yours or someone else's), or personal weakness. Remember the Bible teaches that anxiety and fear are not sins but can lead to sin by undermining trust in God (Ps. 139:23–24; Rom. 14:23). Anxiety can get worse because of the power of your personality to charm you into denying your problems, stress, worries, and fears. You may try to secure your own well-being through getting

Figure 12.1

Cycle of Anxiety

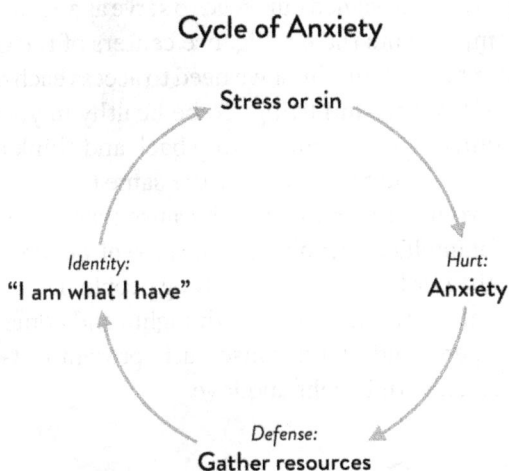

Stress or sin

Identity:
"I am what I have"

Hurt:
Anxiety

Defense:
Gather resources

and controlling resources. Without realizing it, you may develop the unhealthy identity of "I am what I have," which will leave you feeling empty and insecure.

If you are a Head type or have a stress line to Five, Six, or Seven, you are especially vulnerable to loop in obsessive thinking that traps you in a quicksand of increasing fear and anxiety. You may run on a fearful script: "What's going to happen to me? How am I going to survive? How can I prepare myself to keep bad things from happening? How do I move forward in life? How do I cope?"[2] The Head types, which we'll unpack in the next three chapters, get stuck in unhealthy personality habits that perpetuate dysfunctional anxiety.

Fives withdraw in fear by gathering knowledge or money to be self-contained.

Sixes project their fears into problem-solving or following authority for security.

Sevens escape from their fears into idealizing things and seeking pleasure.

Clear Thinking

Our loving Creator designed our Head to serve as an intelligence center that complements the intelligence centers of the Gut and Heart. To be our best self in Christ we need to access each of these three modes of learning and living. To be healthy in your Head center, give yourself permission to step back and think about a situation before speaking or acting. At the same time, be careful you don't deny your fears or anxieties because that will diminish your capacity for intelligent thinking. Instead, seek out empathetic listening from the Lord and from safe, strong people. This will help you to quiet your inner chatterbox of thoughts and come to rest in a calm and open mind that is consciously present to God and others, ready to act with insight and love.

Understanding Anxiety

Some of the most insightful and inspiring words in the Bible are Jesus' teachings on anxiety in his Sermon on the Mount in Matthew 5–7. For instance, he encourages us, "Do not worry about your life. . . . Look at the birds of the air; they do not sow or reap or store away in barns, and yet your heavenly Father feeds them. Are you not much more valuable than they? . . . See how the flowers of the field grow. . . . Therefore do not worry" (6:25–34). In his great sermon the Wonderful Counselor taught on anxiety in 44 percent of the verses! That's more than any other subject. His message is that you'll suffer with anxiety if, instead of finding security in God's kingdom, you try to *secure yourself* in the world by:

Giving, praying, and fasting to impress people (6:1–18)
Stockpiling money for yourself (6:19–24)
Using shopping and eating to make you happy (6:25–27)
Dressing to get attention (6:28–34)
Trying to control people by judging or fixing them (7:1–6)
Relying on false spokespersons to excite you (7:15–20)
Sounding or acting spiritual to impress people (7:21–23)

Anxiety is often embedded in these situations. What is anxiety? You feel it at times, but what defines it? Anxiety is an emotion of nervousness, pressure, or apprehension about a pending event or relational interchange that's not going well. Often people describe feeling anxious as being "stressed out," but really anxiety is being "stressed *in*." It's internalized stress. Often you don't realize you're overstressed until the wild animals of anxiety pounce on you out of nowhere.

Contrary to the stereotype, it's not weaker people who are most likely to suffer from anxiety but *stronger* ones.[3] People who struggle with anxiety are typically earnest, capable, and responsible, and they're anxious because they're trying to control situations and denying their personal needs or emotional struggles. Anxiety is a dis-ease of overcontrol and undigested emotions of fear, anger, shame, or sadness.

To be emotionally whole and relationally loving like Jesus you'll need to care for your anxious emotions and bring your temptations and stress into the Kingdom of God rather than trying to secure yourself by controlling situations, things, or people. The core emotion of anxiety has many different hues. Learning to name anxiety by using the feeling words from the list below will help you to receive empathy and offer it to others.

Feeling Words for Anxiety

Emotions: concerned, troubled, uneasy, stressed, distressed, disquieted, worried, nervous, fretting, bothered, fussy, angsty, overwhelmed, in travail, restless, sleepless, ambiguous, distracted, confused, divided, discombobulated, vacillating, fragmented, hurried, harried, frenzied, miserable

Fear emotions: startled, afraid, scared, apprehensive, suspicious, foreboding, trapped, hypervigilant, terrified, trembling, trepidation, cowardly, panicked, dread

Doubt emotions: doubtful, vascillating, wavering, apprehensive, scrupulous, mistrusting, skeptical, cynical

> *Idioms*: on pins and needles, antsy, ants in my pants, fidgety, jittery, nail-biting, fainthearted, of two minds, on the fence, up in the air, cold feet, cold sweat, shaky, jumpy, heebie-jeebies, butterflies in my stomach, the willies, racing mind, rushing pell-mell, the creeps, chills down my spine, basket case, at the end of my tether, tied up in knots, freaking out, lost my nerve, like a chicken with its head cut off, struck dumb, scared stiff, scared to death, petrified
>
> *Hebrew idioms*: river that floods,[4] darting back and forth[5]

As the Old Testament idioms and many of the English idioms reflect, anxiety and fear are physical. Your brain is busy all the time, and in your body you may experience jitteriness, sickness, tiredness, trembling, shallow breathing, sweating, increased heart rate, dry mouth, tension in your muscles, dizziness, or tossing and turning in bed.

Anxiety, Fear, and Adrenaline

In the Head anxiety mode we may be like the little Dutch boy who tries to plug a leaking dike with his finger. Commitments to people, responsibilities, expectations, relational breakdowns, temptations, decisions, grief, and more surge against the wall of our defense mechanisms. The pressure of the surging water keeps creating more holes in the dike and threatening to burst the dam and flood our village. But we don't have enough fingers to plug all the holes!

It's helpful to distinguish between anxiety and fear. Anxiety is generalized, whereas fear is specific, like being afraid of rejection, public speaking, or spiders. Often anxiety is *repressed fear that's not felt.* (It also can be repressed shame, anger, or sadness.) Many anxious people are not able to say, "I feel anxious. Can you listen and give me empathy?" Instead, they have thoughts or vague feelings of pressure, hurry, restlessness, apprehension, pessimism, self-doubt, irritability, frustration, or worry. Or they may not consciously feel any of those anxiety-related emotions because they're externalizing their anxiety through projection, fixing people, or cleaning.

We clearly see the interplay of fear and anxiety in Donna's story. She developed panic disorder, an anxiety disorder in which a person is overwhelmed by panic attacks that come on suddenly, seemingly out of nowhere, and that can't be controlled. The experience is so frightening that you become afraid of having another one. That's panic—*fear of fear*. But you don't start out being crippled by fear. You're just going through stress and marshaling all your resources to deal with things, not realizing that you are denying fear, which over time generates a flood of anxiety that will burst through the dike in the form of a panic attack.

To some extent every person probably suffers with fear or anxiety at times, even those who are not Head types. Here are the most common fears reported in recent studies:

Most people fear rejection
77 percent fear public speaking[6]
61 percent fear going to the dentist[7]
40 percent fear flying[8]
31 percent fear failure[9]
20 percent admit to fearing death (it's probably much higher)[10]

Additionally, there are specific phobias that many people have, like being afraid of the dark, heights, spiders, or open spaces. And not only do we deny our fears but we tend to avoid the situations that make us afraid, which strengthens the fear and *shrinks our life*. That's what happens with panic disorder and why it often includes agoraphobia, which is a fear of leaving home or another circle of safe places. Effective therapeutic treatments for overcoming fear and anxiety center on taking courage to do what scares you with the support of a therapist or friend. If we could put this into an equation it would look like this:

Courage = Empathy + Action

Anxiety is physical. For instance, Christian psychologist Archibald Hart specialized in helping people with a form of anxiety called "hurry sickness," which includes a strong link between adrenaline and stress. He explains, "We live at a pace too fast for our bodies. This hurried lifestyle creates a persistent internal state of emergency that keeps our stress hormones elevated."[11] This is especially true for type A personalities, which account for as much as 50 percent of the US population.[12] Enneagram Sixes and Sevens are often type A, along with Eights, Ones, and Threes. A hurried lifestyle is called a *sickness* because the elevated levels of adrenaline and cortisol cause heart disease and other health problems, along with eroding the vitality of our soul.

As a type A counselor and pastor, I (Bill) burned out in my late thirties. I discovered that hurry sickness was a main culprit and I had been unconsciously depending on adrenaline because it gave me energy, confidence, speed, and success. I was rushing around, impatient, and had a low frustration tolerance. Whenever I slowed down, like on vacation, I became bored and depressed from adrenaline withdrawal and kept wanting to go back to work. My hectic schedule, doing too much, downing caffeine, and running late—and even the exciting church services that I liked—were all ways I was jacking myself up with adrenaline.

In my spiritual renewal that began at age forty, I learned how to care for my soul in many ways, like enjoying Sabbath rest, setting boundaries, receiving empathy, meditating on Scripture, and purposefully coming down from adrenaline spikes to relax—even when it meant persisting through boredom to get to the other side where I could feel the gentle blessings of peace and contentment in simple things. I was surprised that this approach not only got me unhooked from adrenaline but also cured my chronic anxiety.[13]

Renewing Your Mind

When I (Kristi) was seven years old, I met Corrie ten Boom (Six), the famous Christian who harbored Jews to protect them from the Nazi regime during World War II. She spoke at our church after her bestselling book *The Hiding Place* was published. I liked listening to her Dutch accent and was so impressed with her courage for Jesus (like a virtuous Six). She captivated the respect of our whole church. The best part was that afterwards we hosted her in our home and she slept in my room! My parents told me not to bother her, but I snuck close and was gazing at her from the hallway, admiring her beautiful silver hair that was rolled up into a bun that looked like a halo. Then she let her hair down and it rolled out in waves that fell below her waist. She saw me peeking and invited me to come in. She asked me personal questions and listened to me with interest and warmth. She told me she was the youngest girl in her family just like me. It impressed me how she was so emotionally present, connective, patient, and kind. I decided I wanted to be like her, which is one reason why I have long hair to this day!

When I was older, the movie based on *The Hiding Place* came out, and I was amazed by the whole story of her life and to see that the loving woman I had interacted with was such a great saint. After that, my grandparents took me to Holland and I saw her clock shop, where she was the first woman to become a licensed watchmaker. I walked into the secret room in her house where her family hid eight hundred Jews to save their lives from Hitler's regime. I stood where she, her sister Betsie, and their father had been abducted by soldiers and freighted off like cattle to a concentration camp where they were horribly persecuted and abused. Yet, through all her suffering, Corrie trusted Jesus, kept a good attitude, and served God by helping fellow prisoners, including smuggling in Bibles for them. After the war was over, she happened to meet one of the prison guards from the camp where her dear sister had died, and she forgave him. I came to deeply admire her loyalty to God and her bravery in risking her life to love other people.

A story about Corrie illustrates the source of her positive faith, despite being in dreadful circumstances. It's especially helpful for Sixes like her, other Head types and thinkers, and all of us who struggle with worry. She and Betsie, along with 1,400 women prisoners, were crammed into a barracks at the Ravensbruck

concentration camp in Germany. It was so unsanitary that they could not breathe without becoming nauseous. In her bunk that first night, Corrie sat up with a start and screamed, "Fleas! Betsie, the place is swarming with them! . . . How can we live in such a place?"[14] But Betsie prayed and the Spirit reminded her of that morning's Bible reading on giving thanks in all circumstances (1 Thess. 5:18). So they began to thank their sovereign Lord Jesus for being together, having a smuggled Bible, and even for the fleas that were biting them! Later, they realized it was because of the fleas that the guards never entered their barracks to mistreat them, which was how they were able to keep their Bible.[15] That's one example of how they made the Word of God their lifeline and drew sustenance and strength from it.

For Sixes, reading, studying, and meditating on the Bible are downstream spiritual disciplines that especially draw on the Head intelligence center.[16]

Scriptures for Anxiety

"I sought the Lord, and he answered me; he delivered me from all my fears" (Ps. 34:4).

"Do not worry about your life. . . . Look at the birds of the air; they do not sow or reap or store away in barns, and yet your heavenly Father feeds them. . . . See how the flowers of the field grow" (Matt. 6:25–26, 28).

"Do not be anxious about anything, but in every situation, by prayer and petition, with thanksgiving, present your requests to God. And the peace of God, which transcends all understanding, will guard your hearts and your minds in Christ Jesus" (Phil. 4:6–7).

"Give all your worries and cares to God, for he cares about you" (1 Pet. 5:7 NLT).

SOUL TALK

1. What did you learn about Head types and anxiety?
2. Which feeling words for anxiety do you relate to personally (or for a loved one)?
3. What is an example of a time or situation in which you experienced one of the common fears?
4. What encouraged you from how Corrie ten Boom responded to her stress and persecution?
5. Which Scripture for anxiety especially encouraged you? Why?

Keys to a Healthy Mindset

1. Open your eyes wide to the mercies of God.

2. Give your body to God in "intelligent worship."

3. "Don't let the world squeeze you into its mould."

4. "Re-mould" your mind in God's Word.

5. Put God's good plan into practice to be like Jesus.

From Romans 12:1–2 Phillips

Type Five: Observer

FELT NEED: Think to have resources

KEY TRAITS: always thinking, perceptive, gathering data, intense, self-sufficient, withdrawn

And this is the way to have eternal life—to know you, the only true God, and Jesus Christ, the one you sent to earth.

John 17:3 NLT

"We read to know we are not alone," a student of C. S. Lewis (Five) says in the movie *Shadowlands*.[1] Fives especially relate to this idea. In *The Great Divorce* Lewis describes a Five character, Sir Archibald, who had started out as an intelligent philosopher but became anxiously obsessed with managing his own survival. He ruined his career with silly speculations that sidetracked him into researching, lecturing, and writing strange stories about the psychic realm. He loved the search for knowledge more than he loved God. Tragically, in the end he chose hell over heaven because he wanted to continue his studies. Lewis lamented that Sir Archibald was unable to have a good laugh at himself and become like a simple and trusting child, which would've enabled him to enter into joy.[2]

Sir Archibald got stuck in his head and lost his heart. His story is a warning sign, especially for Fives and thinkers. We may love books and collect them without reading them. We may be fascinated to prove God's existence but neglect to care about God himself. We may be occupied in sharing Jesus with others but not give a thought to our personal relationship with him. We may organize charities but lose our love for the poor.[3]

Living in Your Head

As a Thinker, I (Bill) have a special affinity for C. S. Lewis' writings and his own personal story of making the journey from his head down into his heart. It's a distance of only eighteen inches, but as a friend of mine says, "Pack a lunch—it's a long way from your head to your heart!" That's why when you ask a Five what they feel they will tell you what they *think*. Often they think their thoughts *are* their feelings because when they're aware of a feeling, they have vivid thoughts about it. Psychologist Beatrice Chestnut explains, "Thinking feels comfortable to Fives because when you think, you can hide. Most people can't tell what others are thinking, whereas when we feel strong emotions, it often shows."[4] That's vulnerability, and Fives like Sir Archibald *do not like to be vulnerable*. For self-protection, they can wall off from other people and not realize it. Typically, Fives are the most emotionally detached of all the personality types—it's how they keep a safe distance and guard against people depleting their inner resources with a flood of words, emotions, or expectations. But isolating emotionally because some people are intrusive is like trying not to breathe because the air is smoggy! Fives need care from people as much as anyone else.

When Kristi and I were on a huge ranch in Texas, we saw a herd of bison that reminded us of Fives. They stood still and strong with their huge eyes fixed on us, very deliberately moving their heads to track us as we walked by. Then, all at once, the herd began to slowly move in unison like a long wave that built momentum and caused the ground to rumble! Like those bison, Fives are intensely observant and slow to act but *powerful* when they do act. They like to sit in the back row of our Soul Shepherding Institute retreats, watching, listening, and thinking. Recently, Kristi had two Fives in an Enneagram webinar that she taught for our spiritual direction students. One Five asked great questions that generated insightful discussions, and the other Five sent the class his study notes, which were well organized and thorough. Every Five I know asks insightful questions and doggedly studies their subject from the ground up.

I'll never forget the time I heard a college president who was a Five give a great speech. It was a hot summer day and there was no air-conditioning in the room. He spoke for twenty minutes from carefully prepared notes with beads of sweat dripping down his forehead. The whole time there were flies buzzing around his head and then swooping onto his face for a sip of sweat. Astonishingly, he was unflinching and undistracted! When he finished his talk, he finally looked at the audience and exhaled. "Man, those flies were really something else!" That's how rigorously Fives can focus. Typically, they have the ability to hunker down to work independently, study, research, analyze data, develop complex ideas, and innovate. These are important leadership abilities that are often overlooked.

Personality Development of Fives

Family Formation: Loner

If you ask a Five what their favorite room was in their childhood home, they'll probably say their bedroom or maybe a library. They retreated from their family into their own private space where they stored their books, computer, musical instruments, tools, or other collection. Many Fives became a *loner*, feeling as if their parent(s) did not want them, were not responsive to their needs, or crossed over their boundaries. Other Fives had to move from place to place as children and could not sink their roots into friendships. Some combination of family experiences, choices, and biological makeup shapes Fives to not expect support from others but to want to be left alone to pursue their own interests without anyone "intruding."

Root Sin: Greed

The desert father Evagrius taught that the deadly sin of hoarding resources was like rowing a heavy-laden boat that easily sinks in a storm.[5] Fives don't realize they're sinking their boat with greed; it's a reaction to fear that's hidden in their unconscious shadow self. Some Fives stockpile wealth like the rich man in Jesus' parable (Luke 12:13–21), but others spend all their money to stockpile knowledge or other resources. Fives don't feel safe needing God or people, so they accumulate piles of money, books or seminars, technology gadgets, photographs, silent retreats, or whatever they think will give them enough resources to feel self-contained and secure. Many Fives are selectively ascetic, denying themselves some things but indulging in others. In stress, they have a side of their personality that's like a hedonistic Seven, trying to fill up an empty soul with food, stuff, or stimulation. Other Fives are broadly ascetic, even minimalistic, and denying themselves resources is their way to not feel afraid of being dependent on others for support.

Defense Mechanism: Intellectualizing

A mother told me (Kristi) that whenever she asked her college-aged son (Five) what he was feeling, he invariably replied, "Fine." She'd reply, "How about some more words?" It was like pulling teeth to try to get some feelings from him. Fives tend to shut down their emotions to focus on their thoughts, which is the unconscious defense mechanism of *intellectualizing*. (Sevens, Ones, and other thinkers are also prone to intellectualize.) They often prefer to withdraw from people and isolate so they won't have to emotionally engage with others or have their energy depleted. In an intimate relationship like marriage, they may avoid affection, sex, and emotional communication.

Most Fives are more afraid of intimacy and emotions than they realize. When they participate in personal conversations, they tend to talk about their feelings *without actually feeling them*. The ability to detach from emotions in order to concentrate mentally helps surgeons, computer programmers, and others to do great work. But as an unconscious habit or relational pattern, it's a soul trap that perpetuates scarcity. The Five's paucity of emotions and intimacy can breed a continuing isolation that starves their soul and the souls of others of much-needed love and nurture.

Emotions of Fives

Core Emotion: Anxiety

My (Kristi's) father was a Five who was emotionally distant and in his head. As a Heart type, I felt rejected and insecure around him, until I came to appreciate that he was inhibited by anxiety, self-doubt, and fear and that *in his heart he really did love me*.

One time my aunt was visiting us, and as she watched him in his ritual of picking lint off the carpet, she playfully said something like, "There goes Fred, walking around *Fredding*!" My father cracked a dry smile under his mustache at my aunt's joke. Like a typical Five, he did not think he was anxious, but I know my father's story. As a boy he put up a wall to cope with being verbally and emotionally abused. He grew up poor during the Great Depression and feared running out of resources, so he learned to be smart and save money. He was determined to always provide well for himself and his family, and he did. Fredding around the house was his unconscious way of externalizing his stress. When he picked up the lint, it made him feel a little more in control for a while.

One of my father's best friends was Dave Stoop, who was also a Five. He was a psychologist and helped my family communicate better about emotions. Dave liked to tell the story of the Inuit people in the Arctic who were afraid of dangerous polar bears. They believed that anyone who wanted to survive as an adult needed to face their fear by literally touching a polar bear, and when they did this they'd receive "the gift of the bear," which was an affirmation of their courage. Dave writes, "In the same way, we will be gifted when we deal with the uncomfortable emotions in our lives . . . the raw, pure, and often scary emotions in each of us. Leaning into those uncomfortable emotions is like touching the bear."[6] Fives need to touch their emotions, especially their master emotions of anxiety and fear that influence their anger, shame, and sadness.

Stress Emotion: Anxiety

Fives try to stay in their heads all the time. They don't realize that they're intellectualizing or avoiding emotions of fear, anger, and shame, which increases their anxious emotions. (Recall from the previous chapter that anxiety is repressed emotion.) In stress Fives take on the characteristics of an unhealthy Seven, which is also an anxiety type. Normally very focused and emotionally flat, Fives in stress become like an anxious Seven that's busy as a bee, on the hop, distracted by whatever is exciting, and seeking pleasure in food or entertainment.

Additional Emotion: Anger

Fives may get angry when someone intrudes into their private space, disrespects them, or pressures them to socialize or be more intimate. Usually the Five's anger churns out of sight in the secret citadel of their mind. They are afraid to express anger directly (except the One-to-One subtypes, who are more vocal with their anger). Anger is like fire—it's overpowering, volatile, and unpredictable—so Fives use their thinking like a firehose to douse their anger. But their anger does not wash away—it just goes into their body and leaks out with sarcasm, snarky comments, or criticism. For personal growth, Fives need to incorporate the traits of a healthy Eight, which accepts angry emotions and tempers them with love. Maturing Fives learn to ask for what they need, set wise boundaries, speak the truth in love, and be assertive to offer their knowledge and gifts to other people.

Additional Emotion: Shame

Many Fives struggle with feeling awkward and embarrassed in social situations. They may prefer to be reading, playing a musical instrument, working, solving a problem, or doing crossword puzzles. In their best self they may want to be warm and friendly, but they can't help standing stiffly with their hands in their pockets and can't quite say what they want to. Deep inside, they probably don't believe they are worthy of receiving love. Fives need to understand their shame as an outgrowth of their anxious insecurity that they don't have enough resources to be who they should be.

Underlying Sadness

Fives often present as calm, even emotionless, but inside they may be dealing with quite a bit of anxiety and depression. Being poker-faced is their self-protective defense mechanism of intellectualizing. Surprisingly, on the inside Fives can be *hypersensitive*. As Observers, they notice everything, especially when people are intrusive or disrespectful. There's a *tender heart* inside every strongheaded Five. That's why they are careful not to bring drama or stress to other people—they don't want anyone to feel smothered like they've experienced in the past.

Michael (Five) and Heather (Two), a pastor and his wife, came to our institute. Heather complained to me (Kristi) that every week Michael got lost in his "sermon head" from Thursday till Sunday. She was carrying all the hurt in the relationship, and he stayed in his head. The more she was emotive with him about this, the more he was rational. The more he was rational, the more she was emotive. This is an example of a relational dynamic called *collusion*.

Michael needed to touch the bear of his emotions. To help him, I started by talking his head language. I taught him that it's natural for him to feel stressed and intruded on by Heather's emotional needs. I explained this in the context of his childhood and how he learned to retreat into his head in order to deal with his mother's depression and emotional reactivity. Later, I helped him use feeling words to tell Heather that he felt pressured and tired. At the same time, I helped her to verbalize her emotions of feeling dismissed and hurt. Michael eventually was able to share his sad feelings and tell Heather that he did not want to be isolated from her. This greatly helped Heather to feel safe and facilitated their intimacy.

Emotional Alarm: Staying in Your Head

A book head (or sermon head) is an example of how Fives and other thinkers stay in their heads and isolate. In studies that have compared the Enneagram and the Myers-Briggs, Fives are almost always identified with thinking and introversion.[7] Similarly, a large survey found that Fives are the least likely type to say they want to spend time with other people when they are stressed.[8] When Fives go into the control tower of their mind, their thoughts keep taking off and circling like planes. They trust in their ideas, data, knowledge, rationalizing, or strategies to feel secure, self-sufficient, and strong. The converse of this is they tend to distrust emotions and experience, which can cause them to struggle with doubts, pessimism, skepticism, or cynicism. Often they don't realize when their rational ego has outsmarted and beguiled them until they run into the reality of their wrong assumptions. Intelligent Fives realize the limitations of their mind and pay attention to their emotions also. As the brilliant Blaise Pascal (Five) wrote in his famous *Pensées* (French for "thoughts") in the seventeenth century, "The heart has its reasons which reason does not know."[9] His discipline of mind and heart made him both a mathematician and a mystic.

In Michael's case, he learned to view his sermon head as an alarm to wake him up to his type Five robotic slide into the abyss of being emotionless, which had a large negative effect on the impact of his sermons. When he caught himself overthinking or obsessing, then he could engage his heart with feeling, stories, deep thinking, and prayer. Much to his surprise, that made his sermons better. Plus, he could choose to engage Heather in personal conversation or enjoying an activity together.

Empathy for Beloved Fives

It's important for you to have lots of time to yourself to think.

You don't want to go to that party and have to do small talk.

Inside you're more sensitive than people realize.

You worry about having enough energy (or another resource).

You got a little lost in your head and felt emotionally distant.

You're afraid that person will overwhelm you.

Down deep you want to be in a safe relationship and be loved.

Jesus as the Model Five

Jesus Has Smart Love

Rabbi Jesus is the perfect Five and, as Dallas Willard (Five) pointed out, he is also the smartest person in the universe (Col. 2:3).[10] Jesus' smarts were more than IQ—he also had smart love. At the end of his Sermon on the Mount, "the crowd burst into applause" because "it was apparent that he was living everything he was saying—quite the contrast to their religion teachers!" (Matt. 7:28–29 MSG). Our opportunity is to develop "the mind of Christ" (1 Cor. 2:16).

How do we do this? How can we incorporate Jesus' healthy, holy Five knowledge and wisdom? By following his way of life. He embraced his hidden years in Nazareth, deepening his trust in his Father, working as a carpenter, loving his family and neighbors, and practicing all of the teachings he'd later share with the world. All through his earthly life, he spent large amounts of time in solitude, Bible study, prayer, and other spiritual disciplines. Jesus was known to be so full of God's radiant wisdom, healing power, and love that crowds constantly prevailed upon him, even when he had retreated into a lonely place (Mark 1:35–37; 3:7; 6:32–34).

We see a Five view of Jesus reflected in the life of Gerhard Tersteegen (Five), a German pietist from the 1700s. He was known as "the recluse in demand" because he had a love for solitude with Jesus, yet people flocked to his "Pilgrim's Hut" and to the places where he taught and they experienced revival.[11]

Father Robert Nogosek (Five) sheds further light on our Lord as a Five: "Jesus' own quest for wisdom involved thinking things through for himself. . . . [Then he] waited for the right moment to share his truth . . . [so] the crowds found a freshness and newness in his teaching, in contrast to the rabbis, whose teaching method was to cite various authorities and give formal teachings."[12] From Jesus' deep-welled soul, he engaged people in relaxed conversations over shared meals, walks, and boat trips to teach them how to live in the abundance of the Kingdom of God.

It's the same for us today. When we follow Jesus and make our work part of Jesus' mission, he leads us out of scarcity thinking (like an unhealthy Five) and into abundance thinking (like a healthy Five). He teaches, "Take nothing with you—trust God to provide," and when we return, he smiles and says, "Did you lack anything?

Jesus as a Healthy Five

Jesus often withdrew from the crowds to pray in lonely places (Luke 5:16).

Jesus taught people through stories and conversations about their daily life (Mark 4:33–34).

He asked questions that motivated people to learn and seek God (Mark 8:27).

Under pressure to go to Jerusalem, he waited patiently and prayed (John 7:6–9).

He listened to Mary and Martha's grief, and he wept for them (John 11:35).

Before clearing the temple of greed and abuse, he carefully observed things.[13]

Of course not. My Father is generous!" (Luke 9:3; 22:35, authors' paraphrase).

> ▶ **PRAYER:** *Jesus, give me confidence to share with others the resources you've given me.*

Virtue to Cultivate: Generosity

Lettie (L. B.) Cowman (Five) provides an inspiring example of giving generously to others, which is the virtue that Fives especially need to work on. She wrote *Streams in the Desert* in 1924, and it became one of the bestselling Christian devotionals of all time. Yet, typical of a Five, she didn't want the limelight. She concealed herself, hiding behind the pen name "L. B.," her husband Charles, and her style of compiling quotes and illustrations from other authors, both famous and unknown. She insisted that her writing came from the Holy Spirit. "Materials come to me, fly to me, from all over the world—in an unlikely tract, an old, faded booklet, crumpled church bulletin, a tattered songbook."[14] She cut out her favorite writings and pasted them into her Bible. *Streams in the Desert* is thousands of bits and pieces from poems, hymns, classic books, letters from a friend, or thoughts God gave her—stitched together into a beautiful tapestry.

Lettie and Charles were missionaries in Japan and founders of the Oriental Missionary Society (OMS). Charles became so ill that he could not sleep or lie down comfortably and was chair-ridden for six years before he died. They prayed for healing but it didn't come. When he was in pain and couldn't sleep, Lettie stretched herself as a Five to stay close to him emotionally, providing empathy and encouraging him with her little devotionals. Later, she shared her writings with missionaries and others, calling them "Thoughts for the Quiet Hour" because that's when she and her husband were crying out to God for comfort. *Streams in the Desert* is the fruit of her generosity in sharing God's wisdom.[15]

Key Soul Care Practice: Bible Study as Worship

The go-to spiritual discipline for Fives is Bible study.[16] Dallas Willard modeled the value of study. He often spent extended hours in solitude, studying the Bible and other books by reading, meditating, cross-referencing, and rereading.[17] But it's easy for Bible students to study and get a congested head that leaves them with an empty heart and relationally distant from people—even loved ones and Jesus. So Dallas explains that in Bible study "we place our minds full upon God and his kingdom . . . [we] take its order and nature into [our] thoughts, and even into [our] feelings and actions."[18] His test for the fruitfulness of Bible study is whether it leads us to *worship God*. He teaches us to study meditatively and pray that God would meet us personally and speak to us.[19] Bible study that inspires us to appreciate and adore the Lord strengthens our capacity to be generous with others, which is the virtue that Fives most need to become more like Jesus. In this way Fives can learn to feel and enjoy relational connection with God and others.

I (Bill) did a Bible study on Thomas (Five) as he is portrayed in the Gospel of John. It's especially encouraging for Fives and other thinkers who struggle to trust God. The Holy Spirit can use Thomas' story to help us articulate our questions, worries, doubts, faltering faith, and curiosity and learn to trust God and to feel his love. In John's Gospel we can come alongside Thomas to see Jesus raise Lazarus from the dead (11:1–16), trust our Lord as the way to know the Father (14:5–7), put our fingers into the nail prints in the hands of our resurrected Savior (20:24–29), and enjoy sharing breakfast on the beach with our eternal Friend (21:1–14).

Fives usually struggle with energy, which is why they need to incorporate the traits of a healthy, assertive Eight. Thomas modeled this in his apostolic mission. According to ancient church tradition and recent archaeological findings, he was a successful missionary and church planter in India until he was martyred for Christ.[20]

Instead of calling him "Doubting Thomas," we ought to appreciate him as "Believing Thomas." In faith we join him in praising Jesus, exclaiming, "My Lord and my God!" (John 20:28). This is perhaps the greatest declaration of Jesus' deity in the Bible. Being honest about our doubts and curious to know God personally, like Thomas was, inspires intelligent and heartfelt Bible study that honors God and calms our anxiety and fear.

Soul Care Practices for Fives

OBSERVER

Study the Bible to help you worship God and pray.

Practice asking for what you need, as Thomas learned to do (John 14:14).

Exercise to get out of your head and activate your body, which will help you be more energetic and generous (the Five's growth line is to a healthy Eight, which is a Body type).

Study how Nicodemus (Five) overcame his fear of losing his status and wealth as a Pharisee and gave it all up to assertively defend Jesus (John 3:1–21; 7:45–52; 19:38–42).

Read C. S. Lewis' (Five) autobiography *Surprised by Joy,* which shows a great Christian thinker coming alive emotionally and activating to serve God generously.

Speak out loud this truth: "I don't have to be the smartest person—that's Jesus!" (see Col. 2:3).

SOUL TALK

1. What did you learn about Fives and their challenges with anxiety?

2. What is an example of your hiding your emotions or avoiding being vulnerable with someone? How do you wish things had been different?

3. What do you notice about Jesus as a mature Five? How might this help you?

4. What were your thoughts after exploring the study on Thomas' story as a Five?

5. Which of the soul care practices for Fives seem most helpful for you personally? Why?

How Fives Become Like Jesus

1. Study Jesus' faith that led to action and being a nonanxious doer (like a healthy Eight).

2. Turn from greed (root sin) and rely on Jesus to be generous to others.

3. Pray to not react to stress with anxious pleasure seeking (like an unhealthy Seven).

4. Ask for empathy when you feel lacking in resources or energy.

5. Join Jesus' generosity (virtue) by sharing your resources with others.

Type Six: Loyalist

FELT NEED: Think to have security

KEY TRAITS: dutiful, problem-solving, authority-minded, hypervigilant, indecisive, contrarian

For God has not given us a spirit of fear, but of power and of love and of a sound mind.

2 Timothy 1:7 NKJV

In J.R.R. Tolkien's novel *The Hobbit*, Bilbo Baggins (Six) likes his secure home. He has a nice hole underground with a fireplace, and he likes to put a kettle of tea on the fire and listen to it sing. When the wizard Gandalf recruits him to help a party of dwarves reclaim their home from an evil dragon, Bilbo churns in anxious indecisiveness. On the one hand he's scared to leave his stable and secure home, but on the other hand he feels the pull of duty to rescue the dwarves. Eventually, he does the loyal thing and leaves his home to help the dwarves. On his journey he has to battle scary wolves, goblins, giant spiders, and the evil dragon Smaug, and protect the magic ring from Gollum. He learns to trust his inner wisdom and take courage to complete his mission.[1] In *The Lord of the Rings* trilogy, Bilbo reflects back on that experience: "It's a dangerous business, Frodo, going out your door. You step onto the road, and if you don't keep your feet, there's no knowing where you might be swept off to!"[2]

Ping-Pong Thinking

Sixes are the most common Enneagram type (tied with Nines).[3] They are the pure Head type on the Enneagram, in the center of the Anxiety triad, so they are most defined by unconscious anxiety and a felt need to have enough resources. As Bilbo's story illustrates, their habit of ambivalence can make them like a Ping-Pong ball that keeps being hit from one side to the other, flip-flopping between polar opposites.[4] They can be a bundle of contradictions: confident and unsure, fearful and courageous, trusting and distrusting, aggressive and passive, thinkers and doers, collaborative and independent, tender and tough, generous and petty, serious and funny. Sixes ping-pong because whenever they have a choice to make, they go back to the deliberations of their inner committee. They gather data, discuss options, debate, and then do it all again! Analysis is their strength, but overplayed, they get paralyzed. They keep worrying, "If only. . . ." They keep second-guessing themselves, especially when they're torn between competing responsibilities. They may become like a frightened rabbit that's facing traffic in the road and can't decide which way to go. But when they finally do come to a decision or opinion, they may get dogged in their determination to stick to the plan or adhere to the rule to keep their life, family, or organization predictable, stable, and secure.

The Six is called the Loyalist because they can be steadfastly faithful to people, causes, and organizations. Ruth's (Six) inspiring loyalty to her mother-in-law, Naomi, is a great example: "Where you go I will go, and where you stay I will stay. Your people will be my people and your God my God" (Ruth 1:16).

Healthy Sixes are very dependable—their word is gold, their values are unshakable, their desire to do what is right is trustworthy, they work hard to accomplish important goals, and their ability to effectively handle a crisis is extraordinary. If a loved one is attacked or in danger, Sixes are like a mama bear rushing in and getting big to protect her cubs. They typically do well in gathering data, solving problems, following rules and systems, attending to details (often they are perfectionists like Ones), and collaborating with others.

Personality Development of Sixes

Family Formation: Guardian or Rebel

Sixes tend to take on the family role of the *guardian* to protect others or the family values. Some Sixes, especially the One-to-One countertypes, play an opposite role of the *rebel* who pushes against family rules or norms, or the related role of the *scapegoat* who misbehaves or does not live according to family values. And some Sixes play both sides, ping-ponging between guardian and rebel/scapegoat. They may have felt overprotected, confined by rules, or lacking in consistent support.[5] Or a parent may have been alcoholic, mentally ill, abandoning, violent, or not strong enough to protect them.[6] Whether from family factors, biology, or their own choices, Sixes grew up struggling with fear, insecurity, broken trust, or authority issues.

Root Sin: Fear

There are so many fears in life (as we shared in chapter 12) that can make us like Bilbo, wanting to hide in our little hole. Fear is the root sin of Sixes because it can cripple their ability to love well and accomplish their most important work. Normally, fear defines their personality, but often it's denied and unconsciously put down into their shadow self. So instead of feeling fear, Sixes become overly loyal to others, carefully obey rules, perfectionistically prove themselves to be capable, or worry about what might go wrong. These are ways they anxiously secure themselves. *Anxiety is what a person feels if they repress fear or the other core hurts of shame, anger, and sadness.* Outwardly, Sixes are problem-solving and reach out to people with friendliness and support. But inwardly they are in their heads, overthinking, afraid of making a mistake or being rejected.

Of course, feeling afraid is not a sin, but *fear leads to sin if we distrust God and hide it.* This is the case in Jesus' parable of the talents with the servant who buried his talent and did not put it to work because he was afraid of losing it and being punished by his master (Matt. 25:14–30). As Paul taught, "everything that does not come from faith is sin" (Rom. 14:23). To lack faith is to separate yourself from God and rely on yourself, which is the essence of all sin.

Defense Mechanism: Projection

There's a funny story that provides a caricature of projection as a reaction to fear and anxiety. A man wants to hang a picture in his house but doesn't have a hammer. He thinks to borrow his neighbor's hammer but begins to doubt and fear and ruminate: *Maybe he won't want to help me? Maybe he's upset with me?* The man slowly gets himself riled up. Finally, he runs to his neighbor's house, rings the doorbell, and shouts, "Keep your stupid hammer!"[7]

Projection is the primary defense mechanism for Sixes to cope with their anxieties and fears. Unconsciously, they project their own worrisome feelings and thoughts onto others, which can create a self-fulfilling prophecy. (Whatever our type, we all do this at times.) When you doubt yourself, you may project this onto others so you feel like they are doubting you, then you relate to them as if they doubt you, then they actually do doubt you! If you can catch yourself projecting, then you can choose to let go of the defense, feel your emotions, and rely on God's grace. That's how your personality blossoms in health.

Emotions of Sixes

Core Emotion: Anxiety

Buck was a ranch owner in Texas and a *Counterphobic Six* (One-to-One subtype), which means that his fear and anxiety were hidden under his anger. In fact, he had mistyped himself as an Eight. To help him feel the fear that he denied, I (Bill) suggested he not carry his gun the next time he went out to a restaurant with his wife. He was shocked to realize that he could not stop scanning the doors and rehearsing in his mind what could go wrong and how he would keep his wife safe. Without his gun, he went full tilt into fear, like when he was a boy in his violent home. For the first time he understood that the main unconscious motivation of his life had been anxiety and fear.

Sixes struggle with anxiety and fear more than any other type. They have a radar for trouble, anticipating worst-case scenarios to avoid. They may catastrophize how horrible things are. Their mind may travel down the dark trail from doubt to skepticism to cynicism. A common way that Sixes cope with anxiety is to externalize it. For instance, they may get obsessive about cleaning, but no matter how spotless they can make their outer world, it cannot clean the anxious mess *on the inside*. Anxiety is something we all experience, but it's the dominant emotion of Head types (Five, Six, and Seven).

Stress Emotion: Shame

In stress Sixes not only feel anxiety but they also feel shame for being weak, stuck, or insecure. They feel pressure to be like high-achieving, impressive Threes, which causes them to drop their heads in discouragement. They imagine that if they were more successful and admired, like Threes seem to be, then they would not feel anxious. But comparing themselves makes them feel more overmatched. To relieve their anxious shame, they may become *servaholics* that keep responding to others' "urgent" needs. They are prone to codependency in which they fix other people's problems to feel important, but they can't perform their way out of feeling bad about themselves. Even when someone appreciates and affirms them, it's especially hard for them to receive it because they're suspicious of being tricked.

Additional Emotion: Anger

Normally, Sixes are compliant types who are overly responsible (along with Ones and Twos), and their anger is repressed, hiding under their churning anxiety. But they may ping-pong to anger, especially if they are affected by other people's lack of responsibility. More often their anger leaks out when they're anxious about a problem and they vent by complaining and blaming others. One woman shared, "My Six father let off steam from his workday at the dinner table. He was angry at people who didn't follow the company policies. When he was like that I just checked out." Additionally, Sixes often play the role of contrarian or devil's advocate, which may come with some anger.[8] They like to state an opposite opinion, even if they don't necessarily believe it, just to get at the truth and express their internal ambivalence.

Underlying Sadness

When Buck was a boy and there was fighting in his family, he went outside to find something to do or mess around with his friends so he wouldn't have to feel sad. But his wife got fed up after years of him withdrawing emotionally in their home. He prided himself on being loyal, especially to her, but he was surprised to discover that when he closed off his hurts it felt *disloyal* to her. So he started doing the inner work of growing in self-awareness and learning to connect emotionally with her. The healing path for Buck was to feel and share his inner hurts, longings, and needs. The insecure boy in his heart needed to take courage to reach out for care from others to develop "basic trust" that he was safe in the world.[9]

Expressing sadness makes us vulnerable, and it's a big step of faith for many of us, especially Sixes. A large survey found that in stress Sixes are one of the types that most wants to be alone.[10] The apostle Peter (Six) wrestled with this. He wept with remorse after he denied Jesus, and for a time he isolated himself (Luke 22:62).

But later he gathered with the other disciples and they grieved together (John 20:19). Then he met with the risen Jesus on the beach, where waves of sadness and love mingled and Peter was reconciled and restored (John 21:15–17).

Emotional Alarm: Relying on Safety Nets

When Sixes get revved up with anxiety, they become like a tightrope walker losing sight of the goal and looking to the safety nets below. To feel secure, they fall into a safe mode of following procedures, saving money, fixing problems, or robotically doing what trusted authorities say. When you're anxious, the path to growth is to catch yourself in your unconscious stress reaction, stop to pay attention to what you're feeling, listen for the Holy Spirit's wisdom, and act with purpose.

John, the beloved disciple, challenges us to not be dependent on human voices or methods but to rely on the inner "anointing" of the Spirit of Christ, who is faithful to guide us in what is true and good (1 John 2:27). Sharing and praying with a godly friend along with meditating on the Word help us to attend to this anointing. These are examples of how "perfect love takes away fear" (1 John 4:18 ERV).

Empathy for Beloved Sixes

LOYALIST

It's tiring for you to always be thinking and problem-solving.

When you slow down you feel anxious.

It's hard for you to quiet your mind, stop worrying, and really feel.

It's hard for you to trust your own feelings and intuitions.

In stress you feel pressure to perform, succeed, and be respected by people.

Hidden inside you there's a child part that feels insecure or afraid.

You want people to appreciate you—even if you don't solve their problems.

Jesus as the Model Six

Jesus Is Calm and Courageous

Jesus is the holy and healthy Six for Sixes and all of us. Sixes are tempted to carry out laws, rules, principles, and procedures but miss their higher purpose. Jesus stayed clear of legalism and taught on the weightier matters of the law: justice, mercy, and faithfulness (Matt. 23:23).[11] He emphasized the spirit behind the laws, which is love for God and neighbor (Mark 12:30–31). To put the highest priority on relationships is to be loyal. Our Lord Jesus is loyal through thick and thin—loyal to his Father (Luke 2:49; John 2:13–17), his mother (Luke 2:51; John 19:26–27), the law and the prophets (Matt. 5:17), the poor and needy (Luke 6:20), those who do his will (Mark 3:34–35), and even to his enemies (Luke 23:34). Jesus is loyal to *all of us* who love him. He is preparing our eternal home and will come again to take us there (John 14:1–3). Our Savior's loyal love ministers comfort, truth, and power to help us overcome fear and the damage it does to our personalities and relationships.

Sixes are problem-solvers, which may be why they seem to experience more than their share of trials. Teresa of Avila (Six) writes, "Life is long and there are many trials in it and we have need to look at Christ as our Pattern."[12] Jesus of Nazareth overcame fear and anxiety in trials. For instance, when he and his disciples were sailing on the Sea of Galilee and got caught in a gale that was swamping their boat with water, the disciples were scared to death, but Jesus was *napping* (Mark 4:35–41). He wasn't pretending to sleep to test his disciples, knowing that he'd calm the storm later. He was truly at rest, trusting his Father to care for him and his disciples. Jesus' ability as a human being to sleep peacefully in a life-threatening storm is the hidden miracle in this story. When the disciples began "shouting" in terror, just inches from his face (v. 38 NLT), he stood up and told the wind and waves to be still— and they obeyed! But Jesus wanted his disciples to have the faith in God that he had so they could learn to be calm and courageous in the midst of storms (v. 40).

▶ **PRAYER**: *Jesus, help me to trust your Spirit in me and to act with courage, purpose, and love.*

Virtue to Cultivate: Courage

Courage is the crucial virtue for Sixes to develop. According to C. S. Lewis, it's something we all need because every virtue requires courage in order to manifest under trial.[13] In the famous allegory *Pilgrim's Progress*, John Bunyan (Six) writes about a pilgrim named Christian (Six) who needs to take courage to overcome his fear and indecision. The book opens with Christian's city in danger of being destroyed. Bunyan writes, "I saw a man clothed with rags, standing by a path with a book in his hand and a great burden upon his back . . . he burst out, crying, 'What shall I do to be saved?'" At that very moment, a man named Evangelist shows up to help Christian begin his journey to the Celestial City.[14] He has to overcome enemies like the monster Apollyon, Giant Despair, and Obstinate who chases him. He has to get through dangerous places like the Slough of Despond, Doubting Castle, the Valley of

Jesus as a Healthy Six

Jesus did not let people's needs derail his mission (John 6:15).

He cares for his disciples' practical needs by washing their dirty feet (John 13:1–17).

He refuses to court the world's authorities but trusts in God's authority (John 19:9–11).

When his disciples are afraid for him to leave, he gives them a plan (Luke 24:49).

Jesus is loyal to love Judas as a friend, despite being betrayed by him (Matt. 26:50).

In anxiety and fear, he takes courage from his Abba to embrace the cross (Mark 14:32–36).

Humiliation, and the River of Death. At each step, Christian takes courage from the Lord through prayer, Scripture, and friends like Faithful, Help, and Hopeful, till finally he is welcomed into the Celestial City.

Bunyan wrote his story to overcome his own fears and to grow in faith. As a boy in seventeenth-century England, he had a recurring fear that the huge church bell he liked to ring would one day fall on his head and he'd go to hell! As a young man, he worked as a poor tinker, like his father, and traveled around repairing pots and pans. Later, he became a Christian and a popular lay preacher, but he continued to struggle with fear, doubt, and guilt over his sins. Then he was put in prison for preaching as a nonconformist, outside the official Church of England. For twelve years he lived in a prison that was overcrowded, unsanitary, and dark, and he was fed meager rations. But every day he read his Bible and prayed. That's when he started writing *Pilgrim's Progress*. One man taking courage to face his fears with Jesus has helped untold millions of people find courage and peace in Christ Jesus.[15]

When we're afraid or anxious like Bunyan, it's easy to think that we should just have courage, but actually we need to "*take courage*." Nobody has the virtue of courage by themselves; we need to get it by trusting the Lord Jesus. Bunyan's allegory shows that we can take courage by trusting friends or mentors who help us to feel our anxieties and fears, receive empathy, rely on God's Word, and act with the Spirit of Christ.

Key Soul Care Practice: Scripture Meditation

The discipline for growth that's most helpful for Sixes is meditating on Scripture with quiet reflection, feeling, prayer, and listening to God.[16] Meditation helps Sixes, anxious thinkers, and all of us to clear out the chattering voices in our heads and settle into the quiet mind that enables us to hear the Lord's voice and experience the Spirit's peace. Receiving the word of the Lord is the source of courage, which Sixes especially need for overcoming their fears and growing closer to Christ. Scripture meditation can help them to feel more confident and calm.

Anxiety

Let's try a short meditation now. Ponder with me the story of the disciples getting caught in another terrible storm at sea (Matt. 14:23–33). The disciples are frightened as their boat is being thrashed about. Suddenly, they see what they think is a ghost walking toward them on the water. It is Jesus, who proclaims, "Take courage! I am. Don't be afraid" (v. 27 TLV). Then Peter (Six) steps out of the boat and walks on the water toward Jesus! But when he looks down at the churning waves, he loses his nerve. He starts sinking into the sea and cries out. Jesus reaches down and pulls him back up to stand with him on the water. Eye to eye again, Jesus encourages Peter not to be fainthearted but to have faith in him—the Son of God is the I AM (Exod. 3:14) who can walk on water and calm storms!

Soul Care Practices for Sixes

Practice Lectio Divina by prayerfully rereading a Scripture passage.

Consider the story of Ruth (Six) in the Bible and pray to be loyal to God as she was.

Let yourself break a rule, as Jesus did for Peter (Six) when they picked heads of grain to snack on while walking in a field on the Sabbath (Mark 2:23–28).

Engage your body in exercise to de-stress and think more clearly. (The Six's growth line is to a healthy Nine, which is a Body type.)

Read *The Scandal of Redemption* by Oscar Romero (Six). His courage to defend the oppressed and speak on "the violence of love" led to him being martyred.

Breathe in, "Christ is here . . ." Then breathe out, "Fear not . . ." (see Luke 2:10–11 ESV).[17]

SOUL TALK

1. What did you learn about Sixes and how they deal with anxiety?
2. What is a fear or worry that you struggle with? How do you feel about this?
3. What do you admire about Jesus as the model Six? How might this help you?
4. What were your thoughts after meditating on the story of Jesus walking on the stormy sea to Peter (Six) and the other disciples?
5. Which of the soul care practices for Sixes seem most helpful for you personally? Why?

How Sixes Become Like Jesus

1. Meditate on Jesus' peace in trials to calm anxiety (like a healthy Nine).

2. Turn from fear (root sin) and rely on Jesus to be loyal to others.

3. Pray to not react to stress with shame (like an unhealthy Three).

4. Ask for empathy when you feel anxious or people hurt you with disloyalty.

5. Take courage (virtue) from Jesus to act with purpose and love.

15

Type Seven: Enthusiast

> **FELT NEED:** Think to have pleasure
>
> **KEY TRAITS:** positive, idealistic, spontaneous, unconventional, scattered, hedonistic

Get your head in the game . . . let yourselves be pulled into a way of life shaped by God's life, a life energetic and blazing with holiness.

1 Peter 1:13–16 MSG

The movie *Bonnie and Clyde* tells the story of Bonnie Parker and Clyde Barrow, a famous American crime couple who robbed banks during the Great Depression in the 1930s. When the two met, Bonnie was not quite sixteen and working as a waitress and Clyde was a violent criminal who had just escaped prison. She was stir-crazy in a small Texas town till, on the spur of the moment, she left it all behind to go rob banks with him. So began the wild escapades of Bonnie and Clyde. For two years they traveled through Texas, Oklahoma, Missouri, Louisiana, and New Mexico, robbing banks, stealing cars, evading police on back roads, holing up in hideouts, and taking on accomplices.[1] Even though "the Barrow Gang" shot and killed police officers and others who tried to stop them, the public cheered for them, viewing them more like two young and adventurous lovers than cold-blooded murderers.[2]

In the movie, Faye Dunaway plays the role of Bonnie, portraying her as a larger-than-life Seven who is lively, romantic, sensual, materialistic, and antiestablishment, goes full tilt, flirts with danger, and wants to get out of wherever she was. Bonnie goes from being a cheeky waitress to a hard-as-nails gangster. Along the way she makes herself the center of attention as the newspapers publish stories of the couple's bank robberies. One famous picture shows Bonnie standing beside a stolen Ford with her foot on the bumper, holding a gun, and chomping on a cigar! The public ate it up. If she were alive today, she'd have millions of Instagram followers. But eventually law enforcement caught Bonnie and Clyde in a trap and riddled their bodies with bullets. In death they were glamorized even more and became two of the most famous bank robbers of all time. It's astonishing to see the power of Bonnie's Seven magnetism to make people feel good, despite her being a gangster and killer.

More! More!! More!!!

For Bonnie and other Sevens, *more is always better.* They want more food, more sauces, more drinks, more fun, more parties, more travel adventures, more money, more attention, more projects, more impactful work, more adrenaline, and, above all, more happiness and side-splitting laughter! They want *all the things*! Their passion for more makes them prone to having a monkey mind. Distractible Sevens may have twenty-nine windows open on their computer—while simultaneously talking on their phone, listening to music, and watching a movie! Bob Goff, a famous and funny Christian author and speaker, exclaimed, "I'm a Seven so my brain looks like fireworks!" That's his way of illustrating how he and other Sevens are more likely than other types to have attention deficit disorder.[3]

Sevens are twitchy and want to move double time. They're like a whirlwind of enthusiastic activity. That's because they have a whole Disneyland of desires and want to do them all. As one Seven quipped, "Happiness is having a ticket!" Especially if they have multiple tickets and can bring others along. Giving people a fun time is how they show their love. It's also what they feel they personally need. To not have something fun to look forward to is totally depressing for Sevens. But they are idealists, so the *idea* of more fun is often better than the reality of it.

In the case of Bonnie Parker, her neurological fireworks of happiness were incited by more and more *danger* because she "needed" the thrill of robbing banks and getting in shoot-outs to make her feel more alive. Other Sevens get illicit pleasure hits through compulsive sex, drug abuse, and other addictions. But most Sevens keep a happy mood with innocent fun. Their problem, as with all types, is that they're charmed by their happy personality and don't see where it's causing pain and problems. They are masters at getting people to line up for their fun event or project but then making them wait till the last minute. That's because they may want to change their mind if a better option emerges, as it often does. Similarly, they can make other people feel so special but then later drop them like a hot potato without even realizing it. The main way Sevens hurt others is when they avoid dealing with conflicts and stressors. Pleasure-seeking Sevens hurt themselves most of all when they neglect their own health, stress limits, or emotional needs.

Healthy Sevens have many positive traits like positivity, joy, charisma, spontaneity, zest for life, warmth, and a desire to affirm and bless others. (Many Threes share these traits, but the Head anxiety of a Seven is quite different from the Heart shame of a Three.) Studies have shown that Sevens are usually high in extroversion and intuition.[4] They also tend to be fast learners, strategic thinkers, and inspiring influencers who are eager to take on new challenges, and they are magnetic in gathering helpers for their work. The diverse interests and gifts of Sevens can make them the "quintessential Renaissance person."[5] For me (Bill), my growth line as an earnest One is to incorporate these healthy Seven traits. It's uncanny that long before I learned the Enneagram, I intuitively sought out relationships with Sevens. For instance, my first spiritual director, Ray Ortlund Sr., was an enthusiastic Seven. Like many Sevens, he had chutzpah, which is an old Yiddish word for "audacity." Rabbis today use it to refer to faith in God, and it has come to mean "bold and vivacious, pursuing what [you] want in life with a cheerful determination."[6] Ray cultivated chutzpah in me with holy laughter and daring faith in Jesus.

Personality Development of Sevens

Family Formation: Cheerleader

In their families, Sevens often played the role of *cheerleader* or clown to distract everyone, especially themselves, from underlying tensions, fears, frustrations, or hurt. When things didn't go well, they kept pumping cheer with slogans like, "Don't worry, be happy!" and "Make people happy!" As young children many Sevens experienced a painful disconnect from their nurturing figure that impelled them to try to take care of their own needs.[7] Perhaps another sibling was born, the mother became quite sick, or there was another family problem. Whether because of family wounds, genetics, or their own choices, Sevens feel unsafe and anxious about needing care from others, so they try to stay in control by wooing people with their positivity to help themselves feel wanted, admired, and celebrated.

Root Sin: Self-Indulgence

Rochelle (Seven) met with me (Kristi) for help with overeating. Her mother had died before her third birthday, and she was raised by her busy father and a strict stepmother. Unconsciously, Rochelle rejected her emotional need to be mothered, banishing it into her shadow self. Instead, she sought comfort and pleasure in food. This was reinforced when her family celebrated her successes in school and soccer with special meals and desserts. As an adult she realized, "I'm hungry for nurturing. Food has been a fake mother that fills my stomach and makes me happy for a little while."

I helped Rochelle accept her need for secure attachment, grieve the maternal care she hadn't received, and learn how to receive empathy from Jesus and others. This included having her spend time alone in nature for quiet prayer, meditation, and journaling. At our next session Rochelle beamed. "The Holy Spirit drew me to Jesus weeping over Jerusalem in Luke 13:34. I never thought of Jesus being like a mother to me, taking me under his wing, and feeding my soul. I feel filled up with God's love!"

Rochelle's emotional eating is not unusual. In America, 38 percent of adults admit to overeating because of stress,[8] and the actual percentage is probably much higher since 42 percent of adults in the US weigh in as obese.[9] Indulging ourselves with food makes a god of our stomach (Phil. 3:19), what Evagrius identified as the deadly sin of gluttony. To be gluttonous is to "center our lives on pleasure . . . to supply that pleasure by ourselves, for ourselves . . . to quell our own feelings of need and longing."[10] Food becomes like a drug to fill up an inner emptiness. Of course, the emotional fullness is short-lived, and it's not real soul care because it substitutes food for God's unconditional love. We might do the same thing with work, wine, shopping, codependent relationships, or unhealthy faith. Sevens, along with Twos and Nines, are especially prone to overeating and other addictions.[11] Christian psychiatrist Gerald May defines addiction as "any compulsive, habitual behavior that limits the freedom of human desire. It is caused by the attachment . . . of desire to specific objects [rather than to God]."[12]

Defense Mechanism: Idealization

Whenever something sad or upsetting happened to Rochelle, she would sing a happy song in her mind to not get pulled down. To stay "up" she would also recite positive Bible verses or obsessively plan fun activities for her family or church. But much of her "positive faith" was the defense mechanism of *idealization*, which is seeing people and experiences as better than they really are. It's a form of rationalization, which is a defense of using thinking to set aside unwanted feelings like anxiety so she would not need support from anyone. The problem was that "looking on the bright side" and "making lemonade out of lemons" left Rochelle's inner child parts unknown and unloved. Furthermore, denying her negative emotions blunted her feeling self, diminishing her sensitivity to experience deep love, joy, and peace.

Emotions of Sevens

Core Emotion: Anxiety

"I've got three hamsters in me running on wheels that won't stop," a Seven quipped. Sevens keep their minds busy, juggle lots of balls in the air, stay constantly on the go doing the next fun thing, and do it all with an indomitable spirit of enthusiasm and confidence. Their indefatigable energy and capacity for stress cause others to marvel! However, underneath their life in the fast lane they tend to feel anxious, uncertain, worried, or fearful like the other Head types (Fives and Sixes). They don't realize that their scattershot activity is so loud that it's jamming the radio signals of their emotions. They keep distracting themselves because they are afraid to feel deprived or trapped in any negative situation. But the negative emotions eventually pop up when Sevens run into unavoidable pain, encounter a crisis, take on too many responsibilities, get disappointed by people, find themselves stuck in a bad situation, or become bored. Anxious Sevens need to pause their activity to observe, reflect, quiet their mind, seek empathy, and focus like a healthy Five (their growth line).

Stress Emotion: Anger

Anger can become a prominent emotion for Sevens under stress. They are frustrated idealists (as are Ones and Fours) because the reality of their experiences and accomplishments does not come close to matching their optimistic hopes. So an angsty anger simmers under the happy surface of their personality. When Sevens get disappointed by people, they are prone to stress reactions of being pushy, perfectionistic, angry, sarcastic, resentful, or judgmental, like an unhealthy One. When they're on a team that needs to get work done, they may feel frustrated that others cannot keep up with them or resentful that the results are squarely on their shoulders and they have to overwork. For other people it's quite a switch when a typically happy and affirming Seven suddenly becomes critical or blows a gasket and blurts out their frustrations. On the positive side, a large survey found that the strength of Sevens in stress is that they are the most likely type to be social.[13]

Additional Emotion: Shame

Their cheerful optimism, excited energy, and striving for influence normally keeps Sevens in high spirits and anticipating better things to come, but sometimes they experience a blowout of shame. As with anger, this may happen on their stress line to an unhealthy One. Many Sevens can be surprisingly like Ones by putting excessive pressure on themselves to reach their goals and being self-critical when they fall short. Recall that often shame is anger turned inward against the self (see chapter 7). Sevens may feel shame when they hurt someone they love, indulge sinful pleasures, ignore a problem that comes back to haunt them, fail, or are rejected or mistreated.

Underlying Sadness

Sevens like to say things like, "Look on the bright side," "Keep your chin up," and "Don't worry, be happy!" As one Seven told me, "The glass is half full and the other half is delicious!" They tend to put a positive spin on hurt and sadness. But as the 2015 hit film *Inside Out* so effectively illustrates, if we reject our feelings of sadness, we will lose our ability to feel joy. The buoyant idealism of a Seven makes them especially prone to this mistake. They need to learn to feel and care for their sad emotions to become their most joyful and loving self.

Many Sevens have a hidden grief from feeling that they're only wanted and appreciated when they're blowing up happy balloons for people. When that's the motive for putting on parties, doing work, or making people happy, it means they're not known and loved unconditionally for their true self. Every personality type experiences loss, hurt, injustice, and pain, and it's natural and healthy to grieve and need comfort. Some Sevens find it especially helpful to connect with the healthy Four's emotional authenticity to feel and verbalize sadness.[14]

Emotional Alarm: Wandering Attention

Typically, Sevens are automatically jumping into another new excitement with a project, party to plan, spur-of-the-moment trip, shopping, scrolling on social media, getting a snack, or any fun distraction. They keep wanting the next thing that will make them happier. The wake-up call for Sevens is to catch themselves feeling dissatisfied and thinking that the grass is greener somewhere else.[15] Then they can stop diverting away from what they're doing or who they're with and choose to enjoy the moment with God and people.

To appreciate moments, the ancient Greeks contrasted *kairos*, which means "the opportune time," and *chronos*, which means "the ordinary passing of chronological time." They imagined a god named Kairos who had a great blessing to offer but was slippery to catch because he was naked, completely hairless except for a tuft on his forehead. He stood on his tiptoes and had wings on his feet to zip and zap all over the place. The only way to catch the opportunity he brought was to see him coming and grab hold of the ponytail that hung over his face before he ran by![16]

Paul exhorts Sevens—and all of us—to seize kairos moments: "Wake up from your sleep, climb out of your coffins; Christ will show you the light! So watch your step. Use your head. Make the most of every chance [*kairos*] you get. These are desperate times!" (Eph. 5:15–16 MSG).

Empathy for Beloved Sevens

You like to bring positivity and joy to bless people.

There are so many fun things, and you want to do them all!

You felt quite bored and antsy at that meeting—it was hard to focus.

It's frustrating for you when people don't do what they said they'd do.

You're avoiding that person for fear of getting trapped.

Underneath all these busy activities, maybe you feel restless or anxious.

You feel pressure to be cheerful in order to be accepted and this causes you sadness.

Jesus as the Model Seven

Jesus' Joy Is Contagious!

As the supreme Seven Enthusiast, the Lord Jesus is "full of joy" (Luke 10:21). He brings us "more and better life" than we ever dreamed of (John 10:10 MSG). This joyful life is not a flash in the pan—it produces an enduring contentment that's cheerful, yet sober.

I (Bill) experienced Jesus' joy a number of years ago in watching *The Visual Bible: Matthew*, a movie that has a script taken word for word from the Gospel of Matthew. The film portrays Jesus as winsome, happy, affectionate, spontaneous, playful, and liking to joke around.[17] We see Jesus enjoying his Father's love and that love overflowing to us (John 15:9). This reminded me of my times with Ray Ortlund Sr. (Seven) who exuded Jesus' joy to me. As a One who needs to integrate the joy of a Seven, watching this presentation of the gospel story was truly life-changing for me. I could literally feel the dour and dutiful religiosity getting washed off my heart-level images of Jesus and the Trinity. I couldn't stop smiling!

Inspired by this, I did a fresh reading of Matthew straight through in one sitting. In my Bible I had fun drawing a smiley face to mark instances of Jesus' joy, witty humor, and playfulness (which are Seven strengths that Ones especially need). *I drew sixty-three smiley faces in my Bible!*

Writing to you now, I'm smiling and I feel happy! But it's hard to convey to you just how much joy splashed out from Jesus as I related to him this way. Perhaps this story will help. Our oldest daughter, Jennie, has had a sunny disposition from birth and has since identified as a Seven. When she was a little girl, I took her to preschool two days a week at the church where I served as a pastor. We held hands as we walked from the car to her class, and as soon as she got to the door her whole class would dance as they sang, "It's a Jennie day! It's a Jennie day!" That's because the two

Jesus as a Healthy Seven

Jesus invites us to "leap for joy" with him, even in trials
(Luke 6:23).

At a wedding party he turned water into wine to bless the
celebration (John 2:1–11).

In his teaching he was winsome, witty, and funny (Matt. 7:3–5;
23:23–24).

He enjoyed going to parties to eat, drink, and socialize (Matt.
9:10).

He had Peter catch a fish with a coin in its mouth (Matt. 17:24–
27). That is so funny!

He played happily and affectionately with children (Matt.
19:13–15).

He optimistically believed that "with God all things are possible"
(Matt. 19:26).

Even in taking up his cross to die for our sins, Jesus was joyful
(Heb. 12:2).

days a week she was in class she brought them so much fun and joy! The key to the life you and I have always wanted is to right now exclaim, "It's a Jesus day! It's a Jesus day!"

▶ **PRAYER**: *Jesus, help me be joyful and content here and now with what you've provided for me.*

Virtue to Cultivate: Sober Contentment

In the twelfth century, when Francis of Assisi (Seven) was a youth, he was a party animal, rushing pell-mell into pleasures and making himself popular. He was a jongleur, or minstrel, who entertained people with music, dancing, songs, and stories. But when Francis trusted in Christ, he stripped off his lavish attire (along with his party lifestyle), laid it at his father's feet, and walked off naked to follow in the footsteps of Jesus. He became known as "God's jongleur," singing about the Lord, caring for lepers and the poor, teaching spiritual lessons, and making disciples of Jesus called friars.[18] His testimony illustrates the power of replacing addiction to sinful pleasures with "addiction" to enjoying God. In the words of Paul, "Don't drink too much wine. That cheapens your life. Drink the Spirit of God, huge drafts of him. Sing hymns instead of drinking songs! Sing songs from your heart to Christ. Sing praises over everything, any excuse for a song to God the Father in the name of our Master, Jesus Christ" (Eph. 5:18–20 MSG).

A story from the life of Saint Francis illustrates his sober contentment in Jesus, which is the virtue for Sevens to cultivate. One winter day when he and Friar Leo were walking through the snow and shivering with miserable cold, he taught Leo about perfect joy. It was not in holiness. Not in miracles. Not in great knowledge. Not even in preaching the gospel. Finally Leo pleaded, "Father, I pray you in the name of God to tell me, where is perfect joy?!" Francis answered,

> If we arrive at our host's house soaked by the rain, frozen, muddy, and afflicted with hunger, knock on the door and the doorkeeper

says, "Who are you? I don't know you!" And he closes the door in our faces so that we must stay outside all night long, freezing to death. If we endure this mistreatment without disquieting ourselves and without murmuring, but think humbly and charitably about the doorkeeper, believing that God is in charge. If we bear these injustices patiently and with cheerfulness, thinking on the sufferings of Christ for us. O Friar Leo, write it down that here is perfect joy![19]

Francis trained to have Jesus' joy in trials through the disciplines of fasting and quiet meditation on Scripture. Because Sevens struggle with self-indulgence and a monkey mind, they need to incorporate the self-denial, quiet mind, and contentment of healthy Fives (the growth line for Sevens). These disciplines prompt confession of sin and deeper reliance on God. Dallas Willard explained, "Persons well used to fasting as a systematic practice will have a clear and constant sense of their resources in God."[20]

Key Soul Care Practice: Silence

The spiritual discipline that Sevens especially need is quiet prayer. When they slow down all their activities, restrain their indulgences, and get quiet in God's presence, they can incorporate the centered mind of a healthy Five, which is their growth line. They're surprised to discover that truly *less is more*. Then they are better able to advance in the virtue of sober contentment that is so important for them. We've had lots of Sevens in our Institute join us on retreat and have seen how refreshing and life-changing it is for them when they learn to practice silence. They do this in quiet prayer, self-reflection, and listening to others with empathy. Silence helps them to emotionally savor the many little blessings in their lives that they otherwise would have hurried past.

A woman from Samaria (Seven) traveled to a well alone in the heat of the day, where she met Jesus (John 4:1–42). It seems her village had branded her with a scarlet A for adultery. She probably had been abused at the hands of men. Jesus asked her for a drink of water, and she replied in a condescending and snippy tone. But Jesus' winsome and gracious manner, combined with his supernatural knowledge about her painful and sinful past, softened her heart and drew her into a riveting soul talk. She asked him sincere questions about worship and the Messiah and was quiet to listen. When he offered her heavenly water that would satisfy her deep thirst, she pleaded, "Please, sir, give me this water!" (John 4:15 NLT). In her great enthusiasm, she left her water jar (symbolizing her new self-denial) and ran to her village to invite everyone to go back to the well with her to meet the Messiah! Together they would drink from Jesus' "internal and eternal source of unfailing spiritual, life-giving water."[21]

Soul Care Practices for Sevens

Slow down and be quiet to savor your life with Jesus—even for just a minute.

Give thanks: "The joy of the LORD is your strength" (Neh. 8:10). Instead of having to manufacture happiness, you can appreciate God's joy.

Read Solomon's (Seven) confessions of indulgence in Ecclesiastes to prompt your own confession to God and request for his mercy.

Ask Jesus questions and be patient to listen quietly (growth line to a healthy Five).

Read *The Christian's Secret of a Happy Life*, a spiritual classic by Hannah Whitall Smith (Seven).

Try this three-step Breath Prayer paraphrased from Matthew 2:10–11: (1) Wait to breathe, "King Jesus . . ." (2) Breathe in, "my joy . . ." (3) Breathe out, "I give you my heart."[22]

· · · · · · · · · · · · · · SOUL TALK · · · · · · · · · · · · ·

1. What did you learn about Sevens and how they deal with anxiety?
2. What is a distraction or pleasure-seeking behavior you struggle with?
3. What do you appreciate about Jesus as a model Seven? How might this help you?
4. What are your thoughts about the Samaritan woman's conversation with Jesus?
5. Which of the soul care practices for Sevens seem most helpful for you personally? Why?

How Sevens Become Like Jesus

ENTHUSIAST

1. Practice silence for a quiet mind and to listen well (like a healthy Five).

2. Turn from self-indulgence (root sin) and rely on Jesus to be enthusiastic for others.

3. Pray to not react to stress with angry judging (like an unhealthy One).

4. Ask for empathy if you feel anxious or hurt when others are not celebrating you.

5. Cultivate Jesus' sober joy (virtue) in your relationships, work, and daily life.

16

Help for Anxiety

You keep him in perfect peace
whose mind is stayed on you,
because he trusts in you.

Isaiah 26:3 ESV

eggie (Five) was a single pastor in his mid-thirties who met
with me (Bill) for help with his compulsive behaviors. He
had gotten trapped in a pattern of self-medicating his anxiety
by drinking alcohol excessively and using pornography. He was
plagued with guilt and fear about his double life. He was a careful
and deep thinker, yet under the surface he had emotions of anxiety, worry, and fear that popped up in stress. He liked to be up in
his head thinking all the time. Up there everything was clear and
clean—he knew what he believed and why he believed it and he
could learn whatever else became important. Seminary had been
right up Reggie's alley because as a Head type he loved to read,
study, discuss ideas, and keep learning.

He also had a lot of Seven in him because that was his stress
number. That side of him was rather opposite of his Five. Every
type is like that. Either your stress line or your wing is opposite
in some ways of how you normally function in your type. For

Reggie, his Seven was like a release valve on his monkey mind that wouldn't stop chattering and worrying about his responsibilities for his church. At times he'd suddenly do something exciting. He'd drop his work and go out with a friend or respond to an urgent need of someone in his church. He took last-minute plane trips to visit family. He splurged on nice restaurants or ordering takeout. That was all fine, except the jerkiness added to his stress and he gained quite a bit of weight. It was on this same stress line that he crossed into sin by drinking too much wine and dabbling in soft porn.

Stressed In and Acting Out

It was confusing to Reggie why he couldn't get his drinking under control and stop using porn. Normally he was so disciplined. I showed him that the main reason he did this was because he was anxious from internalizing stress with caring for his related emotions and needs. He denied his emotions and needs and stayed in the safe confines of his thinking by going into his head with study, intellectualizing, and problem-solving. Being *stressed in* led to *acting out* his denied anxiety by self-medicating with drinking and porn. He was trying to feel better and get his needs met without seeking "truth in the inward being" of his heart and mind (Ps. 51:6 ESV).

There are many ways that we might act out unconscious anxiety, like through compulsive cleaning or rescuing people from problems they need to take responsibility for. Anxiety feels out of control, so it feels good to get in control by cleaning a mess or fixing someone's problem. Anxiety is a disease of trying to control people or situations that we're not meant to control.

Without realizing it, Reggie had projected his unconscious shadow personality dynamics into his understanding and teaching of the Bible—something that is very common for every Enneagram type. For instance, here's how he understood Paul's famous teaching in Philippians 4:6–7 that starts out "Do not be anxious about anything":

Stuff your worries and fears. Just believe what's true and pray. You should always look and act calm, happy, and strong. If you feel anxious, insecure, or emotional, you're not a good Christian.

In reality, Paul's message is along these lines:

When you experience stress in your life and work . . . when you have conflict in your relationships . . . when you have pain in your body . . . when you're late and stuck in traffic . . . whenever you feel worried, afraid, frustrated, or insecure, talk to God and a friend about how you feel, sharing your emotions openly. Don't pretend to be strong—be vulnerable. Don't rely on yourself—ask for the grace you need and absorb it by being thankful. Then God's sweet and powerful peace will nourish you and protect you in the way of Christ.

Reggie had learned to use spiritual thoughts to deny his emotions as a child growing up in a large, religious family. He was the youngest by six years and felt on his own and like a loner. His parents provided well for his physical needs but not his emotional needs. His dad was a busy doctor who hardly ever spent time with him and never showed affection. His mom was emotionally reactive, judgmental, and always worrying about what the neighbors thought. He had to always look and act "like a responsible Christian."

Inflows and Outflows

Usually, when someone is overstressed, their inflows and outflows are out of balance. Stress and pain are coming into their soul but not being released. The inflow is being stressed in, like we just talked about. The other half of the problem is that lack of outflow or release. It's often thought that you can release stress by having fun, watching a movie, or taking a bath. Those types of things are good, but they don't go nearly deep enough to help with anxious rumination and compulsive behavior. The cycle of anxiety from chapter 12 illustrates the problem with stress and sin getting internalized as anxiety, then worsening through obsession, and then forming an unhealthy identity of "I am what I have."

Reggie oscillated between ruminating about his problems and distracting himself with the stimulation of seeking knowledge, drinking wine, or using porn. In the excitement phase they felt like stress relievers, but they were making his anxiety worse by denying it and adding in stressful consequences such as guilt, weight gain, and reinforcement of unhealthy habits. He wasn't meeting his needs for empathy, acceptance, and affirmation because he wouldn't even let himself feel vulnerable. He didn't realize it, but despite all the positive Scriptural affirmations he professed to believe about his identity, his operational identity was built on the lies that his security was based on having more fun, more knowledge, or more money. He had a scarcity mindset of anxiously preserving his resources to take care of himself. But he couldn't see this because he thought his personality was helping him.

In Reggie's early therapy sessions, I helped him feel his emotions. I gave him lots of empathy, drawing from some of the feeling words for anxiety and depression that we've shared with you, like *stressed, worried, apprehensive, alone, fearful, bored, restless, guilty, regretful,* and *empty.* Our lists of empathy statements illustrate this. Receiving empathy facilitates the outflow of stress, pain, and sin. This is called *catharsis,* which is an emotional release that gives your soul more space to breathe and helps you to be your true self.

I had Reggie go to AA and work the steps with a sponsor. I've learned that addicts need to be with fellow addicts in recovery to hear their stories and receive support and accountability. Sober addicts are quick to know when a fellow addict is putting up a front.

Talking to Jesus in an Empty Chair

I knew that a primary aspect of Reggie's anxiety and addictive behavior related to his relationship with God. So I invited him to have a conversation with Jesus in an empty chair. I guided him to express himself with emotional honesty. He confessed with brokenness: "Lord Jesus, I serve you as a pastor, but I don't really believe in you anymore. I don't turn to you for comfort and help—I drink wine and look at porn. Being a Christian feels dutiful. It's hard to always do what's right and good. I'm tired of caring for so many people and having to be a leader and an example. What's in it for me?"

Then I had Reggie change chairs. I asked him, "What do you suppose the Lord Jesus might say to you about this?" He was quiet. Then he imagined Jesus confronting him angrily: "Reggie, I'm so disappointed in you. How can you say, 'What's it in for me?' That's so selfish! Nobody would want you as a pastor or even as a friend if they knew about your sins. You're a hypocrite!"

I could see the anxiety, anger, shame, and sadness on Reggie's face. "I'm really sad for you," I responded. "Your understanding of God is that he's very harsh with you. There's no compassion for how you're hurting or how tired you are. There's no mercy and forgiveness for your sins and struggles."

The next week Reggie missed his appointment. But he rescheduled. Then he missed that one and rescheduled. *Seven times he scheduled and missed his appointment!*

I knew that Reggie needed me to fight for him the way I had for my son David when he was five years old and scared of the ocean. As David watched the waves swell and rush toward shore and heard their thunderous crash just a few feet away, it frightened him. I wanted to build his confidence and courage, so I turned it into a game. We found sticks on the beach and pretended they were swords. I told him that we were going to fight those bad waves and tell them they couldn't hurt him. So I took his hand and as the waves receded into the ocean we chased them back, thrusting our swords and yelling, "Go back! You can't hurt us!" Then, as the waves reversed and came into shore, we'd run ahead to safety, still holding hands, as we screamed with excitement, "Ahhhh!" Again and again we did this. Then David wasn't scared anymore. He took courage from me. Today he enjoys surfing those waves!

At this point, fighting for Reggie looked like praying for him and leaving supportive voicemail messages. I was afraid I wouldn't see him again. I was afraid that I'd gone too deep too soon by having him talk to Jesus in the empty chair.

Then, after *seven* missed appointments, Reggie showed up at my office without an appointment. Fortunately, I was available. He handed me a big check, sat down, and reported, "I'm ready to continue my conversation with Jesus."

Right there, to use the language of step 3 in AA, he turned his will and his life over to God.[1] In the weeks that followed, he did further inner work to talk through his anxious emotions with caring people rather than acting them out in compulsive behavior. He also renewed his image of God and enjoyed a fresh experience of God's grace.

Jesus Is Your Anxiety Bearer

In his prayer in the garden of Gethsemane, Jesus kneeled in the shadow of his coming cross and felt overwhelmed with anxious feelings. He felt fear and the temptation to get out of a painful trial, so he asked his friends to pray for him, but they let him down. He was rejected and alone, bearing more stress than a human being can handle. He cried out to his Papa in the heavens. In anxiety and fear he took courage and was faithful (Mark 14:32–42). Then, going to the cross, Jesus took up our sins and our diseases (Isa. 53:4; Matt. 8:17), including our dis-ease of anxiety.

Throughout the Gospels we can see Jesus as our Anxiety Bearer. When you are anxious, you are not alone; Jesus is with you and feels for you. He gives you help and courage in your storm (Matt. 14:22–33).

> In Mary's womb, baby Jesus felt the distress of her trials (Matt. 1:19; Luke 2:1–7).
>
> As a little boy, he and his parents had to escape at night and flee for their lives to Egypt (Matt. 2:13–15).
>
> He was pressured by his mother to fix the problem of running out of wine (John 2:1–4).

He felt the stress of crowds pressing him with needs and expectations (Mark 3:7–8; 5:24).

At times Jesus was so busy in ministry that he didn't have time to eat (Mark 3:20; 6:31).

He was triangled into people's conflicts and pressured to fix them (Luke 12:13–14).

When Jesus faced his cross at the Passover his soul was troubled (John 12:27).

Silence for a Quiet Mind

Head types need silence in order to turn down their inner noise and *really listen* to God, others, and their own self.[2] Quiet prayer is the main discipline that helps them to abandon their anxious programs for securing themselves through having resources. It fosters their self-awareness of anxiety, fear, and sin so they can release their distress to Jesus and cultivate his virtue for their type.

Fives see their anxious hoarding, release it to God, and share their resources.

Sixes let go of worry and fear and take courage from Christ to love faithfully.

Sevens stop pursuing happy distractions and savor God's presence.

Reggie's daily practices of silent prayer and Scripture meditation were part of him working on step 11 of Alcoholics Anonymous.[3] These quieting disciplines surfaced his inner fears, worries, insecurities, and doubts, which he processed by venting with his sponsor and in therapy. Receiving empathy further reduced his anxiety and reinforced his developing a quiet mind. This is called *mindfulness*. To be mindful is "training your attention to achieve a mental state of calm concentration and positive emotions."[4] It's to be fully present in the moment, appreciating whatever is good in your experience. It's what Paul describes as "filling your minds

Mindful Prayers for Anxiety

To grow in mindfulness, it's important not to hurry, analyze, or judge what you see, but rather to simply observe and appreciate. These practices of mindfulness can help reduce your anxiety:

Slowly recite a Scripture you've memorized, like Psalm 23 or the Lord's Prayer.

Pray Psalm 46 or another psalm that offers comfort for anxiety and fear.[5]

Relax in God's creation to appreciate the sounds, colors, shapes, and movements.

Look at a cross and quietly repeat the name of Jesus (John 19:25).

Listen to a waterfall sound on your phone and pray to the Living Water (John 7:38).

Recall one memory of God guiding you as you breathe in and out slowly.

Smile as you receive Julian of Norwich's (Five) famous words as a gift of grace: "All shall be well and all manner of things shall be well."[6]

and meditating on" whatever is true, noble, gracious, and beautiful (Phil. 4:8 MSG). The ultimate expression of mindfulness is to live with the "mind of Christ" (1 Cor. 2:16).

Mindfulness enables Head types to make better use of their thinking strengths. Whatever your personality, you benefit from tapping into your thinking intelligence center through quieting your mind. Mindfulness helps you experience a calm mind that's relaxed, open, observant, insightful, able to feel, focused, and ready to act with love for others. A review of two hundred research studies on mindfulness found that it was an effective treatment for reducing stress, anxiety, depression, pain, and addiction.[7]

One time Dallas Willard (Five) told me that if he could use only one discipline for a spiritual life in Christ, it would be memorizing Scripture passages. Since that day in 2006 I have memorized dozens of paragraphs and chapters of the Bible, particularly the ones he called "the electric Scriptures" because they're especially life-giving.[8] "This is the primary discipline for the thought life . . . to memorize [the passages] and then constantly turn them over in our minds as we go through the events and circumstances of our life (Josh. 1:8; Ps. 1)."[9] You may not think of memorizing Scripture as a practice for mindfulness, but I have found that carrying Scripture in my mind to ponder, feel, and pray calms my worries, brings God's peace, and helps me to be more fully present to love God, others, and myself.

Steps to Help with Anxiety

The following action steps describe the process for reducing anxiety:

1. *Identify anxiety.* Stress overload, irritability, hurry, and worry are signs that you may be struggling with anxiety. The first step to receiving help is admitting your need.

2. *Ask for empathy.* Repressed feelings of anxiety, fear, or another emotional distress may get acted out in compulsive behavior. Asking for empathy from the Lord and a spiritual director or friend brings comfort, calming, and clarity. The feeling words list in chapter 12 will help you get started.

3. *De-stress.* When you are anxious, stress is getting into your mind and body but not getting out. Empathy facilitates cathartic release. Additionally, you need to set boundaries to limit the stress you are internalizing.

4. *Practice silence.* It's challenging for Head types and other thinkers and multitaskers to practice silence. Being quiet on a walk, in meditation, or during a retreat can surface your emotions. This enables you to open yourself deeper to God's peace.

5. *Be secure in Christ.* Soul care practices like Scripture meditation, mindfulness, thankfulness, and Breath Prayers can calm down monkey mind. It can help you affirm the identity-strengthening truth: "In Christ I am secure."

SOUL TALK

1. What did you learn from Reggie's story of getting help for his anxiety and compulsive behavior?
2. What interests you about mindfulness or Scripture memory as a help for anxiety?
3. What makes it difficult for you to meditate on Scripture in a way that relieves anxiety?
4. What do you appreciate about Jesus as your Anxiety Bearer?
5. Which of the mindfulness practices for anxiety seem most helpful for you personally? Why?

Check out our free bonus resources for more help with anxiety. You can also talk with one of the spiritual directors or coaches who have earned a certificate in our Soul Shepherding Institute. Just scan the QR code or go to SoulShepherding.org/enneagram.

PART 4

SADNESS

A HEALING PATH

Sadness as Good Grief

Blessed are you who are grieving, for the Lord's comfort is available to you.

Matthew 5:4 (authors' paraphrase)[1]

(Kristi) am grieving while we are writing this book. My mother (Eight) is dying from cancer. Based on the life span of her parents, we had anticipated having her with us another fifteen years. I cry at times because I can't imagine my life without her. She prays for me and my family every day. She also prays for the ministry of Soul Shepherding, which she helped us start. When she's no longer here, there will be many things I will wish I could talk to her about. She's one of the few people in the world who is *totally for me*. I'm thankful I've had the opportunity to tell her how much I'll miss her and to draw her out to talk about her grief.

Emotions are a new language for my mom. Our best con-versations are when she is able to take courage, be honest and vulnerable, and share what she is feeling. She's experiencing all the emotional phases of grief we discuss below. All in the same day she might believe she'll get stronger and beat the cancer, then feel discouraged, then feel angry at a loved one, then enjoy being with family, then feel sad that she's dying. Whatever she's feeling, I've noticed that as I listen, seek to understand, mirror back to her what I hear, and validate her emotions with empathy, she feels better and her body returns to peace. This is the gift that comes to all of us, whatever our type, when we are willing to face the underlying sadness and grief.

As her daughter and one of her caregivers, I've also needed empathy. Often I reach out to Bill, a friend, my sister, or my spiritual director to ask them to listen to me process what I'm feeling and to pray for me. When I finish sharing, I literally feel as if thirty pounds of weight has been lifted off me. Of course, it doesn't feel good in the moment to face the sadness and grief, but when I get help accepting the pain then I am able to return to joy.

From Depression to Sadness

At times on this journey, my mother and I have felt depressed. That's natural when you're grieving, but the danger is you can sink down into a depressed condition that's like being stuck in the Slough of Despond, the dreadful bog of depression in *Pilgrim's Progress*. Treating acute or chronic depression usually requires a combination of therapy, medicine, and spiritual care. Psychologically, depression can often be understood as *ungrieved grief*. In the history and heart of someone who is depressed there are usually painful losses, traumas, or other hurts that have not been grieved, comforted, and adjusted to.

Some well-intentioned but poorly trained helpers may try to pull you out of discouraged or sad feelings with advice, cheery reassurance, Bible insights and promises, or other quick fixes. But those tactics invalidate your emotions and tend to exacerbate depression. When you're depressed, struggling emotionally, or grieving, it's important not to isolate but rather to find safe and wise friends and guides who will provide you with empathy. The "Feeling Words for Depression" list below can get you started on articulating your emotions and needs.

Feeling Words for Depression

Emotions: discouraged, lonely, low, bummed out, whining, despondent, dispirited, somber, melancholy, bleak, glum, dismal, moody, joyless, numb, pessimistic, hopeless, despairing

Idioms: blue, droopy, down in the dumps, down and out, cast down, a downer, shuffling my feet, out of sorts, the doldrums, wallowing, in a pit, stuck in a bog, in the slough of despond, sunk, at the wall

Hebrew idioms: face falls,[2] eyes fail,[3] hands fall limp[4]

Usually depressed emotions relate to shame and underlying sadness. Recall our adage from chapter 11: "Don't feel bad, feel sad." Shaming yourself is "worldly sorrow" that exacerbates depression and distance from God, but expressing sadness is "godly sorrow" that opens you to receive God's love and grace (2 Cor. 7:10–11). To help you differentiate and understand these two sorrows, we've provided feeling words and phrases for each in the figure below:

Feeling Words for Worldly Sorrow and Godly Sorrow

Worldly sorrow: shame, insignificance, unworthiness, bad, self-reproach, self-rejection, self-hatred, hiding, isolating

Godly sorrow: sad, convicted, sorry, conscience-stricken, regretful, apologetic, remorseful, contrite, asking for mercy, seeking reconciliation

Worldly sorrow is *bad grief*; it's shaming and isolating. When I'm enticed by worldly sorrow about my mom's cancer, my internal thoughts and feelings sound like this: "I am not a very loving daughter. I should be doing more for her. . . . Why am I afraid of losing her? I should have faith, not fear. . . . I need to stop feeling sorry for myself and just be grateful I still have her here now." If I give in to guilt and shame, it blocks my flow of grief that needs comfort and keeps me from being able to enjoy my mom now.

In contrast, godly sorrow is *good grief*; it's a healthy combination of emotional honesty, personal responsibility, trust in God and others, and asking for what you need. When I am in godly sorrow about my mom's cancer, I pray about my internal thoughts and feelings, which sounds like this: "Jesus, I confess I want to avoid the pain of this journey with Mom through the valley of the shadow of death. I want to focus on happy things and not be exposed to her pain and suffering and the mess that her decaying body makes. Give me strength, Jesus, to trust you when I am weak, tired, sad, distressed, hurting, and afraid. Help us look to you to shepherd us in this dark and painful valley."

It's been helpful to my mom and me that I know the emotional language of godly sorrow and grieving. The "Feeling Words for Sadness" list below elaborates on godly sorrow:

Feeling Words for Sadness

Emotions: hurt, unhappy, disappointed, distressed, troubled, sorrowful, longing, yearning, deep desire, teary, tearful, grieving, mourning, lamenting, agony

Idioms: melting, down in the mouth, lump in my throat, rainy day, crying on the inside, brokenhearted, emotionally hungry, heavy-hearted, heartsick, falling to pieces, beating my breast, in sackcloth and ashes, baptism of fire, cross to bear

Hebrew idioms: heavy,[5] pain like childbirth[6]

Caring for the sad feelings that tend to hide behind depression, shame, anxiety, or anger will strengthen your emotional and spiritual health. As John Townsend explains, "Grief is God's solution for accepting what we cannot change. Sadness allows our heart to let go of what it can't have and prepare for what it can."[7]

The Emotional Phases of Grief

Grief is a deep sorrow reaction to all kinds of losses: death, aging, trauma, abuse, rejection, abandonment, separation from a loved one, being hurt by a loved one, loss of intimacy, loss of health, loss of job, loss of finances, loss of home and neighborhood (e.g., moving), loss of tradition, loss of church, or loss of feeling God's loving presence. It's important to say that grief is not something to just get over—it's a journey. Denying your grief emotions adds to the pain and puts you in an increasingly unhealthy state. When you experience a loss, you can't change what happened, but you can change your response to it by seeking the comfort and care of a friend, counselor, or spiritual director.

Grief is painfully disorienting, so it's important to have a map. As we've discussed, your personality type predicts important aspects of how you'll uniquely respond to grief and other emotions. Additionally, it's helpful to have a general map of the grief journey that gives the lay of the land for all the types. The grief process was illuminated by Elisabeth Kübler-Ross, a Swiss-American psychiatrist who in 1969 did extensive research and famously identified five stages of grief.[8] When you're grieving, you experience these stages as *emotional phases* that you go in and out of in a back and forth way. While there is a general developmental progression to the phases, they are not orderly and linear but messy emotional reactions that most people experience after a painful loss. Grief emotions are a muddle because, as we've said, our core hurts stack, with emotions hiding under each other.

Denial

A common reaction to a painful loss is emotional shock: "I can't believe this happened." It's a God-given cushion to absorb a gut-punching blow. In my mom's grief journey with terminal cancer she has often commented, "I can't wait till I get better and can get back to life as usual!" We both feel the temptation to be in denial and pretend she isn't dying. After all, she is very much alive right now, and we are enjoying time together. Mom is an Enneagram Eight—she's strong, confident, and assertive. Her pastor's wife sent her a card that says, "You are strong and then some!" I asked Mom's counselor if she was doing any grief work and the counselor replied, "No. She is soldiering on. She is doing what has worked for her: fight and survive." That's a mixture of her Eight denial and strength of personality.

Anger

In grief we tend to be irritable and prone to angry reactions. You may get angry at loved ones, doctors, someone connected to your loss, God, yourself, your sickness, a clerk at a store—or even your pet! In my mom's grief journey, she got angry when we told her we didn't think it was safe for her to drive and then when we transitioned her to hospice. Her anger was triggered when she experienced losses of freedom and control.

Bargaining/Anxiety

"What if . . . ?" and "If only . . ." are part and parcel of grief and loss. We feel out of control and afraid in suffering and so we replay scenarios to a better conclusion. We may get obsessive and be anxious. In my mom's journey, even though her cancer was advanced and terminal, her anxiety and bargaining manifested in debating chemo and alternative treatments, trying to control her health and many aspects of her care, and steeling her will to live.

Depression/Guilt/Shame

The depression of losing a loved one—or your health, job, or something else that's important to you—can be unbearable. It cuts deep into your heart. It feels terribly lonely. At times you may feel guilty, ashamed, empty, or hopeless. You may blame yourself for some aspect of the loss, even if it's not rational. My mom's increasing needs for physical care and personal support have led her to offer guilty apologies several times a day. She apologizes for having needs and she apologizes after sharing her emotions. She also confessed regrets to me and asked my forgiveness. In the first year of COVID many people were tired and lethargic and didn't know it was grief from all their losses. As we pointed out above, depressed emotions are normal in grief, but they can slip into an unhealthy condition of being stuck in depression.

Acceptance/Sadness

Underneath the grief reactions of anger, anxiety, and shame is sadness. You dearly miss your loved one(s) or the blessed experience that you lost. But in healthy grief you come to accept this reality through a process of being emotionally honest, receiving empathy, and trusting God. The big losses for my mom have been losing the ability to travel to see her family and great-grandchildren, losing control over her body and health, and losing the opportunity to teach Bible studies and mentor younger women. Through all these losses and more, my mom has given me the gift of trusting me with her emotions. This has helped me to feel close to her, understand her, and grieve with her. Of course, it has also helped her to not feel alone and to trust that God is with her and caring for her.

I asked my mom what is helping her in her grief, and she was quick to reply:

> Being honest! Sharing my fears, frustrations, and longings. This helps me to be more realistic and accept reality. The first time I heard I had cancer it was such a shock; I accepted what I was told intellectually, but accepting it emotionally has been a work in progress. Knowing where I am going when I die and being secure in my faith in Christ gives me hope and comfort. Being with family is helping me accept my death, as I see them accept it. Having them journey with me helps me be secure in their love and I'm grateful for that. Prayer is helping me entrust my family to God. I talk to the Father and know he is there and I am connected with him. I remind myself that my life is not my own; I am just passing through.

Meaning

Grief expert David Kessler added a sixth stage to grief: rediscovering new meaning and purpose in life.[9] The suffering of grief can produce persevering faith, virtue, hope, and the outpouring of God's love (Rom. 5:3–5). Jesus wants to comfort us in our loss, which in time can set us up to become a comfort and help to others (2 Cor. 1:3–7). Even though my mom and I are both sad and grieving, we've enjoyed having meaningful conversations. It's also been encouraging to see that through her suffering, her trust in Jesus has been deepening and she keeps offering blessings to me and others. I'm getting a front-row seat to watch her faith in action! It is also meaningful for me to be able to share a little of my experience with you now with the hope that it brings you Good Shepherd's comfort and guidance.

In your experience of sadness and in the phases of grief, it's important to differentiate between good and bad complaining. Bad complaining blocks healthy grieving and perpetuates getting stuck in depression, wallowing in self-pity. But good complaining facilitates healing grief as you process your emotions, trust God's comfort, return to joy, and act with wisdom.

The following comparison between the Old Testament example of the Israelites grumbling against God in the wilderness (Exod. 16:1–3; Num. 14:1–4) and the psalms of lament highlights some sharp distinctions:

Bad Complaining vs. Good Complaining

Bad Complaining	Good Complaining
Grumbling	Lament
Blaming God or others	Taking responsibility for yourself
Repressing emotions	Being emotionally honest
Relying on self	Receiving help
Spoiling what's good	Appreciating what's good
Trying to control things	Abandoning outcomes to God
Stuck in depression	Processing grief

Good Grief and Joy

Our Master Teacher Jesus closes his best sermon with four "pictorial contrasts" featuring two gates, two trees, two people at the final judgment, and two houses (Matt. 7:13–27).[10] They evoke our longing to join with him to become the kind of person who loves God and people well. Or they might make us sad because we're missing out on that true and full life. Our Lord is inviting us to live from the Kingdom of the Heavens. Knowing this spiritual reality immerses us in God's love. Thomas Aquinas taught that "love follows knowledge"; it's more than right beliefs and right actions, it's "an emotional response aroused in the will by visions of the good."[11]

There are two ways that people grow: *pain pushes* and *vision pulls*. The pain of sadness over what hurts us pushes us to seek help, and the vision of longing for a better life can pull or woo us to take steps of growth. But most of the time we need to be activated by distress to seek God's love. In the spiritual allegory *Hinds' Feet on High Places*, Much-Afraid wants Joy and Peace to be her companions always, but the Shepherd tells her that the only way to reach the high places of God's beauty, love, and glory is to take the hands of Sorrow and Suffering and let them lead her.[12] Wise is the person who is motivated to grow from vision rather than needing to be besieged with painful trials! We can pray to soften our hearts to God right now.

In the *Philokalia*, the ancient Russian masterpiece on prayer of the heart, the Eastern Church Fathers emphasized the value of tears to heal our soul of sin and strain and draw us to love God. In the seventh century, Abba Isaac of Syria wrote that through "the grace of contemplation" (or quiet prayer) the flow of tears purifies us and promotes deeper intimacy with God.[13] When we set our heart on the Lord, our tears become a spring of new life (Ps. 84:6). That was the case for the town harlot who rained tears on Jesus' feet (Luke 7:36–50 MSG).

Along these lines, C. S. Lewis defined joy as a combination of grief and longing for the presence of God. He reported experiencing this from time to time through nature, reading poetry, talking with a friend, or trusting God to work a miracle after the death of his mother.[14] Maybe that's evidence of Lewis' healthy Four (Lewis was a Five with a Four wing). Fours remind us that there is a *happy-sad* feeling, a good grief. The psalms of lament often pair sadness over losses with warmhearted longing for God. They can be a model for us of how prayer supports healthy grieving. In the *Philokalia* the ancient prayer masters draw on the Psalms and teach us to *incite* our souls to long for and love God with tears.[15]

Psalm 42 features a stream of water and tears, which makes it an especially helpful prayer to cry out to God for comfort and renewed intimacy when you're in grief. The psalmist is in a crisis, and he's separated from the sanctuary of the Lord and his community. When you feel this grief, you can join with the psalmist and cry out to God:

> As the deer pants for streams of water,
>   so my soul pants for you, my God.
> . . .
> My tears have been my food day and night.
> . . .
> Why, my soul, are you downcast?
>   Why so disturbed within me?
> Put your hope in God,
>   for I will yet praise him,
>   my Savior and my God. (vv. 1, 3, 5)

The psalmist leads us to cry with sadness and yearn for God's loving presence. You can find comfort and courage by grieving in a community that consists of the authors of the psalms, God's people in history, your church, a friend you can share with, and most of all the Trinity, surrounded by angels and saints. Here, as Thomas Merton discovered, "Everything is compassion and I am swimming in it."[16]

Scriptures for Sadness

"The LORD is close to the brokenhearted and saves those who are crushed in spirit." (Ps. 34:18)

"There is . . . a time to weep and a time to laugh, a time to mourn and a time to dance." (Eccles. 3:1, 4)

"The tears stream from my eyes . . . Until you, God, look down from on high." (Lam. 3:49–50 MSG)

Jesus wept, "How often I've ached to embrace [you], the way a hen gathers her chicks under her wings, and you wouldn't let me." (Matt. 23:37 MSG)

"Don't let your hearts be troubled. Trust in God, and trust also in me." (John 14:1 NLT)

· · · · · · · · · SOUL TALK · · · · · · · ·

1. What did you learn about grief and your need for empathy?
2. Which feeling words for depression or sadness do you relate to for yourself (or a loved one)?
3. What helps you to feel desire or longing for God? What distracts you from appreciating the Lord's loving presence?
4. What is one key to healthy grieving that you'd like to try to foster emotional and spiritual health?
5. Which Scripture for sadness especially encouraged you? Why?

Help for Sadness

Be sad with those who are sad.

Romans 12:15 NLV

S ome years ago, George (Three) came to me (Bill) for counseling because he was buried in depression. He was a pastor
with a seminary degree and had been leading his church for
thirty years. He was stuck at The Wall in his journey of the soul.
"I feel like I've lost my faith in Christ," he admitted. "I can't go
on . . . Why doesn't the message of faith in the Lord that I preach
to other people hit home for my own reassurance?"

George felt depressed and bad about himself all the time. He
couldn't relax or concentrate on his work. In fact, it was hard
for him to get out of bed and get through the day. Every step felt
like slogging through a thick bog. Especially preaching—it was a
chore he hated. His church was dying—it had declined from 125
members to 25. He felt like a total failure every time he walked into
the church. Furthermore, his negativity had beaten down his wife
and adult son. He was so isolated that no one except his doctor
and me knew how deeply he was suffering.

Empathy for the Four Hurts

Failure is not an option for Threes, so George was overwhelmed with shame and depression. As a Three, he was under pressure to be a hero, but in recent years he'd been anything but that. To escape from feeling so much shame, he shut down emotionally and avoided difficulties (at his stress line to an unhealthy Nine).

My guiding principle with George was that his shame-filled depression was ungrieved grief, and he needed to learn to feel sad, not bad, and to receive comfort. Often sadness is hiding under shame and needs to be drawn out and cared for. But, as with many people, it was hard for him to be vulnerable to share sadness because in the past that had led to people distancing from him, giving him advice, or judging him.

Many people judge their sadness or hurt as too needy, so it gets converted into shame and buried in the shadow self. That was George's experience, and it was a big part of why his personality was shot through with gloomy shame. His depression was like a long, dark tunnel, and he could not see the light on the other side—*but I could see it*. The light in his depression was for him to not withdraw and isolate but feel his emotions and receive God's empathy through me. He needed to grieve his hurt from his father, the decline in his church, and the harm his cantankerous spirit had caused his family and himself. He needed to feel his underlying sadness and seek comfort.

The way to begin helping someone is to empathize with where they are at that time. For George that meant delving into his depression. I drew out from him some of the feeling words for depression (see chapter 17) and the feeling words for shame (see chapter 7). He needed to feel and articulate his emotions and receive God's empathy through me. That would pave the way for the additional soul work he needed to do.

After building rapport and trust around my empathy for his depression and shame, I focused on his repressed anger (from his stress line to an unhealthy Nine in the Anger triad). In other words, his angry emotions were hiding under his depressed emotions.

As is typical of depression, George had internalized anger against himself, which converts anger into shame. From a comment he made at the outset, I sensed that his anger issue was about his father. It's difficult to be angry at someone you love and need, even if it's not directly expressed to them or they've died. So before going there, I empathized with his anxiety and fear about uncovering his relationship with his father.

To understand your deeper emotions and struggles, it's helpful to remember the important role that family formation plays in spiritual formation and personality development. George reported that when he was a boy he asked his father, who was a pastor, about having a relationship with God and he got a lecture. It was the same when he went to college and told him he wanted to be a PE teacher. His father barked, "Why would you do that? Your older brother is a pastor like me, and you should do the same." His father was always so confident as he led his church of two thousand, and George was afraid to cross him, so he became a pastor too. Decades later, George was still trying to please his father, laboring under his furrowed brow. He kept his father's "hellfire and brimstone" sermons alive in his heart by listening to podcast preachers who blasted away on the wrath of God and the reality of hell.

To help George bring his anger out of hiding, I guided him to verbally confront his father in a loud, angry voice. He needed to feel in his body the force of his aggression. Ultimately, this would become part of his forgiveness process. Because he had emotionally internalized his father, George carried his father's negative judgments of him as if they were his own. To help him shift out of his shame posture, I led him in a type of role-play called "psychodrama." On one side of the couch I put "Preacher George," who was shaming him, and on the other side I put "Rebel George," who had been silent and passive-aggressive. He had a good and bad split. He thought that Preacher George was good and Rebel George was bad, so he tried to live up to the standards of the preacher and he repressed the anger of the rebel. He made his personal weaknesses bad, and this is why he felt so much shame.

It was easy for him to verbalize for Preacher George: "If you don't confess your sins and trust Christ you'll go to hell! . . . You're not a successful pastor like your father. . . . God is going to give up on you. He probably already has."

But I suggested to him that Preacher George was as bad as Rebel George. And that Rebel George wasn't so bad—especially if he could vent his anger to me rather than unconsciously converting it to shame that got stored in his body. His anger was also seeping out in cynicism and self-hatred, and sometimes he reacted to people with his own angry judgments. So I prodded him along to give Rebel George a voice and to fire back at Preacher George. He was able to get free with his anger: "I'm sick of your religious crap! . . . You're a hypocrite like my dad! . . . Stop judging me!"

In all my conversations with George, when he shared I'd volley the ball back to him with an empathetic statement, inviting him to hit the ball back to me by sharing more of his feelings. One time I noticed that when I asked him about how he was doing in his relationship with his wife, he got a little teary-eyed. The same thing happened when I asked about his relationship with God. At that point, I realized that he was ready to go deeper emotionally, to get underneath his anger to explicitly feel and express his underlying sadness. His verbalizations and my empathy helped him start learning to receive comfort without feeling bad about his emotions and needs. His heart was starting to thaw from being frozen in shame, and he was realizing how much he needed God's love.

Sadness and Longing for God

Prior to his counseling, pretty much the only ways George knew to engage God were in Bible study and ministry to others, but in recent years even those activities fell flat. In his words, he was "a dried-up person." But now the Spirit of Jesus was helping us get underneath all his good doctrines and duties to find his broken heart of sadness. I spent a lot of time empathizing with him. I helped him feel and verbalize the different shades of his sad emotions like disappointment, loss, rejection, loneliness, and grief. We connected his emotions with concrete examples from his life, like the decline in his church, emotional distance in his marriage, his son growing up, and wounds from his father.

The deepest, most painful sadness that we all feel is in our unfulfilled longings for God. Yet, it can be an example of *happy-sadness* because great hope is mixed in. In my conversations with George, I looked for his repressed heart desires for connecting with God. Since he was a Heart type, this was especially important. I found lots of little treasures, like him offering kindness to a woman in his church who was dying, feeling loved by his wife when they were in the pool and she looked at him with twinkling eyes and spoke to him in a sweet voice, enjoying golfing with his brother on a beautiful day, and being proud of his son as he led worship at their church. I made a big deal about these things as being God's gift to him. "This is how much God loves you!" I'd say. "You're experiencing the presence of the living Christ!"

George thought he had no desire for God, only doubt, distrust, and duty. But *longing for God is the breath of the soul*, which meant he was suffocating. The place to start was to help him see that even though he was not feeling longing for God, he *longed* to long for God. He wanted to desire God like he had in the past, but he was being shut down by his depression.

I knew that our treasure hunt for his heart was working when George emailed me between appointments: "Thanks for your prayers. As I'm seeking God, *I find myself hoping for a revealing moment with Jesus.*"

Jesus Is Your Sadness Comforter

Connecting personally with Jesus is the ultimate help for sadness or any other need. It's a blessing to tune in to the loving presence of the Spirit of Jesus. The place to start may surprise you: it's to identify something in your life that you feel sad about. Then you turn your attention to appreciating Jesus' human journey of faith and how he relates to you today, through the Holy Spirit. He feels your loss. He is with you and caring for you.

Our Savior is the "Man of sorrows and acquainted with grief" (Isa. 53:3 NKJV). Jesus knows the pain of losing a loved one. His father Joseph died, probably when Jesus was young. This pain is called *attachment pain*, and it's the worst loss. He felt sad for his mother, his siblings, and himself. They lost their provider and rock. Joseph's chair at the dinner table was empty. There were probably things Jesus enjoyed doing with his dad like fishing or working side by side in the carpenter shop. Maybe he missed the way his dad laughed. Joseph knew Jesus from birth and held his history. He was surely a champion for Jesus and the call on his life. As the oldest son, Jesus probably felt an increased weight of responsibility to provide for his family after Joseph died. Losing his father may have restricted his own freedom and opportunities. Is this why he waited till age thirty to start his public ministry? Is it why his mother and brothers pressured him to stop his ministry and come back home (Mark 3:31–32)?

Jesus saw people grieving and hurting and had empathy for them (Heb. 4:15). He feels your sadness, and his heart is open to you. Whatever loss or hurt you experience, Jesus is your Sadness Comforter:

Jesus felt sad for the widow of Nain who lost her only son (Luke 7:11–15).

He sighed with sadness when people didn't want him, just his miracles (Mark 8:11–12).

When Mary and Martha's brother Lazarus died, we read that "Jesus wept" (John 11:35).

Jesus cried for Jerusalem because they said no to God's mercy (Luke 19:41–44).

He felt crushing grief when he anticipated dying on the cross (Mark 14:34).

Falling Back into Jesus' Arms

Looking at his personality map as a type Three helped George understand what was helping him in counseling and how to be intentional about this in his life. He learned to appreciate that his growth line was to a healthy Six. The key for him was to take courage to be emotionally honest, trust Jesus and caring people, and be loyal in his relationships. This path enabled him to cultivate his Three virtue of authenticity.

At my office one day, George told me that the night before he'd had a recurring dream in which he saw himself walking on a path to Jesus but running into a brick wall. Spontaneously, I led him in a time of healing prayer. I helped him to be quiet and present to God. Then I directed him to recall the image and ask the Lord Jesus to reveal himself in George's imagination. After about five minutes of shared, silent prayer, I asked him if he saw or felt anything. He replied, "In my mind I hear Jesus from the other side of the wall saying, 'Come to me, George.' It's like I can see through the wall and his arms are open to me. But I can't get through the wall. I can't get around it. I can't reach Jesus!"

I saw hope in his experience and affirmed, "You're feeling desire for Jesus." Even though a wall separated George from Jesus, I could tell that his heart was warmed by sensing the Lord's loving presence with him. We continued praying quietly. Then the Holy Spirit showed *me* a picture of Jesus stepping around the wall, unseen by George, and standing right behind him. Jesus' arms were open as he whispered in his ear, "Fall back into my arms, George. Let me hold you." I felt the Lord leading me not to tell George about my experience but to instead use what I had discerned to guide his next step. I suggested he continue to pray about his image and keep redirecting his thoughts away from self-recrimination and to the mercy of Christ. "Stop *trying* to believe in God," I urged. "Jesus is believing for you. Just let yourself fall back into his loving arms."

That week George prayed and imagined himself falling back into Jesus' arms. He told me it was "a turning point . . . that I will remember for the rest of my life. I came to peace . . . I have a real relationship with Jesus Christ!" The pivot in George's care and spiritual renewal was shifting from depressive grumbling and self-hatred into lament about his losses and longing for Jesus' comfort and love, which he began to experience. Then the joy of Jesus started flowing into him.

Steps to Help with Sadness

Here is a summary of the steps that help with sadness.

1. *Identify sadness.* Notice if you feel anger, shame, anxiety, or another distress. Usually these are warning lights that you have underlying sadness from a hurt or loss. For instance, depression is often due to ungrieved grief. Getting in touch with your sad feelings can open you to receive the care and guidance you need.
2. *Ask for empathy.* Sadness, hurts, and other emotions are tender, so it takes courage to ask for empathy from the Lord and a friend, but it can bring comfort, insight,

Soul Care for Sadness

Jesus and others can help you care for your hurts, losses, unmet needs, and longings. Consider which of the following soul care practices that helped George with hidden sadness are valuable for you.

Take a gratitude shower to thank God for as many blessings as you can!

Meditate on Gospel stories of Jesus comforting people who were sad.[1]

Pray (and sing) psalms of lament.[2]

Disrupt worry by writing down your emotions.

Fast as you pray Psalm 63 to feel your heart-longing for God.[3]

Pray the Jesus Prayer: "Lord Jesus Christ, have mercy on me."

Talk with a spiritual director for empathy and guidance.

and new energy. The feeling word lists help you get started.

3. *Process grief.* When a loved one dies or you experience another loss, it's natural to go through the phases of grief in a back and forth way. Learning this gives you a map of emotional places you're likely to visit. The most important thing is to trust that your distressed emotions are natural, even a blessing, and to engage the process of grieving with a spiritual director or grief group. In God's time, you can get to the final phase of establishing new meaning, purpose, and joy.

4. *Cultivate longing for God.* Losing relationship with a loved one surfaces a deep need for loving attachments with other people. At the center of this is your *deepest longing for God's love.* Grief is an opportunity for receiving healing and developing a new intimacy with Jesus and others.

5. *Be joyful in Christ.* It's surprising how God can make joy out of loss and sadness. Participating in the healing process for grief helps you to affirm the identity-strengthening truth, "In Christ I am joyful."

SOUL TALK

1. What is one thing you learned about sadness? How might this help you?

2. How do you relate to George's story (personally or for a loved one)?

3. What helps you to long for closeness with God?

4. What do you especially appreciate about Jesus as your Sadness Comforter?

5. What is a life situation in which it would be helpful for you to stop straining and fall back into Jesus' arms?

Check out our free bonus resources for more help with sadness. You can also talk with one of the spiritual directors or coaches who have earned a certificate in our Soul Shepherding Institute. Just scan the QR code or go to SoulShepherding.org/enneagram.

Conclusion

Help for Your Hurt

Jesus explained, "Here on earth you will have many trials and sorrows. But take heart, because I have overcome the world" (John 16:33 NLT). We all have hurts in our soul that we want to fix. But your soul is not like a broken car that can be fixed by a mechanic. *The cure for a hurt soul is care.*

In our thirty years as therapists and spiritual directors we've found that the key to emotional and spiritual growth is for your broken personality to reach out for Jesus' loving touch. The best way to do this is to go on an inner journey of identifying and feeling your hurt of sadness that underlies anger, shame, anxiety, and the stressors in your life and sharing this with other followers of Jesus who are emotionally honest and gracious.

In this book we've shown you how to use the Enneagram to understand your type's family formation, root sin, and damaged emotions of anger, shame, anxiety, and sadness, which show you the deeper care that you need from the Lord. Furthermore, learning your type's emotional alarm, needs for empathy, perfect image in Jesus, virtue, and soul care practices charts out a path of soul care. As you absorb more of Jesus' grace in your personality, it enables you to better care for and guide others.

The best learning is relearning at a deeper level, so you'll find it helpful to reread the chapters on your type, wing, stress line, growth line, and core emotions. Reading a chapter to better understand, support, and pray for others is a great gift of love.

Empathy Prayer

In closing, we want to share with you *Empathy Prayer*, which is a resource that we teach in Soul Shepherding Institute retreats and that our senior spiritual directors use with their clients.[1] Whatever you or your friends are feeling, Empathy Prayer is a resource that will help you. It guides you with simple steps for receiving Jesus' empathy for your hurt emotions. You express appreciation to Jesus, share a personal situation that you need help with, and pay close attention to five specific ways that Jesus cares for you with empathy.

Just use each prompt below to journal, pray, or share with a friend. Best of all is to do all three!

Talk to Jesus

Dear Jesus, my [identify a favorite name for Jesus, like Shepherd or Lord] . . .

I appreciate how you have cared for me when [share a memory of experiencing God's blessing] . . .

Today, I need your help with [briefly describe a specific situation or need] . . .

Listen to Jesus' Empathy

Dear [your name],

I see your physical demeanor of [e.g., rushing around, carrying heavy responsibilities, tossing and turning in bed, clenching your jaw, slumping your shoulders, frowning, crying] . . .

I hear what you are saying (or thinking in your mind) . . .

I understand you are feeling [*e.g., anger, shame, anxiety, sadness, and other emotions*] . . .

I know this is really big for you because you need . . .

I enjoy being with you and affirm you as a person who is [*e.g., emotionally honest, trusting, courageous, kind, persevering, faithful*] . . .

I want to encourage you by sharing a Scripture [*e.g., a Bible promise*] . . .

Give Thanks

Jesus, in this prayer time I appreciate how you cared for me by . . .

Acknowledgments

The journey to writing this book started fifteen years ago when our friends Jane Willard and John and Margaret Snyder introduced us to the Enneagram. Thank you, Jane, John, and Margaret. It's been so helpful in our lives, relationships, and the ministry that we and our staff offer. It's become our go-to coaching tool.

Our board has provided enthusiastic support for this project. Thank you, John and Margaret, Steve and Joan Graham, Lance Wood, and Steve and Jayne Watts. Your friendship, prayers, wisdom, and investments make our ministry possible.

The Soul Shepherding staff prays and works alongside us every day, which enables us to give most of our time to ministry, including using the Enneagram in speaking and coaching for over a decade and then writing this book. We appreciate each of you! Special thanks to Briana Gaultiere for being an early adopter of our approach to the Enneagram and emotions and for offering your talents as a graphic designer.

The vision for this book was shaped by our literary agent, Don Gates, and our editor, Vicki Crumpton, and it was supported by Revell, a division of Baker Publishing Group. Amy Nemecek's expert editing provided clarity in the wording and accuracy in many details. Thank you, Don, Vicki, Amy, and the rest of the team at Revell.

The inspiration for this book came from the pastors, missionaries, leaders, spiritual directors, counselors, and coaches that we serve. Thank you for sharing your lives with us.

This is more than a book—it's part of the Soul Shepherding curriculum for emotional and spiritual growth. We are thankful for the team of spiritual directors and coaches we've trained who serve alongside us.

Diagram of Enneagram Types

Summary of Types and Emotions

For easy reference, on the next page we have included a chart summarizing the key features for each of the nine types and four emotions.

	Felt Need	Family Formation	Root Sin	Defense Mechanism	Core Hurt	Stress Emotion	Emotional Alarm	Stress Type	Growth Type	Virtue to Cultivate	Key Soul Care Practice	Positive Emotion to Nurture
GUT												
Eight (Challenger)	Act with power	Fighter	Lust for power	Denial	Anger	Anxiety	Toughening up	Five	Two	Mercy	Spiritual friendship	Gentleness
Nine (Peacemaker)	Act to avoid conflict	Lost child or peacemaker	Lethargy	Emotional numbing	Anger	Anxiety	Accommodating others	Six	Three	Self-activation	Spiritual direction	Liveliness
One (Reformer)	Act to be perfect	Parentified child	Resentment	Reaction formation	Anger	Shame	Personal obligation	Four	Seven	Serenity	Abandoning outcomes to God	Joy
HEART												
Two (Helper)	Feel wanted	Enabler	Pride	Repression	Shame	Anger	People-pleasing	Eight	Four	Humility	Solitude	Self-esteem
Three (Achiever)	Feel successful	Hero	Vainglory	Identification	Shame	Anger	Conditions of worth	Nine	Six	Authenticity	Emotional honesty	Free of pressure to perform
Four (Individualist)	Feel special	Victim or special	Envy	Introjection or artistic sublimation	Shame	Shame	Stirring up emotions	Two	One	Emotional balance	Thankfulness	Enjoying God's blessings
HEAD												
Five (Observer)	Think to have resources	Loner	Greed	Intellectualizing	Anxiety	Anxiety	Staying in your head	Seven	Eight	Generosity	Bible study as worship	Relational warmth
Six (Loyalist)	Think to have security	Guardian or rebel	Fear	Projection	Anxiety	Shame	Relying on safety nets	Three	Nine	Courage	Scripture meditation	Calm confidence
Seven (Enthusiast)	Think to have pleasure	Cheerleader	Self-indulgence	Idealization	Anxiety	Anger	Wandering attention	One	Five	Sober contentment	Silence	Savor little blessings

Enneagram Subtypes and Countertypes

Subtypes

There are three subtypes or modifiers for each of the nine personality types (which makes twenty-seven different types). Learning these can prevent mistyping. For most people one subtype is prominent, but you may have two or three, and your main subtype may change over time. The subtypes express themselves somewhat differently in each of the nine types.[1]

Self-Preservation

Called "Self-Pres" for short, they are often warm and friendly, but also reserved and cautious. They are sensitive and protective, taking care of practical needs like safety, security, and well-being for themselves and their loved ones. They tend to feel more anxiety.

Social

The Socials are not necessarily extroverted—they're focused on belonging, recognition, and everyone getting along in a social group. They can be winsome and charismatic to influence others positively and garner admiration. They tend to feel more shame.

One-to-One

The One-to-Ones are also called the Intimacy or Sexual sub-type. They are intimacy-oriented, strong-willed, directive, can be seductive, and like to assume a stance of power or align with a person who has power. They tend to feel more anger.

Countertypes

The most important thing to know about the subtypes is that for each of the nine types, one is the countertype that seems contrary to the type because they're strongly resisting the root sin and weaknesses of their type. Mistyping is often due to not realizing that you (or another person) are the countertype.

Eight: Social Eights resist their challenging, rebelling nature and seek to be protective and loyal.

Nine: Social Nines resist their lethargy to pursue group interests and strive for accomplishments.

One: One-to-One Ones try to avoid resentment by directly expressing their anger.

Two: Self-Pres Twos are less self-effacing to help others and act to take care of their own needs.

Three: Self-Pres Threes try to avoid their vainglory by being good and securing others' well-being.

Four: Self-Pres Fours hold back their emotiveness and seek to endure pain more stoically.

Five: One-to-One Fives seek intimacy and express their emotions more than typical remote Fives.

Six: One-to-One Sixes are *Counterphobic*, resisting fear by taking risks and being aggressive.

Seven: Social Sevens seek to replace hedonism with compassion and distractibility with focus.

Scripture Permissions

Unless otherwise indicated, Scripture quotations are from THE HOLY BIBLE, NEW INTERNATIONAL VERSION®, NIV® Copyright © 1973, 1978, 1984, 2011 by Biblica, Inc.® Used by permission. All rights reserved worldwide.

Scripture quotations labeled CEV are from the Contemporary English Version © 1991, 1992, 1995 by American Bible Society. Used by permission.

Scripture quotations labeled ERV are from the HOLY BIBLE: EASY-TO-READ VERSION © 2014 by Bible League International. Used by permission.

Scripture quotations labeled ESV are from The Holy Bible, English Standard Version® (ESV®), copyright © 2001 by Crossway, a publishing ministry of Good News Publishers. Used by permission. All rights reserved. ESV Text Edition: 2016

Scripture quotations labeled KJV are from the King James Version of the Bible.

Scripture quotations labeled MSG are from *THE MESSAGE*, copyright © 1993, 2002, 2018 by Eugene H. Peterson. Used by permission of NavPress. All rights reserved. Represented by Tyndale House Publishers, Inc.

Scripture quotations labeled NCV are from the New Century Version®. Copyright © 2005 by Thomas Nelson. Used by permission. All rights reserved.

Scripture quotations labeled NEB are from the New English Bible, copyright © Cambridge University Press and Oxford University Press 1961, 1970. All rights reserved.

Scripture quotations labeled NIrV are from the Holy Bible, New International Reader's Version®. NIrV®. Copyright © 1995, 1996, 1998, 2014 by Biblica, Inc.® Used by permission. All rights reserved worldwide.

Notes

Chapter 1 Where's Your Hurt?

1. Bill and Kristi Gaultiere, *Journey of the Soul: A Practical Guide to Emotional and Spiritual Growth* (Grand Rapids: Revell, 2021), 115–41.

2. A review of 104 empirical studies on the Enneagram found some positive evidence of reliability and validity and partial alignment with the Myers-Briggs Type Indicator and Big Five. Joshua N. Hook et al., "The Enneagram: A Systematic Review of the Literature and Directions for Future Research," *Journal of Clinical Psychology* 77, no. 4 (December 2020), 1–19, https://doi.org/10.1002/jclp.23097.

3. Rebecca Konyndyk DeYoung, *Glittering Vices: A New Look at the Seven Deadly Sins and Their Remedies* (Grand Rapids: Brazos, 2009), 34.

4. In the late 1960s, Oscar Ichazo started teaching the modern Enneagram with the nine root sins. See Richard Rohr and Andreas Ebert, *The Enneagram: A Christian Perspective* (New York: Crossroad, 2007), 10–14.

5. C. S. Lewis, *The Voyage of the Dawn Treader* (New York: Collier Books, 1970), 90–91.

6. Gerald May, *Addiction and Grace: Love and Spirituality in the Healing of Addictions* (New York: HarperCollins, 1988), 117 (italics in original).

7. Beatrice Chestnut, *The Complete Enneagram: 27 Paths to Greater Self-Knowledge* (Berkeley: She Writes Press, 2013), 358.

8. John Townsend, *Hiding from Love: How to Change the Withdrawal Patterns That Isolate and Imprison You* (Colorado Springs: NavPress, 1991), 30.

9. *Shadow self* is a Jungian term for your unconscious self that is usually in the dark or hidden from you but follows you around like your shadow. It contains the unwanted or denied aspects of your personality that resist the grace you need.

10. C. S. Lewis, *Mere Christianity* (New York: HarperCollins, 2001), 192.

11. Bill Gaultiere, "How to Feel Your Emotions with Jesus," Soul Shepherding, https://www.soulshepherding.org/how-to-feel-your-emotions-with-jesus/.

Chapter 2 Anger as Broken Boundaries

1. In instances like this, we identify the Enneagram type to help you reference the personality behind the story, illustration, or quote.

2. Don Richard Riso and Russ Hudson, *The Wisdom of the Enneagram* (New York: Bantam Books, 1999), 54.

3. Jesus' teaching on anger in his great sermon is found in Matthew 5:21–32, 38–48; 6:12; 7:1–6.

4. Dallas Willard, *The Divine Conspiracy* (New York: HarperCollins, 1997), 147.

5. Willard, *Divine Conspiracy*, 151.

6. Daniel Goleman, *Emotional Intelligence: Why It Can Matter More Than IQ* (New York: Bantam Books, 1995).

7. Brené Brown, *Atlas of the Heart: Mapping Meaningful Connection and the Language of Human Experience* (New York: Random House, 2021), xx–xxi.

8. Brown, *Atlas of the Heart*, 222.

9. In this feeling words list and the ones in later chapters, the emotive words generally intensify from left to right in each category.

10. *Haron* is a Hebrew word for "anger" that means "red-hot neck." Translated by Old Testament scholar Jeff McCrory in a personal conversation.

11. *Qatsaph* is a Hebrew word for "anger" that literally means "snorting with your nose." Hence the phrase "snorting like a bull." McCrory, personal conversation.

12. *Akzari* is a Hebrew word that is usually translated "cruel," even for God, as in Isaiah 13:9, but it's connected to the word for "valiant" or "courageous." It's like a mama bear protecting her cubs. Chaim and Laura Bentorah, "Hebrew Word Study: Cruel, Wrath, Anger," Chaim Bentorah Biblical Hebrew Studies, July 1, 2018, https://www.chaimbentorah.com/2018/07/hebrew-word-study-cruel-wrath-anger/.

13. *Haron* is an Old Testament Hebrew word that is usually translated as "wrath" but literally means "raging fire" or "consuming passion." Bentorah, "Hebrew Word Study."

14. *'Evrah* is an Old Testament Hebrew word that means "fierce anger," and its root word (*'ever*) refers to a river overflowing its banks. It bursts through boundaries because it's overwhelming and all-encompassing. Bentorah, "Hebrew Word Study."

15. Michael Mangis, *Signature Sins: Taming Our Wayward Hearts* (Downers Grove, IL: InterVarsity, 2008), 36.

16. DeYoung, *Glittering Vices*, 142.

17. Heather Murphy, "A Man Demanded His Final Paycheck. The Auto Shop Delivered 91,500 Greasy Pennies," *New York Times*, March 25, 2021, https://www.nytimes.com/2021/03/25/business/auto-shop-pennies.html.

18. Chestnut, *Complete Enneagram*, 97.

19. Willard, *Divine Conspiracy*, 148.

20. Henry Cloud and John Townsend, *Boundaries: When to Say YES, When to Say NO, to Take Control of Your Life* (Grand Rapids: Zondervan, 1992), 31–32.

21. Ten times the Bible explicitly praises God as compassionate, gracious, *slow to anger*, and abounding in love and faithfulness: Exodus 34:6; Numbers 14:18; Nehemiah 9:17; Psalms 30:5; 86:15; 103:8; 145:8; Isaiah 48:9; Joel 2:13; and Nahum 1:3.

Chapter 3 Type Eight: Challenger

1. Wikipedia, s.v. "Fritz Perls," last modified July 24, 2022, https://en.wikipedia.org/wiki/Fritz_Perls; Jodi Clarke, "What Is Gestalt Therapy?," VeryWellMind, July 31, 2021, https://www.verywellmind.com/what-is-gestalt-therapy-4584583.

2. Kenneth Wong, "What Is the Rarest Enneagram Type and the Most Common Enneagram Type?," The Millennial Grind, June 11, 2022, https://millennial-grind.com/what-is-the-rarest-enneagram-type-and-why/.

3. There are three subtypes for each of the nine Enneagram types: One-to-One, Self-Preservation, and Social. Appendix 3 offers a brief summary of the three general subtypes and identifies the countertype for each of the nine types.

4. George S. Patton's exact quote is, "A good plan, violently executed now, is better than a perfect plan next week." "Quotes by General George S. Patton Jr.," General Patton, accessed December 16, 2022, http://generalpatton.com/quotes/.

5. Chestnut, *Complete Enneagram*, 96.

6. "Fritz Perls Biography," IMDb, accessed December 16, 2022, https://www.imdb.com/name/nm2841759/bio.

7. Wikipedia, s.v. "Fritz Perls"; Clarke, "What Is Gestalt Therapy?"

8. Hook et al., "The Enneagram," 11.

9. Blair is not her real name. Throughout this book, whenever we tell someone's personal story, we change their name and identifying details to protect their confidentiality.

10. Stephanie Barron Hall, "Most Common Stress Responses of Each Enneagram Type and How to Manage Them," *Truity's Personality and Careers Blog*, July 11, 2021, https://www.truity.com/blog/most-common-stress-responses-each-enneagram-type-and-how-manage-them.

11. Chestnut, *Complete Enneagram*, 128.

12. Rohr and Ebert, *The Enneagram*, 168.

13. Every Enneagram type is loved by God, but we rarely talk to someone who finds it easy to love their own type. Hence, the affirmation "beloved Eights." For each type, we will at times identify them as beloved by God and others. This follows the example of Adele and Doug Calhoun and Clare and Scott Loughrige in *Spiritual Rhythms for the Enneagram: A Handbook for Harmony and Transformation* (Downers Grove, IL: InterVarsity, 2019).

14. Mother Teresa, *No Greater Love* (Novato, CA: New World Library, 2002), 34.

15. Wikipedia, s.v. "Caspar Milquetoast," last updated September 1, 2022, https://en.wikipedia.org/wiki/Caspar_Milquetoast.

16. Robert J. Nogosek, *Nine Portraits of Jesus: Discovering Jesus through the Enneagram* (New York: Paulist Press, 2018), 95 (italics in original).

17. John 8:1–11 is missing from some early manuscripts, probably because it was such a scandal in the early church.

18. José Luis González-Balado, *Stories of Mother Teresa* (Liguori, MO: Liguori Publications, 1983), 13.

19. Mother Teresa, *A Simple Path* (New York: Ballantine Books, 1995), 93–94.

20. Mother Teresa, *A Simple Path*, xxi.

21. Brian Kolodiejchuk, ed., *Mother Teresa: Come Be My Light—The Private Writings of the "Saint of Calcutta"* (New York: Doubleday, 2007).

22. Herbert Lockyer, *All the Women of the Bible* (Grand Rapids: Zondervan, 1967), 40–42.

23. Mother Teresa, *A Simple Path*, xxviii.

24. Bill Gaultiere, *Breath Prayer Guides* (Irvine, CA: Soul Shepherding, 2019), 34.

Chapter 4 Type Nine: Peacemaker

1. *Oblomov* was published in 1859 by Ivan Goncharov. Rohr and Ebert give a summary of the novel in *The Enneagram*, 188–89. See also Wikipedia, s.v. "Oblomov," last updated September 23, 2022, https://en.wikipedia.org/wiki/Oblomov.

2. Wong, "What Is the Rarest Enneagram Type and the Most Common Enneagram Type?"

3. Hook et al., "The Enneagram," 11.

4. Wikipedia, s.v. "Meh," last edited November 14, 2022, https://en.wikipedia.org/wiki/Meh.

5. Rohr and Ebert, *The Enneagram*, 180.

6. Archibald Hart, *Adrenaline and Stress* (Nashville: Thomas Nelson, 1995), 149–50.

7. Abigail Abrams, "Nine Sleep Habits from Around the World," *Time*, April 27, 2017, https://time.com/4713813/sleep-habits-napping-siesta.

8. You can learn about the Soul Shepherding Institute or talk with a spiritual director or coach at SoulShepherding.org.

9. Quoted in Rohr and Ebert, *The Enneagram*, 191.

10. Chestnut, *Complete Enneagram*, 58–59.

11. Riso and Hudson, *Wisdom of the Enneagram*, 333.

12. Margaret Frings Keyes, *Emotions and the Enneagram: Working Through Your Shadow Life Script* (Muir Beach, CA: Molysdatur, 1992), 72.

13. Riso and Hudson, *Wisdom of the Enneagram*, 322.

14. Richard Foster, *Prayer: Finding the Heart's True Home* (New York: HarperSanFrancisco, 1992), 8.

15. Jesus shares with us what he learned by experience, "Blessed are you who are caught in the middle of a conflict for you can be at peace as God's child" (Matt. 5:9, authors' paraphrase). Jesus is not giving us an imperative, "Be a peacemaker so you can be blessed." The blessing is not in the *condition* but in the *Kingdom* of God. See Bill Gaultiere, *Your Best Life in Jesus' Easy Yoke: Rhythms of Grace to De-Stress and Live Empowered*, updated edition (Irvine, CA: Soul Shepherding, Inc., 2020), 62.

16. John Woolman, *The Journal and Major Essays of John Woolman*, ed. Phillips P. Moulton (Richmond, IN: Friends United Press, 2001), 53–54.

17. Woolman, *Journal and Major Essays*, 58.

18. Riso and Hudson, *Wisdom of the Enneagram*, 316.

19. Eugene Peterson, *Under the Unpredictable Plant: An Exploration in Vocational Holiness* (Grand Rapids: Eerdmans, 1992), 100–101.

Chapter 5 Type One: Reformer

1. Rebecca Keegan, "Is 'Saving Mr. Banks' Too Hard on 'Mary Poppins' Creator?," *Los Angeles Times*, December 28, 2013, https://www.latimes.com/entertainment

/movies/moviesnow/la-et-mn-disney-mary-poppins-saving-mr-banks-travers
-20131228-story.html.

2. Amy Henderson, "How Did P. L. Travers, the Prickly Author of Mary Poppins, Really Fare against Walt Disney?," *Smithsonian*, December 20, 2013, https://www
.smithsonianmag.com/smithsonian-institution/how-did-pl-travers-the-prickly
-author-of-mary-poppins-really-fare-against-walt-disney-180949052/.

3. *Saving Mr. Banks*, directed by John Lee Hancock (Walt Disney Pictures, 2013).

4. Gaultiere, *Your Best Life in Jesus' Easy Yoke*, 62.

5. Chestnut, *Complete Enneagram*, 400.

6. Rohr and Ebert, *The Enneagram*, 50.

7. Hook et al., "The Enneagram," 11.

8. Bill and Kristi Gaultiere, "Enneagram & Emotions" course, SoulShepherding
.org/enneagram.

9. Riso and Hudson, *Wisdom of the Enneagram*, 101.

10. Charlton Heston, interview by King Watson, *Meet the Press* (Australia), December 6, 1960, accessed January 25, 2023, YouTube, https://www.youtube.com
/watch?v=BH3UXBj_sfs.

11. Dante Alighieri, *The Divine Comedy: Inferno*, canto VII. See Beatrice Chestnut, *The Complete Enneagram* (Berkeley, CA: She Writes Press, 2013), 403.

12. Brown, *Atlas of the Heart*, 141.

13. Thomas Kelly, *A Testament of Devotion* (1941; repr., New York: HarperCollins, 1992), 92.

14. The Greek word *oligopistos* is translated as "little-faith," a word that Jesus coined (Matt. 6:30; 8:26; 14:31; 16:8; 17:20; Luke 12:28). Some people imagine Jesus calling his disciples "little-faiths" with a scowl of angry judgment. Instead, imagine hearing Jesus chuckle and say, "C'mon guys! Think about it. I know you can learn this."

15. Watchman Nee, *The Normal Christian Life* (1957; repr., Fort Washington, PA: CLC Publications, 2020), 238–39.

16. Gaultiere, *Your Best Life in Jesus' Easy Yoke*, 34–40.

17. Priscilla provided hospitality for Paul for two years and helped him in his ministry (Acts 18:18; 1 Cor. 16:19), corrected Apollos' teaching (Acts 18:26), and served as a house church pastor (Rom. 16:3–5; 2 Tim. 4:19).

18. "Jesus delights in me" is inspired by Psalms 18:19; 34:5; 37:4. Gaultiere, *Journey of the Soul*, 72–74.

Chapter 6 Help for Anger

1. The American Psychological Association found that half of drivers admit to responding aggressively to the careless acts of other drivers. Taylor Covington, "Road Rage Statistics in 2022," The Zebra, updated July 7, 2022, https://www
.thezebra.com/resources/research/road-rage-statistics/.

2. Todd W. Hall and M. Elizabeth Lewis Hall, *Relational Spirituality: A Psychological-Theological Paradigm for Transformation* (Downers Grove, IL: InterVarsity, 2021), 85.

3. Christopher L. Heuertz, *The Sacred Enneagram: Finding Your Unique Path to Spiritual Growth* (Grand Rapids: Zondervan, 2017), 177.

4. Heuertz, *Sacred Enneagram*, 177.

5. Henry Cloud and John Townsend, *How People Grow* (Grand Rapids: Zondervan, 2001), 180–81.

6. Heuertz, *Sacred Enneagram*, 181.

7. Other examples of facedown prayer include Judges 13:20; Ezekiel 9:8; 11:13; 43:3; Daniel 8:17; Matthew 17:6; 18:26.

8. Cursing Psalms include Psalms 35, 59, 69, 70, and 109.

9. This is adapted from Jesus' prayer on the cross, "Father, into your hands I commit my spirit" (Luke 23:46).

10. Saint Dominic, a twelfth-century Spanish priest, used many other bodily postures in prayer, like bowing before an altar as if Christ were actually there, repeatedly kneeling and rising while looking at a cross, lifting his hands open like a Bible, cupping his hands around his ears to listen to God, and standing straight to be like an arrow flying in the heavens. Simon Tugwell, ed., *Early Dominicans: Selected Writings* (Mahwah, NJ: Paulist Press, 1982), 94–103.

Chapter 7 Shame as Self-Rejection

1. Goleman, *Emotional Intelligence*. See also Bill Gaultiere, *Emotional Intelligence: 5 Steps with Jesus to Better Living & Leading* (Shop.SoulShepherding.org).

2. Willard, *The Divine Conspiracy*, 102 (italics in original).

3. In Matthew 5:8 Jesus is not saying, "Be pure in heart so you can be blessed by God." He's pronouncing a blessing on a group of people who don't feel blessed. "Pure" can mean absolutist, perfectionist, thorough, or earnest. I (Bill) understand Jesus to be saying, "Blessed are you who pursue seemingly unattainable ideals, for you can find God" (Gaultiere, *Your Best Life in Jesus' Easy Yoke*, 62).

4. Willard, *The Divine Conspiracy*, 222. In Matthew 6:1–7:12, Jesus especially speaks to people who are earnest about practicing their faith and struggling with shame and anxiety.

5. Quoted in Brown, *Atlas of the Heart*, 135. Biographical information is from Wikipedia, s.v. "Antwone Fisher," last updated November 26, 2022, https://en.wikipedia.org/wiki/Antwone_Fisher.

6. Research studies cited in Brown, *Atlas of the Heart*, 147.

7. Wikipedia, s.v. "Antwone Fisher."

8. Willard, *The Divine Conspiracy*, 222.

9. The Hebrew word *bosh* is the most common Old Testament word for shame, used nearly two hundred times, and can be translated as "dropping your head." Personal conversation with Old Testament scholar Jeff McCrory, MDiv, PhD.

10. Isaiah connects shame (*bosh*) with licking the dust in Isaiah 49:23: "with their faces to the ground; they will lick the dust." McCrory, personal conversation.

11. The Hebrew word *qalal* is often translated as "lightened" or "despised" as in Sarah's treatment of Hagar (Gen. 16:4). It's the opposite of the Hebrew word *kavod*, which means "glory" or "weight." See NAS Exhaustive Concordance, s.v. "7043," Biblehub.com, https://biblehub.com/hebrew/7043.htm.

12. Leanne Payne, *Restoring the Christian Soul through Healing Prayer* (Wheaton: Crossway, 1991), 26–27.

13. Gaultiere, *Your Best Life in Jesus' Easy Yoke*, 169–70.

14. C. G. Jung, *The Collected Works of C. G. Jung, Vol. 7: Two Essays on Analytical Psychology*, ed. and trans. Gerhard Adler and R. F. C. Hull (New York: Pantheon Books, 1953), 158.

15. D. W. Winnicott, *The Maturational Processes and the Facilitating Environment: Studies in the Theory of Emotional Development* (New York: Routledge, 2018), 140–52.

16. The New Testament Scriptures teach self-denial in many places (Matt. 19:21; Luke 5:27–28; 9:23; John 12:23–25; Rom. 13:14; 1 Cor. 6:12; Gal. 5:16; Titus 2:12–13; James 4:7; 1 Pet. 2:11; 4:2).

17. Jeremiah teaches us that the human heart *apart from God* is deceived and sinful. Jesus taught us to hate our life that is *opposed to him* and to deny our self that is *proud* or *self-sufficient* (John 12:25; Luke 9:23).

18. Pss. 26:2; 51:6; 139:23; Prov. 14:8; 2 Cor. 13:5; and 1 John 1:9 teach the importance of self-awareness.

19. Ephesians is one source of affirmations for your identity in Christ. See 1:3, 7, 13; 2:7, 13; 3:12; 5:8.

Chapter 8 Type Two: Helper

1. Thorton Wilder, *The Angel That Troubled the Waters: And Other Plays* (New York: Coward-McCann, 1928), 145–46.

2. Wilder, *Angel That Troubled the Waters*, 149.

3. Wilder, *Angel That Troubled the Waters*, 149.

4. Riso and Hudson, *Wisdom of the Enneagram*, 128.

5. Rohr and Ebert, *The Enneagram*, 71.

6. Rohr and Ebert, *The Enneagram*, 71.

7. Chestnut, *Complete Enneagram*, 364.

8. Hook et al., "The Enneagram," 11.

9. Brené Brown, *Dare to Lead: Brave Work, Tough Conversations, and Whole Hearts* (New York: Random House, 2018), 132.

10. Henri J.M. Nouwen, *The Inner Voice of Love: A Journey through Anguish to Freedom* (New York: Doubleday, 1996), xiv.

11. Nouwen, *Inner Voice of Love*, 86.

12. Nouwen, *Inner Voice of Love*, 42.

13. Rohr and Ebert, *The Enneagram*, 64, 81.

14. Michael Hollings, *Thérèse of Lisieux: An Illustrated Life* (Ann Arbor, MI: Servant, 1981), 35.

15. Brother Lawrence, *Practicing His Presence* (Jacksonville: SeedSowers, 1985), 59.

16. Brother Lawrence, *Practicing His Presence*, 70.

17. This prayer is inspired by Psalm 131:2. See Gaultiere, *Breath Prayer Guides*, 17.

Chapter 9 Type Three: Achiever

1. Adapted from Doug Lipman, "Why Weren't You Zusia?," Hasidic Stories Home Page, https://hasidicstories.com/Stories/Other_Early_Rebbes/zusia.html.

2. DeYoung, *Glittering Vices*, 45. Contemporary lists of the seven deadly sins often do not include vainglory.

3. Carl G. Jung, *Man and His Symbols* (New York: Doubleday, 1964), 287.

4. Riso and Hudson, *Wisdom of the Enneagram*, 164.

5. Chestnut, *Complete Enneagram*, 316.

6. Riso and Hudson, *Wisdom of the Enneagram*, 160.

7. *The Chosen*, season 2, episode 3, "Matthew 4:24," directed by Dallas Jenkins, aired April 13, 2021.

8. George Müller, *Answers to Prayer* (Chicago: Moody Press, 1896), 30. His exact words are, "I have sought to encourage myself in God, by laying hold in faith on His mighty power, His unchangeable love, and His infinite wisdom, and I have said to myself: God is able and willing to deliver me if it be good for me."

9. Bill Gaultiere and Sheridan McDaniel, *Souls on Fire: Black Heroes Who Inspire Our Devotion to Jesus* (Irvine, CA: Soul Shepherding, 2022), ebook on SoulShepherding.org.

10. Jarena Lee, *Religious Experience and Journal of Mrs. Jarena Lee: Giving an Account of Her Call to Preach the Gospel* (Philadelphia: Pantianos, 1836), 94.

11. Lee, *Religious Experience and Journal*, xi.

12. Lee, *Religious Experience and Journal*, 21.

13. Lee, *Religious Experience and Journal*, 105.

14. Lockyer, *All the Women of the Bible*, 65.

15. Gaultiere, *Breath Prayer Guides*, 13.

Chapter 10 Type Four: Individualist

1. C. S. Lewis, *The Great Divorce* (New York: HarperCollins, 1946), 83.

2. Lewis, *Great Divorce*, 85–87.

3. Riso and Hudson, *Wisdom of the Enneagram*, 201.

4. Hook et al., "The Enneagram," 12.

5. Bill and Gloria Gaither, "You're Something Special" (Gaither Music, 1974).

6. Brennan Manning, *Ruthless Trust: The Ragamuffin's Path to God* (New York: HarperCollins, 2000), 4.

7. Manning, *Ruthless Trust*, 13–14.

8. DeYoung, *Glittering Vices*, 68.

9. Alice Fryling, *Mirror for the Soul: A Christian Guide to the Enneagram* (Downers Grove, IL: InterVarsity, 2017), 18–19.

10. Quoted in DeYoung, *Glittering Vices*, 79.

11. Chestnut, *Complete Enneagram*, 274.

12. Gaultiere, *Journey of the Soul*, 115–42, 219–20.

13. Hall, "Most Common Stress Responses of Each Enneagram Type."

14. Curt Thompson, *The Soul of Shame: Retelling the Stories We Believe about Ourselves* (Downers Grove, IL: InterVarsity, 2015), 34.

15. Brennan Manning, *Abba's Child: The Cry of the Heart for Intimate Belonging* (Colorado Springs: NavPress, 1994), 106.

16. Manning, *Abba's Child*, 106–7.

17. Nogosek, *Nine Portraits of Jesus*, 56.

18. Nogosek, *Nine Portraits of Jesus*, 56.

19. Saint Augustine, *The Confessions*, trans. Henry Chadwick (New York: Oxford University Press, 1991), 180.

20. Jesus was loving when his disciples had "little faith" in him (Mark 4:35–41), were slow to understand spiritual reality (8:14–21), and abandoned him at the cross (14:50).

21. "Sadhu Sundar Singh: Indian Christian Missionary," Christian Classics Ethereal Library, https://www.ccel.org/ccel/singh.

22. Sadhu Sundar Singh, *At the Master's Feet*, trans. Arthur and Rebecca Parker (New York: Fleming H. Revell Co., 1922), 49.

23. "Giving Thanks Can Make You Happier," Harvard Health Publishing, August 14, 2021, https://www.health.harvard.edu/healthbeat/giving-thanks-can-make -you-happier.

24. Brennan Manning, *The Furious Longing of God* (Colorado Springs: David C Cook, 2009), 22.

25. Manning, *Abba's Child*, 168.

Chapter 11 Help for Shame

1. Townsend, *Hiding from Love*, 30.

2. Manning, *Ruthless Trust*, 13–16.

3. Brennan Manning, *All Is Grace: A Ragamuffin Memoir* (Colorado Springs: David C Cook, 2011), 19.

4. Paraphrased from Jesus' Beatitudes in Matthew 5:3–10. For a fuller interpretation and application, see Bill Gaultiere, *Jesus' Greatest Teaching* (Irvine, CA: Soul Shepherding, n.d.).

5. Jesus died for our sins to forgive us, heal us, and reconcile us to God. This includes healing our shame, which he experienced on his cross journey (Isa. 53:5; Heb. 12:2; 1 Pet. 2:24). See Bill Gaultiere, *Unforsaken: Journey with Jesus on the Stations of the Cross* (Irvine, CA: Soul Shepherding, 2020, 48–50).

6. Heuertz, *The Sacred Enneagram*, 182.

7. Henri J.M. Nouwen, *Spiritual Direction* (New York: HarperCollins, 2006), 34.

8. Psalms to help with shame include Psalms 25, 31, 32, 34, 44, 51, 69, and 71.

9. Nouwen, *Spiritual Direction*, 36.

Chapter 12 Anxiety as Repressed Emotion

1. National Institute of Mental Health, "Any Anxiety Disorder," https://www .nimh.nih.gov/health/statistics/any-anxiety-disorder.

2. Riso and Hudson, *Wisdom of the Enneagram*, 57.

3. Hart, *Adrenaline and Stress*, 47.

4. *Yare'* is a Hebrew word for "fear" that alludes to a river that floods, as in Psalm 46:2 (with the idiom continued in verse 3). Strong's Old Testament Hebrew Lexical Dictionary, s.v. "Strong's #03372," StudyLight.org, https://www.studylight .org/lexicons/eng/hebrew/03372.html.

5. *Da'ag* is a Hebrew word for "anxious" that means the darting around of fish; Old Testament Hebrew Lexical Dictionary, s.v. "Strong's #1672," StudyLight.org, https://www.studylight.org/lexicons/eng/hebrew/1672.html.

6. Lisa Fritscher, "Glossophobia or the Fear of Public Speaking: Symptoms, Complications, and Treatments," VeryWellMind, updated July 16, 2021, https:// www.verywellmind.com/glossophobia-2671860.

7. DentaVox, "Study Finds More Than 60 Percent of People Suffer from Dental Fear," Dental Products Report, September 13, 2018, https://www.denta lproductsreport.com/view/study-finds-more-60-percent-people-suffer-dental -fear.

8. Sarah Vander Schaaff, "Lots of Americans Have a Fear of Flying. There Are Ways to Overcome the Anxiety Disorder," *Washington Post*, October 12, 2019, https://www.washingtonpost.com/health/lots-of-americans-have-a-fear-of-flying -there-are-way-to-overcome-the-anxiety-disorder/2019/10/11/d4746d84-d338-11e9 -86ac-0f250cc91758_story.html.

9. Peg Moline, "We're Far More Afraid of Failure Than Ghosts: Here's How to Stare It Down," *Los Angeles Times*, October 31, 2015, https://www.latimes.com /health/la-he-scared-20151031-story.html.

10. Angela Morrow, "When Your Fears about Dying Are Unhealthy," VeryWell-Mind, updated June 9, 2022, https://www.verywellmind.com/scared-to-death-of -death-1132501.

11. Hart, *Adrenaline and Stress*, 36.

12. Melissa Heisler, "Have You Become a Type A Personality?," HuffPost, January 19, 2015, https://www.huffpost.com/entry/have-you-become-a-type-a-personal ity-_b_6508920.

13. I (Bill) wrote extensively on anxiety and adrenaline dependence, along with soul care and "hurrying up to be still," in *Your Best Life in Jesus' Easy Yoke*.

14. Corrie ten Boom, *The Hiding Place* (Grand Rapids: Chosen, 1971), 198.

15. Ten Boom, *The Hiding Place*, 199–205.

16. AJ Sherrill, *The Enneagram for Spiritual Formation: How Knowing Ourselves Can Make Us More Like Jesus* (Grand Rapids: Brazos, 2020), 74–75.

Chapter 13 Type Five: Observer

1. *Shadowlands*, directed by Richard Attenborough (Price Entertainment, 1993).

2. Lewis, *Great Divorce*, 73.

3. Lewis, *Great Divorce*, 74.

4. Chestnut, *Complete Enneagram*, 239.

5. DeYoung, *Glittering Vices*, 129.

6. David and Jan Stoop, *SMART Love: How Improving Your Emotional Intelligence Will Transform Your Marriage* (Grand Rapids: Revell, 2017), 76.

7. Hook et al., "The Enneagram," 12.

8. Hall, "Most Common Stress Responses of Each Enneagram Type," 3.

9. Quoted by A. Kenneth Curtis and Dan Graves, *In Context: The Stories Behind Seventy Memorable Sayings in Church History* (Worcester, PA: Christian History Institute, 2012), 96.

10. Willard, *The Divine Conspiracy*, 94. Note that we experienced Dallas Willard as a Five, but he did not use the Enneagram or identify himself as a Five.

11. Gerhard Tersteegen, *Recluse in Demand: Life and Letters* (Shoals, IN: Old Paths Tract Society, 1990). He spent his adult years until age thirty in "the Pilgrim's Hut" in solitude, study, prayer, and weaving. After this crowds of people came to him to hear his teaching, and revival broke out in the cities around him.

12. Nogosek, *Nine Portraits of Jesus*, 66.

13. Mark gives the detail that Jesus went into the temple to observe and then came back the next day to drive out the hucksters and clear space for people to pray, worship, and be ministered to (Mark 11:11, 15–17).

14. Lettie Cowman and Ed Erny, *The Story behind Streams in the Desert* (Greenwood, IN: OMS International, 1994), 17.

15. Michelle Ule, "Who Wrote *Streams in the Desert*?," OMS International, https://onemissionsociety.org/detail-page/who-wrote-streams-in-the-desert.

16. Sherrill, *Enneagram for Spiritual Formation*, 74.

17. Willard, *Divine Conspiracy*, 356.

18. Willard, *Divine Conspiracy*, 361.

19. Dallas Willard, *The Spirit of the Disciplines: Understanding How God Changes Lives* (New York: HarperCollins, 1988), 177.

20. Timothy Tennent, "Saint Thomas, Not 'Doubting Thomas,' Preaches the Gospel in India," Seedbed, December 4, 2016, https://seedbed.com/saint-thomas-preaches-the-gospel-in-india.

Chapter 14 Type Six: Loyalist

1. Wikipedia, s.v. "Bilbo Baggins," last updated December 9, 2022, https://en.wikipedia.org/wiki/Bilbo_Baggins.

2. J.R.R. Tolkien, *The Fellowship of the Ring: Being the First Part of The Lord of the Rings* (Boston: Houghton Mifflin Harcourt, 2012), 60.

3. Wong, "What Is the Rarest Enneagram Type and the Most Common Enneagram Type?" Sixes and Nines tied as the most common type, each accounting for 16 percent of 189,957 people.

4. Riso and Hudson, *Wisdom of the Enneagram*, 236.

5. Riso and Hudson, *Wisdom of the Enneagram*, 237.

6. Chestnut, *Complete Enneagram*, 187–88.

7. Paul Watzlawick, quoted in Rohr and Ebert, *The Enneagram*, 134.

8. Helen Palmer, quoted in Rohr and Ebert, *The Enneagram*, 134.

9. Erik Erikson, *Childhood and Society* (New York: W.W. Norton, 1985), 247.

10. Hall, "Most Common Stress Responses of Each Enneagram Type."

11. Nogosek, *Nine Portraits of Jesus*, 80.

12. Teresa of Avila, *Interior Castle* (New York: Doubleday, 2004), 174–75.

13. C. S. Lewis, *The Screwtape Letters* (New York: Macmillan, 1982), 137.

14. John Bunyan, *Pilgrim's Progress*, retold by James H. Thomas (Chicago: Moody Press, 1964), 11–12.

15. Ken Curtis, "John Bunyan," Christianity.com, https://www.christianity.com/church/church-history/timeline/1601-1700/john-bunyan-11630083.html.

16. Bill Gaultiere, *Lectio Divina Guides: Listen to God in Scripture* (Irvine, CA: Soul Shepherding, 2019).

17. Gaultiere, *Breath Prayer Guides*, 29.

Chapter 15 Type Seven: Enthusiast

1. Wikipedia, s.v. "*Bonnie and Clyde* (film)," last updated December 28, 2022, https://en.wikipedia.org/wiki/Bonnie_and_Clyde_(film).

2. Jennifer Rosenberg, "Biography of Bonnie and Clyde, Notorious Depression-Era Outlaws," updated January 30, 2020, https://www.thoughtco.com/bonnie-and-clyde-1779278.

3. Bob Goff's presentation at the Mental Health Collective sponsored by Chick-fil-A, Atlanta, Georgia, April 19, 2022.

4. Hook et al., "The Enneagram," 12.

5. Riso and Hudson, *Wisdom of the Enneagram*, 262.

6. Riso and Hudson, *Wisdom of the Enneagram*, 262.

7. Riso and Hudson, *Wisdom of the Enneagram*, 264–65.

8. American Psychological Association, "Stress and Eating," accessed January 4, 2023, https://www.apa.org/news/press/releases/stress/2013/eating.

9. Centers for Disease Control and Prevention, "Adult Obesity Facts," updated May 17, 2022, https://www.cdc.gov/obesity/data/adult.html.

10. DeYoung, *Glittering Vices*, 185–86.

11. Rohr and Ebert, *The Enneagram*, 151.

12. May, *Addiction and Grace*, 24–25.

13. Hall, "Most Common Stress Responses of Each Enneagram Type."

14. The theory of the Enneagram Harmony Triads gives all nine types a growth line into each triad. For Sevens this gives them a positive line to the Four, the type that is most able to articulate feelings of sadness. See Calhoun and Loughrige, *Spiritual Rhythms for the Enneagram*.

15. Riso and Hudson, *Wisdom of the Enneagram*, 269.

16. Wikipedia, s.v. "Caerus," last modified January 24, 2023, 14:22, https://en.wikipedia.org/wiki/Caerus.

17. *The Visual Bible: Matthew*, directed by Regardt van den Bergh (Visual Bible International, 1993). The film uses the NIV text and Bruce Marchiano plays the part of Jesus. It's available on streaming services or you can watch clips on YouTube.

18. G. K. Chesteron, *St. Francis of Assisi* (1924; repr., New York: Dover, 2008).

19. Ugolino di Monte Santa Maria, *The Little Flowers of St. Francis of Assisi*, ed. W. Heywood (New York: Vintage Books, 1998), 19–21.

20. Willard, *Spirit of the Disciplines*, 167.

21. Lockyer, *All the Women of the Bible*, 238.

22. Gaultiere, *Breath Prayers*, 19.

Chapter 16 Help for Anxiety

1. Step 3 of AA's Twelve Steps is: "Made a decision to turn our will and our lives over to the care of God as we understood Him." Alcoholics Anonymous, "The Twelve Steps," accessed January 4, 2023, https://www.aa.org/the-twelve-steps.

2. Heuertz, *The Sacred Enneagram*, 182–83.

3. Step 11 of the Twelve Steps of AA is: "Sought through prayer and meditation to improve our conscious contact with God as we understood Him, praying only for knowledge of His will for us and the power to carry that out." Alcoholics Anonymous, "The Twelve Steps."

4. American Psychological Association, "Mindfulness Meditation: A Research-Proven Way to Reduce Stress," October 30, 2019, https://www.apa.org/topics/mindfulness/meditation.

5. Psalms for anxiety and fear include Psalms 23, 27, 37, 46, 55, 91, 121.

6. Julian of Norwich, *Revelations of Divine Love* (New York: Penguin Books, 1998), 80.

7. American Psychological Association, "Mindfulness Meditation."

8. See Bill Gaultiere, "Electric Bible Passages for Scripture Memory," Soul Shepherding, https://www.soulshepherding.org/electric-passages-of-the-bible-to -memorize/.

9. Dallas Willard, *Renovation of the Heart: Putting on the Character of Christ* (Colorado Springs: Navpress, 2002), 113.

Chapter 17 Sadness as Good Grief

1. Jesus' point is not, "Grieve so you get a blessing." He's saying that, even in grief, which is so painful, you can receive the blessing of God's comfort by joining with Jesus in the Kingdom of the Heavens. Gaultiere, *Jesus' Greatest Teaching*, 17.

2. *Wayyippelu* is a Hebrew expression for "shame" and means the face or countenance falling in depression, as in Genesis 4:5; Strong's Lexicon, s.v. "Genesis 4:5," Biblehub.com, https://biblehub.com/strongs/genesis/4-5.htm.

3. *Mikka'as* is a Hebrew word for "grief" that makes our eyes fail, as in Psalm 6:7. Strong's Lexicon, s.v. "Psalm 6:7," Biblehub.com, https://biblehub.com/strongs /psalms/6-7.htm.

4. *Yirpu* is a Hebrew expression for "discouraged" and means the hands go limp, as in Zephaniah 3:16; Strong's Lexicon, s.v. "Zephaniah 3:16," Biblehub.com, https://biblehub.com/strongs/zephaniah/3-16.htm.

5. *Sar* is a Hebrew word for "heavy" or "sad," as in 1 Kings 21:4. Strong's Lexicon, s.v. "1 Kings 21:4," Biblehub.com, https://biblehub.com/1_kings/21-4.htm.

6. *'Atsav* is a Hebrew word for "hurt," "pain," or "grief" and is connected to the Hebrew word for a mother's labor pains in childbirth. Yaakov Ariel, "Deeper Hebrew Meanings from the Garden of Eden," Hebrewversity, https://www.hebrew versity.com/deeper-hebrew-meanings-garden-eden/.

7. John Townsend, *Hiding from Love: How to Change the Withdrawal Patterns That Isolate and Imprison You* (Grand Rapids: Zondervan, 1996), 127.

8. Elisabeth Kübler-Ross, *On Death and Dying* (New York: Macmillan, 1969).

9. David Kessler, *Finding Meaning: The Sixth Stage of Grief* (New York: Scribner, 2019).

10. Willard, *Divine Conspiracy*, 275.

11. Willard, *Divine Conspiracy*, 323.

12. Hannah Hurnard, *Hinds' Feet on High Places* (Wheaton: Tyndale, 1984), 66.

13. *Writings from the Philokalia: On Prayer of the Heart*, trans. E. Kadloubovsky and G. E. H. Palmer (London: Faber and Faber, 1992), 229.

14. C. S. Lewis, *Surprised by Joy: The Shape of My Early Life* (San Francisco: HarperOne, 1955), 17–23.

15. *Writings from the Philokalia*, 153.

16. Quoted in Manning, *Ruthless Trust*, 159.

Chapter 18 Help for Sadness

1. Jesus comforted many people who were sad, including a leper (Matt. 8:1–4), children who had been rejected (Mark 10:13–16), a rich man (Mark 10:17–31), a

grieving widow (Luke 7:11–17), Mary and Martha when their brother died (John 11:17–44), and Peter after he had denied him (John 21:1–19).

2. The lament psalms include Psalms 3, 13, 22, 25, 31, 44, 57, 77, 86, 90, 142.

3. We call this the spiritual discipline of "taking heart." See Gaultiere, *Journey of the Soul*, 157–60.

Conclusion

1. Empathy Prayer is inspired by Sungshim and John Loppnow, Anna Kang, and Jim Wilder, who developed Immanuel Journaling, a more in-depth process of "interactive gratitude" and "thought rhyming" that they teach in their book *Joyful Journey* (East Peoria, IL: Shepherd's House, 2019). To learn more, you can also visit the Loppnows' ministry, presenceandpractice.com.

Appendix 3 Enneagram Subtypes and Countertypes

1. For detailed descriptions of the twenty-seven subtypes see *The Complete Enneagram* by Beatrice Chestnut.

Drs. BILL and KRISTI GAULTIERE have been counseling and ministering to people for thirty years. Bill is a psychologist who has served in private practice, co-led a New Life psychiatric day hospital, and pastored churches. Kristi is a marriage and family therapist who has also served in private practice and church ministry. Together they are the founders of Soul Shepherding, a non-profit ministry to help people discover their next steps for growing in intimacy with Jesus, emotional health, and loving relationships. They are authors of *Journey of the Soul* and a number of other books and resources. Bill and Kristi live in California.